A Study of Vasyl' Stefanyk

A Study of Vasyl' Stefanyk:

The Pain at the Heart of Existence

D. S. Struk

University of Toronto

With Foreword
by

G.S.N. Luckyj

1973

Ukrainian Academic Press

Library of Congress Card Number 72-89110
International Standard Book Number 0-87287-056-1

UKRAINIAN ACADEMIC PRESS
A Division of
Libraries Unlimited, Inc.
P.O. Box 263
Littleton, Colorado 80120

TABLE OF CONTENTS

Foreword by George S. N. Luckyj 7
Introduction 9
Chapter I: "From Writer to Politician to Gazda"
    1871 to 1905 15
    1905 to 1916 24
    1916 to 1936 25
Chapter II: Critical Approaches to Stefanyk 34
Chapter III: Definition of Genre
    Novella in General 62
    Features of Stefanyk's Novella 70
Chapter IV: Structure of Stefanyk's Novella 87
Chapter V: The Pain at the Heart of Existence 107
Conclusion 139
Appendix: Novellas in Translation 142
    "Loss" 143
    "A Stone Cross" 145
    "Suicide" 155
    "Sons" 158
    "Children's Adventure" 163
    "All Alone" 165
    "The Agony" 167
    "The Thief" 169
    "Sin" 176
    "Les' Family" 178
    "News" 181
    "Mother" 184
    "The Pious Woman" 186
Bibliography 189

To my wife Roma
in gratitude for all of the
encouragement, help and
understanding

FOREWORD

Although virtually unknown in the West, Vasyl' Stefanyk is a Ukrainian prose writer whose work merits much greater attention. Recently, English translations of his stories have appeared in Canada* and were well received by the critics. But his work remains little known and is often misunderstood even by Slavic specialists. This is partly due to the fact that much of it is written in the Pokuttya dialect of Ukrainian which is almost untranslatable. Ukrainian critics, too, have so often labelled Stefanyk as a peasant writer that, quite unwittingly, they have thus robbed him of universal significance. As frequently happens in literature, readers and interpreters of a writer may find his art elusive and are satisfied with superficial impressions.

The present study attempts to get to the core of Stefanyk's art. It rejects the standard ideological interpretations of his work, originating in either nationalist or socialist doctrine. It tries to assess Stefanyk as a craftsman and artist. Yet it avoids a purely formalist approach. In fact, it combines several approaches and does not ignore the social and national background. In that sense it helps to establish a perspective on Stefanyk's place in the literature of his time as well as his meaning today. Finally, it offers the reader a sampling of Stefanyk's stories in English translation. Perhaps it attempts to do too much in the pages of one book, but it should fulfill the vital function of introducing an English speaking student to a first-rate writer.

There is no doubt about the high quality of Stefanyk's work. That it could have been created in a remote and culturally isolated part of Europe early in this century proves the extraordinary vitality of the region from which Stefanyk came. However, the local oral tradition, rich in folklore and poetry, was rejected rather than accepted by the young writer. His stories are not idealizations of peasant life; they are intensely realistic. They reach down into a stark and naked

* Vasyl Stefanyk, *The Stone Cross*, Toronto, 1971.

7

human existence. Stefanyk's regionalism, like Giovanni Verga's, has general significance. His peasants are not quaint, exotic types but suffering human beings. Their predicament is everybody's concern.

Essentially, Stefanyk's art is the result of an interaction between native talent and the influence of outside forces. Stefanyk came into contact with these outside forces during his student days in Cracow. He did not fall completely under the sway of Polish Modernism. It might even be argued that he rejected it. But from it he did learn the most important lesson a writer can learn—that it is the form of his work which matters. Stefanyk's form is strikingly original. It reveals a sensitive man successfully laying bare those realities which, in Mr. Struk's words, reveal the "pain at the heart of existence."

— George S.N. Luckyj

INTRODUCTION

Vasyl' Stefanyk belongs to those writers who produce a striking, but not always an understandable, effect on the reader. This Ukrainian writer, master of the novella, is more read than analysed, more often appreciated than understood. The reasons for this are several. He is read and appreciated for his laconic style, for his dramatic stories couched in a lyrical and imagistic language, enriched by a pithy Ukrainian dialect. For the very same reasons, he is seldom analysed and studied. The dialect spoken by his peasant characters is at times too "local" for general comprehension; the dramatic story is at first glance too easily understood to merit further elucidation.

Because Stefanyk used Ukrainian peasants as characters and their lives as themes, he was often misunderstood by his readers, critics and translators. As one critic remarked, "The peasants don't like Stefanyk, for they think that he is making fun of them; the intelligentsia does not like him for it thinks that he is weeping over the [plight] of the peasants."[1] Most critics, being a part of the intelligentsia, have acclaimed Stefanyk as the bard of the peasant life, and Soviet critics in particular see in him the delineator of the latent "class consciousness" of the "noble proletariat of the fields."

This "peasant" image is what, perhaps, has stood in the way of Stefanyk's due recognition outside of Ukrainian literature. His virtual obscurity in world literature is certainly not the result of a lack of translations of his works: from the moment of his first appearance in print, he has been translated into almost every major language.[2] The reason, therefore, for his lack of due recognition must lie, at least partially, in the fact that critics have overemphasized Stefanyk's treatment of peasant life and have thus presented him to the world either as a typical nineteenth-century *narodnyk-khlopoman* (a populist) or, as in the case of the majority of Soviet criticism, as the typically class-conscious sociologist hoping to "show and tell" of the exploitation of the peasant class and thus bring it one step closer to the realization of its unavoidable struggle for its class rights.

9

Yet the question of Stefanyk being a "peasant" writer or not is essential not only because its resolution might attain for Stefanyk his world recognition but also because, as I. Myronets' has pointed out:

> ... [the question] whether Stefanyk is first of all the bard of pauperized Galician peasantry, an artist of economic destitution, or if these are secondary moments in his work—this question has a profoundly principal, methodological significance and is one of the basic questions in the discussion of all of Stefanyk's work.[3]

A careful reevaluation of Stefanyk's novellas helps one resolve this question by revealing an artist more concerned with the anguish of man's life than with the portrayal of social mores; an artist more attuned to the slightest tremors of man's soul than to major social upheavals. Perhaps as important as the reevaluation of the novellas is the realization that the writer and the man are not necessarily synonymous, that a work of art and a private letter or a speech, or political essay, are not all one and the same in regard to the presentation of "truth," that there is such a thing as "artistic reality" which is not necessarily identical to reality *per se*. The flaw of most critical studies of Stefanyk lies in the inability or unwillingness to remember these basic distinctions. It is often misleading and even dangerous to judge a work of art on the basis of what the author himself says or writes about it. Yet most critics so far have concentrated on why Stefanyk wrote, what he based his impressions on, and what he supposedly tried to achieve. Of what importance is it that Shakespeare wrote for a specific group of actors, keeping in mind certain characters he could use in writing quickly so that he would have a play ready to perform? The question basically lies in whether the product is universal in value and study should concern itself first with what makes the work universal and not with motives and sources. At best these can help to elucidate the main question, but can never serve as answers to it. Mykola Zerov correctly remarked in one of his critical essays:

> ... the wide panorama of *War and Peace*, without comparison, gives more food for thought, than the historiosophic theories and strategic contemplations of Tolstoy. A work of art nourishes the reader more with its images, its emotional coloring than with the most detailed presentation of the formula of the author's design.[4]

It is, therefore, imperative, even when dealing with an author's biography, to filter out the author from the man. In the case of Stefanyk, the author himself has begun the process. There is a distinct division in the life of Stefanyk between Stefanyk the author, Stefanyk the *gazda*,[5] and the politician. It is as if Stefanyk were incapable of mixing the various facets of his life and lived each out separately.

Although a new biographical study of Stefanyk would be most welcome, such a task is beyond the scope of this work, nor could it be undertaken with much profit without an access to archival materials—an impossibility for a scholar outside of the Soviet Ukraine. A short biographical sketch, however, seems appropriate to provide the most essential factual information about Stefanyk and to illustrate the marked three-fold division of his life.

The fact that Stefanyk the writer acted quite separately from Stefanyk the politician helps to support the thesis of this monograph—namely, that although Stefanyk was interested in socio-economic problems, he was so mainly in his role as a politician and not as an artist. As a writer, his interest lay primarily in an artistic portrayal of human anguish. And although the anguish often resulted directly or indirectly from adverse economic and social conditions, Stefanyk's artistic eye focused not on these conditions, nor on their amelioration, but on the profound, often devastating, psychological dramas in the lives of his heroes. Although these heroes were for the most part common peasants from his native Pokuttya, in the depiction of their anguish Stefanyk managed to portray the universal pain that lies at the heart of existence.

That this was his main interest is further supported by his highly effective and unique artistic technique. Were he primarily interested in the delineation of social classes and condemnation of social and economic injustices, as some critics maintain, he would undoubtedly have chosen a less artistic and less dramatic narrative than his novella—an extremely condensed prose genre, most effective in the presentation of the brief, often violent, upheavals in man's soul.

It seemed appropriate, moreover, to provide the reader with a survey of the main critical approaches to and the evaluations of Stefanyk. This was done in the hope that the reader, armed with a sketch of Stefanyk's life and with a survey of the previous critical evaluations of his work, will then be able to judge the validity of the present interpretation, as presented in the chapters dealing with an analysis of Stefanyk's genre, his method of construction, and the content of his novellas. To facilitate this even further, especially for the reader with no knowledge of Ukrainian, translations of several representative novellas were provided in the appendix.

One must be aware, however, that even though this is the first, and therefore introductory, study of Stefanyk in English it is nevertheless limited in scope since it is devoted to the study of the universality of Stefanyk's works. Only the most important aspects of Stefanyk's life, work, and peculiarities of style as well as language,[6] aspects directly pertaining to the thesis, are treated in this monograph. Still it is hoped that this study of Stefanyk's work will help to alter the interpretation of Stefanyk from the over-simplified belief that he is a "peasant" writer to a more proper evaluation of him as a master artist in the depiction of human anguish. Furthermore it is also hoped that this book will serve as a stimulus for a further study of other facets of the life and work of one of the foremost writers of modern short prose.

FOOTNOTES

[1]Mykhaylo Rudnyts'ky, *Vid Myrnoho do Khvyl'ovoho* (L'viv, 1936), p. 249.

[2]Vasyl' Kostashchuk, *Volodar dum selyans'kykh* (L'viv, 1959), pp. 110-11, writes:

Besides the translations, already mentioned, of Wacław Moraczewski into Polish, of Ivan Franko, Ol'ha Kobylyans'ka, and Yurko Moraczewski into German, in 1905 there appeared in Warsaw *Klonowe liście* [Maple Leaves] in the translation of M. Moczulśki.

The same year in Prague there appeared *Powidky* [Stories] of Stefanyk in a Czech translation of K. Ripachka. Stefanyk's novellas, written after 1916, were translated into Czech by Rudolf Hulka. . . .

In 1907 appeared in St. Petersburg *Rasskazy Stefanyka* [Stories of Stefanyk]. In 1910 *Doroha* [The Road] appeared in Bulgarian, and in 1912-1914 . . . 32 novellas of Stefanyk were translated into Croatian.

In 1926 *Klenovi lystky* [Maple Leaves] appeared in the Italian translation of M. Lypovets'ka.

Mykhaylo Rudnyts'ky translated the novella "Zlodiy" [The Thief] into French. Several Stefanyk novellas have been translated into English and Spanish. . . .

[In English as early as 1914. See also O. P. Kushch, ed., *Vasyl' Stefanyk. Bibliohrafichnyy pokazhchyk* (Kiev, 1961, pp. 16-65 for bibliographical data on translations of Stefanyk's works. Also Richard Lewanski, *Slavic Literatures: The Literature of the World in English Translation* (New York, 1967), pp. 440-41. Moreover, a new collection of Stefanyk's novellas in English translation, *The Stone Cross* prepared under the editorship of Prof. C. H. Andrusyshen, was published by McClelland & Stewart, Toronto, 1971 in commemoration of the centenary of Stefanyk's birth.]

Stefanyk's novellas appeared in a separate collection in People's China in the translation of Li-M-e.

[3]Iv. Myronets', Review of V. Stefanyk, *Tvory* (peredmova V. Koryaka, 3 vyd. DVU, 1929), in *Krytyka*, No. 6 (June 1929), p. 158.

[4]Mykola Zerov, *Vid Kulisha do Vynnychenka* (Kiev, 1929), p. 174.

[5]*Gazda*—a West Ukrainian dialectal word not translatable into English directly. It often appears in Stefanyk's novellas and is left in this work in the original form throughout. It implies a master of one's home and property; a propertied peasant as opposed to one who is not. The female counterpart is *gazdynya*.

[6]Stefanyk's use of the Pokuttya dialect is only metioned. This very important and interesting aspect of his novellas deserves a separate linguistic study.

CHAPTER I

"FROM WRITER TO POLITICIAN TO GAZDA"

In a curious way, a study of Stefanyk's life is not really necessary for the understanding of his novellas. More than most authors, Stefanyk, save for a few atypical autobiographical pieces, stayed out of his creations. He is quoted[1] as having said that although he would like to have written in verse for it affords a permanence not available to prose (he felt that the poem by its very structure does not allow for reader alterations; every word remains the way it was written and in the order composed by the poet), he could not write verse for people do not speak in verse. He maintained that in order to write in verse he would have to write about himself as all poets do (actually his two autobiographical novellas are written in highly stylized poetic prose). Being concerned not with himself but with people, he chose prose. A study of his life, therefore, cannot serve as much as a key to his novellas, but as a general background to his work.

For the purposes of this work some biographical guidelines are necessary, if for no other reason than to place Stefanyk in a chronological context. Also, the biography is necessary to see what formative influences there were on his work, if any, and to show that there is a distinct separation between Stefanyk's artistic and socio-political aspirations. The last reason prompted the division of this chapter according to dates which correspond to the various activities of the author.

1871 to 1905

Stefanyk's life divides itself into three distinct periods. The first of these is perhaps most important, as it is not only the formative period of his life, but also the time in which he presented himself to the reading public. Stefanyk was born on May 14, 1871,[2] in the village of Rusiv, Snyatyn district of Western Ukraine, the second child in a family of a wealthy peasant. As the first male child in the family (he had an older sister Mariya, and two younger brothers and a sister) he was sent to school against the wishes of his mother and sister Mariya, two members of the family most beloved by the young Stefanyk. School was by no means a happy experience for Stefanyk. Both in the elementary school at Snyatyn, which he attended until completion of the fourth grade in 1883, and in the Polish gymnasium (high school) in Kolomyya, where he stayed till 1889, Stefanyk endured various forms of scorn and derision—something which he could never forgive or forget. The bitter memories of these years found their way into his autobiography as the time when he "felt a great contempt from the teachers for ... all that was peasant."[3] This hurt pride produced lasting dislike of the city and its inhabitants.

While in the gymnasium, he joined a secret society of students where he read various proscribed books and met Les' Martovych and Lev Bachyns'ky, two friends who had a considerable influence on his life. The society was discovered and Stefanyk, together with his friends, was expelled from the gymnasium and had to transfer to another in Drohobych, from which he graduated in 1892.

Just as his membership in the secret society and his friendship with Bachyns'ky led to the beginnings of his political life, so the friendship with Martovych led to the beginning of his literary life. Though in later life Stefanyk, with his powerful stories, quite overshadowed Martovych, a writer with a distinct wit and a bend for irony, it was the opposite while they were still in the gymnasium. As Stefanyk admits in his autobiography, Martovych, older of the two, was extremely gifted and wrote "poems against the teachers and God, full of bile and mockery."[4] Stefanyk, too, began writing while still in high school, but Martovych's talent so overwhelmed him that he would not admit it at the time.[5] The two of them, however, formed a partnership under the cryptonym "L. M." and wrote two little stories, "Nechytal'nyk" (The Non-Reader) and "Lumera" (Lumbers—a peasant mispronunciation of the word "numbers").[6] It is striking that "L. M." are the initials of Les' Martovych. This in itself reveals how the weights were balanced in this partnership. Stefanyk's contribution to the composition of these stories must have been minimal, for they bear the distinct mark of Martovych. V. Lesyn's contention that this literary alliance served as Stefanyk's schooling in the art of satire[7] is rather doubtful. Equally questionable is Yuriy Hamorak's statement that, thanks to Martovych, Stefanyk overcame his early tendencies toward lyricism.[8] If anything at all, the alliance with Martovych, as well as Stefanyk's great respect for Martovych as a talented writer, probably taught Stefanyk how not to write if he ever wanted to become a writer in his own right.

In 1892 Stefanyk enrolled at the University of Cracow to study medicine. The same year brought the first of a series of deaths with a profound influence on Stefanyk. His beloved sister Mariya died at the age of 24. The death of this sister who, like his mother, would rather have seen him at home than at some far away school was almost an omen; he never became a doctor. "That whole medicine of mine," as he later wrote, "was a useless venture, for neither did I like those studies, nor could I in any way torture the sick with my knocking and feeling."[9]

Far from being wasted, the years in Cracow were perhaps the most important in his life. Here he met and was befriended by Wacław Moraczewski, an erudite Polish doctor, and his Ukrainian wife Sofia, née Okunevs'ka. The Moraczewskis introduced Stefanyk to contemporary European culture and their friendship provided him with that necessary sophistication without which he could never have become more than a peasant story teller. Through Moraczewski, Stefanyk met the foremost literary figures of Poland, S. Przybyszewski, W. Orkan, and other members of the decadent group *"Młoda Polska"* (Young Poland) which centered around the paper *Życie*.

Life in Cracow soon became hectic and exciting for Stefanyk. Writing to his friend L. Bachyns'ky, he describes a typical day in his "university" life:

> For 7 hours I sit among corpses, then I save the world with politics, ethics (Spencer, Zola, Dumas), I run around various literary circles . . . and I go to the cafe for a glass. . . .
> I am writing this letter at 2:30 A.M., having just come home . . .[10]

As is evident from this letter and other letters of the time, Stefanyk was voraciously consuming West European literature.[11] In letters to his friends he mentions various books which he read at the time, sometimes seeking and sometimes giving advice, or sending the books on to his friends, or even discussing literary theory as in this letter to Ol'ha Hamorak, a friend who later became his wife:

> But today we are reading Lenau, Musset, and Zola, and the Goncourts. Will the same type of naturalism return, as Zola predicts—it is hard to judge, we can only go on facts, *per analogiam* we can say, that as the romanticism of Byron is different from the

17

romanticism of Jacobsen, so the naturalism of the future will be different from the naturalism of Zola.[12]

Scattered throughout his letters are also references to works of such modernist authors as Baudelaire, Keller, Verlaine, Maeterlinck, Bourget, Luys, Hauptmann and others. Stefanyk's awareness of the latest trends in literature can be seen in statements like the following:

> ... a book, which represents a true achievement of contemporary literature. In my opinion, such a book is *Die versunkene Glocke* of Gerh. Hauptmann.[13]

Yet reading, discussions, literary circles, and personal friendships with writers, were not the only things which formulated young Stefanyk's literary future. Actually, in his reminiscences, Lepky observed that Stefanyk disliked discussing both literature and philosophy: a discussion of literature, Stefanyk claimed, was no more than a "pouring from a vacuity into a vacuum," whereas a philosophical discussion was futile. Since the eternal questions could not be solved, there was little point in "knocking one's head against the wall."[14]

When one recalls Stefanyk's statement that he wrote about people it becomes not at all surprising that he spent much of his time observing people and listening to them. One of his favorite pastimes in Cracow was visiting taverns where he saw "so many people, so much temperament, grief, and laughter as there is in private apartments."[15] Lepky also recalls how Stefanyk used to go to the railway station and watch the trainloads of peasants emigrating to Canada.[16] What he witnessed there, he described vividly in a letter to Bachyns'ky:

> ... the women are giving birth to children under the railway's cloacae, ... yellow as wax, green as grass, they die like flies on the benches of the III class, ... the peasants weep and say that they are no longer Ruthenians, but gipsies. A sea of tears, a hell full of torture! ... Not Ruthenians but gipsies *morituri*; but even they are people. Oh, human fate, how bitter you are and how endlessly bad![17]

These scenes left an indelible mark on Stefanyk.

Such visits to the station, the hectic bustle of the city life he loathed,[18] constant longing for his mother and home, the pressure of studies he disliked, an incessant flood of new impressions both from reading and from social contact—all this soon exhausted the young and very impressionable Stefanyk.

He developed neurasthenia. Whether Stefanyk often sought solace in the use of morphine and whether he developed an addiction is not known, but at least on one occasion he admits to having taken an overdose and being sick from it.[19] His real solace, however, was in writing to his friends, especially to the Moraczewskis, Lev Bachyns'ky, and Ol'ha Hamorak. It is in these letters that Stefanyk begins to emerge as a writer.

First, under the influence of modernism, Stefanyk's letters are full of poetic prose, mystical, slightly tinged with symbolism, always very lyrical, quite often dark, and self reflecting. Very often, as Lesyn pointed out, he assumed "the pose of a great sufferer"[20] and reveled in his suffering and self-deprecation as a typical decadent. In this self-critical vein, Stefanyk wrote a long letter to Bachyns'ky in which, while showing why he cannot possibly marry his friend's sister,[21] he presents quite an interesting analysis of his own "faulty" character:

> . . . I am a visionary. This *genus* of my character has the following subdivisions: plans which cannot become reality, little lies and real lies which I can spread and even believe in myself, a certain type of optimism. The second *genus* is that I am an idealist; the subdivisions are such: I am very sensitive to misfortune and hurt, new impressions keep forming time after time and clouding over the former ones, and this causes a lack of determination and decisiveness; I hate the lack of toleration and I love all people for I can often cry at their misery. The third *genus* is the heritage of all peasant children—I am taciturn and secretive. Subdivisions: jealousy, love of intrigue, sacrifice and quiet ignoring of people.[22]

Although this serves as an example of what Stefanyk thought about himself, it is by no means representative of the majority of his letters, in which he was much more artistic and lyrical. A good illustration of these poetical letters is one Stefanyk wrote to Moraczewski on April 22, 1896. It must be quoted in full for it not only shows Stefanyk as the writer of poetic prose but also presents him in a stage of transition—a transition to the type of writing which would later make him famous. The letter in full reads as follows:

> Dear Ones!

> I am a bit ill, but quite better now. I cannot write you about the state I'm in. My soul has boiled over with so much of something, so sad and endless, that the scratching of the pen pushes this sadness down

even further than before. Words are lacking. Perhaps Verlaine will tell you, at least in part, what I cannot. Quiet weepings. Sadly wet Autumn weeps, Chills embrace the heart, Wild despair plays on it. I wander anguished, Over a world in anguish. All emaciated, As if beaten by the wind. Over empty fields a withered leaf.

"Tomorrow is Easter! Today I had work and more work! I baked some Easter-bread, swept the yard, washed the benches . . . There's no end to it! I can't tear myself to pieces. Even if he'd beat me, I couldn't manage. I call Anychka. I comb out her braids, like little mouse tails, I take and wash her little head, comb her, and braid her. I think to myself: here, here and she'll grow up and you'll finally get yours, Oksana. You'll be sneaking it from your husband and you'll be placing in front of her eyes flowers, and bangles, and beads — you'll take whole bunches of them from the stores. Ivan will look and; 'Look, Oksana, how pretty our Anychka is.' 'Eh, my dear one,' I think, 'if you only knew how much money I gave away for those bangles and flowers, then you'd finish me off right here and now. But it's always like that with husbands.'" The young woman flew about ten years ahead in time. In a year she flew off into strange worlds. She sat at a railway bench, exactly on Easter Saturday. She sat there and talked to herself. "What's the matter with you, woman? Why are you talking to yourself? Get a hold of yourself. Anychka is over there sleeping, black as a crow. You're no longer a *gazdynya*, but a gipsy and I'm a gipsy too. Now such a time has come for Ruthenians that they turn into gipsies." So spoke Ivan.

"Oh, I'll be, here I'm puttering around this wind-blown child, and work stands still. Will I ever get it from Ivan! The axel grease hasn't been brought in, the shirts have not been mangled, the collars have not been sewn on . . . I still have to run and still give the cow something to eat." "All's not well with the wife," thought Ivan, "she's talking to herself, I might have to bury her somewhere on the way. If only she'd last till we get there. What will I begin with the children?" And they travelled, travelled to America—the promised land.

I greet you heartily.
Stefanyk[23]

The translation in the letter from the paraphrasing of Verlaine, so reminiscent of Stefanyk's own poetic prose, to the little story is quite apparent. The story, although quite crude, has all of the characteristics of a Stefanyk novella, as will be seen later on. The importance here lies in the fact that Stefanyk was still not sure of his own path. He was still experimenting. He had written several pieces of poetic prose and had tried to have them published, but they disappeared in the editorial offices of various papers. Finally he gathered several of them into a collection and called it *Z oseny* (From Autumn), but found no one interested in having it publishhed. The collection consisted of seven short poems in prose and Stefanyk presented all of them to his friend Moraczewski together with a diatribe against utilitarian publishers who want works which are of some practical use.[24]

Like any young writer who wants to be published, Stefanyk was understandably upset. What he did not realize was that, thanks to a built-in reading public—the recipients of his letters—and thanks to the narrow-mindedness of some editors, when he finally did appear in print it was as a full-grown artist. For even though the replies of his friends to his stories in letters[25] are unavailable for the most part, these replies must have contained constructive criticism and a certain reader reaction, necessities without which Stefanyk could not have developed as a writer.[26]

When not writing his stories to his friends, Stefanyk liked to narrate them in person. Once he told some of his stories to a friend of his, V. Budzynovs'ky, who was then the editor of the paper *Pratsya* in Chernivitsi. Budzynovs'ky promised Stefanyk that if they were written down exactly the way he told them, they would be published in his paper.[27] Thus in 1897, in *Pratsya*, numbers 14-17, appeared the first seven novellas of Stefanyk. Although Stefanyk was afraid of the reception these stories would meet and had Budzynovs'ky publish them under the pseudonym "S," they were an immediate success. In 1898 the *Literaturno-naukovyy vistnyk* (LNV), the most prestigious magazine in Ukraine at the time, published three more of Stefanyk's stories. Not completely understanding the novelty of Stefanyk's method, the editors of the *LNV* had some reservations, but Stefanyk stood his ground, and even though his novellas were not published as "novellas," but as "photographs from life," they were published nonetheless without any changes.[28]

Only a year later, in Chernivtsi, appeared Stefanyk's first collection of novellas, *Synya knyzhechka* (The Blue Book), published by Professor S. Smal'-Stots'ky and with a short introduction by him. With the appearance of *The Blue Book* (named after the first novella in the collection), Stefanyk entered the ranks of Ukrainian literature as a new, exciting, and already proficient writer. The general reaction to the collection was similar to that of Ol'ha Kobylyans'ka (1865-1942),[29] who befriended Stefanyk in 1898. She was ecstatic over the depth of feeling which rang from Stefanyk's novellas like a "shout of sorrow" over fields.[30]

Everything, however, did not proceed as smoothly with Stefanyk's personal life. He fell in love with a married woman, seven years his senior, Yevheniya Kalytovs'ka, the sister of his friend and wife-to-be O. Hamorak. The love affair was a bitter one for Stefanyk. He declared himself in 1899 while visiting the Kalytovs'kys for Christmas and urged her to leave everything and go with him. She refused on account of the children. Even though Stefanyk eventually married her sister, he never really stopped loving her and later in his life in one of his autobiographical poems in prose, "Sertse" (The Heart, 1926), he called her his "highest ideal of a woman."[31] At the time of his greatest passion he wrote two autobiographical stories: "Confiteor," 1899, which later he reworked and published as "Moye slovo" (My Word, 1901), and "Doroha" (The Road, 1900) and sent them to Kalytovs'ka on her birthday in the given years.

With these stories, and especially with "Confiteor," Stefanyk paid his debt to the influences of Polish modernists, in particular Przybyszewski.[32] At the same time, as further proof of his early fascination with West European modernism, Stefanyk translated a story by Arne Garborg, "Den Burtkomne Faderen" (The Lost Father) and "Solide Köpfe" (Hard Heads) as well as "Das Sterben" (Death) by Ludwig Thoma. These were published in the *LNV*, Garborg in 1902 and Thoma in 1900.

1900 was a difficult year in Stefanyk's life. His father, angered by prolonged and seemingly fruitless but expensive studies, cut him off financially. His neurasthenia grew progressively worse. By 1899 he complained to O. Hamorak of such severe nervous disorders that he had to resort to morphine.[33] In 1900 he wrote of complete, though temporary, nervous exhaustion.[34] Matters were not helped any by the frustrating love affair with Kalytovs'ka nor by the fact that the year began with a tremendous blow, for on January 1st his mother died. Since writing did not come easily to Stefanyk, as attested by many of his contemporaries,[35] and since each novella was born accompanied by severe emotional labour pains during which Stefanyk relived the anguish of his characters, it is quite surprising that this was one of the most creative of his periods.

Thus, the only consolation of that year was the publication of his second collection of novellas, *Kaminnyy khrest* (The Stone Cross), published in L'viv by M. Yatskiv. The collection is again named after the first novella which, along with the whole collection was dedicated to his friend and later father-in-law Kyrylo Hamorak. The collection contained nine stories, three of which were published for the first time; the rest had appeared previously either in the *LNV* or in *Pratsya*.

His relationship with his father worsened even more when the father remarried only a few months after his wife's death. Fundless and nervously exhausted, Stefanyk no longer attended lectures but still stayed on in Cracow. Ivan Franko (1856-1916), one of the editors of the *LNV*, a scholar and the leading Ukrainian writer of the time, suggested that Stefanyk switch over to the Faculty of Arts at the University of L'viv and study on a scholarship offered him from the Shevchenko Scientific Society, but this did not materialize since Stefanyk lacked the stamina to continue.

With the financial help of a friend, in 1901 Stefanyk went to the mineral baths at Pistan, Hungary, and although his health was very poor, in the same year the third collection of his novellas *Doroha* (The Road), appeared in L'viv. Having as its title story the autobiographical novella which Stefanyk wrote for Kalytovs'ka in 1900, the collection contained thirteen stories of which all but two were published for the first time. In his article "Z ostannikh desyatylit' XIX viku" (From the Last Decades of the XIX Century), Franko praises Stefanyk as the most talented artist to have appeared in Ukrainian literature since the time of Shevchenko.[36] Franko was not the first of the major writers to recognize Stefanyk. In 1900, Lesya Ukrayinka (1871-1913), a foremost Ukrainian poetess, attempted an analysis and a characterization of Stefanyk's writings in comparison to other writers who came out of the Bukovyna region of Western Ukraine.[37]

In 1903 Stefanyk, already as a recognized writer, took part in the unveiling of a monument to Ivan Kotlyarevs'ky (1769-1838), the father of modern Ukrainian literature, in Poltava. This was Stefanyk's first trip to Eastern Ukraine and his presence at the unveiling allowed him to meet the foremost writers of Ukraine proper: Mykhaylo Kotsyubyns'ky (1864-1913), Lesya Ukrayinka,[38] Mykhaylo Staryts'ky (1840-1904), and others. All of them had read at least some of Stefanyk's novellas and praised him very highly, especially the renowned Ukrainian impressionist, Kotsyubyns'ky.

1903 was the apex of Stefanyk's first period. In 1904 he married Ol'ha Hamorak and the couple began to live with her father in the village of Stetseva. In 1905 his fourth collection of novellas *Moye slovo* (My Word) appeared, but it consisted of only two previously unpublished novellas—the title novella "My Word" (previously written for Kalytovs'ka in 1899) and "Sud" (Judgment). The rest consisted of reprints of all the novellas which appeared in the first two collections with the exception of "Portret" (A Portrait). After this, Stefanyk the writer gave way to Stefanyk the politician.

1905 to 1916

The second period in Stefanyk's life is a period of creative silence. M. Kotsyubyns'ky writing to Stefanyk typified the feeling of many at the time when he wrote:

> It cannot be that Stefanyk, our, and especially my, beloved writer, the beauty of our anemic literature, the fortunate oasis, has fallen silent forever.[39]

O. Kobylyans'ka, however, as early as 1899, felt that "sometimes he [Stefanyk] repeats himself and is weaker . . ." and that "a time will come and he will fall silent."[40] Some critics almost in agreement with Kobylyans'ka's prognosis explained Stefanyk's silence as an emotional catharsis, an exhaustion which arose from the fact that, as M. Dan'ko put it:

> The human psyche cannot forever react only to pictures of suffering; either they lose their freshness of impression, dulled by the repeated excitement, or they destroy it by taking away the psychological impact and not replacing it by positive experiences [feelings].[41]

Others, however, blamed recent misfortunes (the death of his mother, his father's remarriage, a tragic love affair) which, they argued, served as catalysts triggering in Stefanyk an ideological crisis and a "disquietude of the soul."[42]

All of these are partially true, as is the fact that Stefanyk, like Thoreau "had other lives to lead." One of such "lives" has its roots in the time when Stefanyk was still in the gymnasium. His membership in the secret student society led to a fascination with the then-current and proscribed "socialism." Stefanyk and his friend Bachyns'ky soon joined the Ukrainian Radical Party which espoused the cause of the peasants and proposed an anti-government program based on the principles of socialism.[43] Although Stefanyk "was not a politician in the broad sense of this word, [although] he did not form any

24

political program, he was a regular member of the Radical Party all his life."[44] His concern for various social inadequacies in the government revealed itself even sooner than his artistic talent. As early as 1890 there appeared the first of a series of publicistic essays[45] revealing a youthful earnestness, concern, and indignation.

Although Stefanyk had often campaigned among peasants still during the first part of his life (he was even jailed for it several times),[46] he now devoted himself to serious community work. As a result of various speeches at community functions, in 1907 Stefanyk was elected as a substitute for the representative to the Austrian parliament, Volodymyr Okhrymovych. A year later Okhrymovych stepped down in favor of Stefanyk and the latter himself became an MP (*posol*) for the Radical Party. Stefanyk remained at his post until World War I, but, although he conscientiously sat through innumerable sessions of Parliament, he never said a word.[47] He did a lot more for his constituents when he lived among them, for he tried to help them with their daily problems in any way possible as attested by the numerous memoirs written after his death.

Meanwhile, Stefanyk was establishing himself as a *gazda*. Until the relations between him and his father improved, Stefanyk lived with his father-in-law. Life would have been quite comfortable, if it were not for the fact that Stefanyk was continually haunted by death. In 1906 his beloved Yevheniya Kalytovs'ka died. In 1910 his father-in-law followed. Luckily the relationship between father and son had improved greatly, and Stefanyk's father deeded him 18 acres of land. Thus with the death of his father-in-law Stefanyk moved to his native village of Rusiv to his own house.

Misfortune again befell Stefanyk. In 1914 his wife died, leaving him a widower with three small sons. When the War broke out and the Russian armies invaded Galicia (autumn of 1914 to spring of 1915) Stefanyk at first stayed behind. When the Austrian armies reoccupied the territory he was arrested on a false charge of spying for the Russians. Only his having been an MP saved him from a hangman's noose. In 1916 Stefanyk emigrated to Vienna. The horror of what he saw on the way stirred his muse and in 1916 he wrote his first story after a silence of nearly 14 years.

1916 to 1936

The last twenty years of Stefanyk's life were, in a way, anticlimactic. Politically, he had reached the height of his development in becoming a Member of Parliament. Artistically, he had a difficult time living up to the success of his first stories. P. Murashko is, at least partially, correct when he claims that:

> . . . the tragedy of Stefanyk as a writer is that after a long pause he could no longer continue the line of development which he began earlier, and his creative heritage has remained only a foundation of that literary edifice which Stefanyk could have created.[48]

Murashko's criticism is a bit too harsh for there are stories in this period in which Stefanyk manages to continue "the line of development"; what he could not do was to surpass that line. Although some of his "war" stories contain all of the elements of his early stories, although they are just as powerful, they are in no way better.

His former political life had but one small encore. During the period of Ukrainian self-rule in Western Ukraine, as a former MP, he was called to be a Vice-Head of the *Natsional'na Rada* (National Council) and in 1919 went as a delegate to Kiev for the signing of the Act of Unification of the East and West Ukraine.[49] In 1922 he became the district head of the Ukrainian Radical Party.

The rest of his life was punctuated by deaths and unified by poverty. In 1919 his brother Volodymyr died; in 1920 his father died, followed by another brother in 1924. As the years progressed, Stefanyk's poverty increased and his health deteriorated. In his letters of this period he often complained of his poverty,[50] but the true state of affairs can be seen very well from a letter written by a close friend and writer, Marko Cheremshyna (pseudonym of Ivan Semaniuk, 1874-1927).[51] Cheremshyna was a lawyer by profession and had his practice in the town of Snyatyn, very close to Stefanyk's village. He wrote:

> . . . he [Stefanyk] is now undergoing an extremely difficult situation with his property and is directly faced with total loss (by forced court auction) of his already small real estate and he has no means for living while he must support one son at the university in L'viv and two at the gymnasium in Kolomyya, as well as his wife's niece studying with the artist Novakivs'ky in L'viv.[52]

A partial solution to these financial difficulties came from the recently formed Ukrainian Soviet Socialist Republic.

Although Soviet critics constantly claim that the government of the Ukrainian S.S.R. decreed a pension for life for

Stefanyk and published his works because he was a sympathiser attuned to the struggle of the masses, the more probable reason for the magnanimity of the Soviet government was given by Yu. Hamorak:

> Russia at the time was triumphantly greeting Maksim Gorky as its cultural prophet. The Ukrainian cultural circles also began to look for a writer who could be such a figure for Ukraine. Franko, Kotsyubyns'ky and Lesya Ukrayinka were no longer among the living, therefore their choice fell on the last one of the great guard, on Stefanyk.[53]

Be that as it may, there was in the Soviet Ukraine a genuine interest in Stefanyk's work and a desire to make him as popular as possible. Partially because of financial difficulties, but also because of an earnest desire to cooperate with the Ukrainian literary and cultural revival, Stefanyk cooperated as best he could with the demands of Soviet literary circles. He authorized an edition of his collected works (1927) under the editorship of Ivan Lyzanivs'ky, which was not only the fullest so far, but also had some of the dialecticisms corrected into literary Ukrainian, so that the work could be more comprehensible to the general East Ukrainian reading public.

The 1927 *Works* also contained stories which Stefanyk had written since 1916, and which previously had appeared in his last collection of novellas, *Vona—Zemlya* (She—The Earth, L'viv, 1926), also under the editorship of I. Lyzanivs'ky. This collection contained eight novellas, all written and published previously; three of them in the Soviet Ukrainian journal *Chervonyy Shlyakh.* Stefanyk wrote only twelve more novellas, which never appeared in a separate collection, but were published individually, and some of them in Soviet Ukrainian periodicals. Although Stefanyk published his novellas in Soviet Ukrainian periodicals and had his works published in Soviet Ukraine, he was not, contrary to the opinion of all of the Soviet critics, a sympathiser of the Communist regime. He never submitted any of his novellas for publication in any of the Sovietophile journals in Western Ukraine and limited himself to the journals in Soviet Ukraine which were openly advocating a Ukrainian cultural revival, such as *Chervonyy Shlyakh* and *Vaplite.*

When in 1927 Stefanyk wrote to the editors of the journal *Svit* to thank the Communist elements in Western Ukraine and the writers and cultural workers in Soviet Ukraine for the greetings and celebrations of his fifty-fifth anniversary he specified to whom his greetings should be sent:

To all the organizations and friends from Soviet Ukraine: *Pluh* [The Plough], Hryhory Kosynka, Ivan Lyzanivs'ky, . . . Mykhaylo Hrushevs'ky, Serhiy Yefremov, and A. Kryms'ky.[54]

It is not hard to discern where Stefanyk's sympathies lay. All the persons mentioned in his greeting were soon repressed and some even liquidated. Stefanyk was, of course, aware of the tightening of party controls in Soviet Ukraine and refused to go there even though he was invited and even offered the title of a member of *VUAN* (*Vse Ukrayins'ka Akademiya Nauk*—The All Ukrainian Academy of Sciences). Soviet sources to this day claim that Stefanyk did not visit Soviet Ukraine because of the repressive tactics of the Polish government, that is, because the government refused to issue him a passport. A more plausible reason, however, is given by Yuri Hamorak (pseudonym of the author's youngest son) who maintained that Stefanyk did not trust the Soviets and was deathly afraid of them.[55]

Not only did Stefanyk not want to go to Soviet Ukraine, but also, prompted by the sad state of affairs at the time of the first wave of repressions, he renounced his pension and wrote a sharp letter of protest to the Soviet consul in L'viv—a fact which is never mentioned in any Soviet sources.[56] Finally in 1932—on the eve of hunger in Eastern Ukraine, caused by forced collectivization, he broke off all relations with Soviet Ukraine.

In 1930 Stefanyk became partially paralyzed, a fact which forced him to dictate the last stories of his life to his youngest son. In 1931 the literary community in L'viv marked his sixty year jubilee, and preparations were made to publish the author's collected works. *The Collected Works* appeared in 1933, containing all Stefanyk had written so far with the addition of three novellas which he wrote for this edition. Stefanyk still lived long enough to see the dramatic quality of his works recognized when he witnessed the Zahrava Theater presentation of stage adaptations of his works in 1934 under the direction of actor and director V. Blavats'ky. On December 7, 1936 Stefanyk died.

After his death, Stefanyk's works appeared in several editions. The first of these was the Regensburg 1948 émigré edition edited by Stefanyk's son Yuriy Hamorak. Not to be outdone, the Soviets began a three-volume Academy edition in 1949 and completed it in 1954. Although it is certainly not a scholarly edition due to many purposeful omissions and some doctoring of certain texts, it still is the most complete edition of Stefanyk's works, letters and unpublished materials to date.

28

Some of the most blatant errors in the 1949-54 edition were corrected in the 1964 edition of Stefanyk's works under the editorship of V. Lesyn and F. Pohrebennyk. This one-volume edition is not complete enough to stand alone but is a welcome addition to the three-volume set.[57]

FOOTNOTES

[1] Bohdan Lepky, *Try portrety: Franko, Stefanyk, Orkan* (L'viv, 1937), pp. 105-6.

[2] In almost all of the sources consulted, Stefanyk's date of birth is given as May 14, 1871. There are two exceptions. Although in his autobiography Stefanyk gives the above date as his date of birth, in a letter to M. M. Mochul'sky, dated December 14, 1901, he writes:

... I have but one date till now, that I was born in the village of Rusiv, Snyatyn District, on the 15th of May, 1971. [In Vasyl' Stefanyk, *Tvory* (Kiev, 1964), p. 458].

The other discrepancy comes in the work of Toma Kobzey, *Velykyy riz'bar ukrayins'kykh selyans'kykh dush*, Shevchenko Scientific Society Ukrainian Studies, Vol. XXI (Toronto, 1966), p. 7, where Kobzey states that Stefanyk was born on May 19, 1871. The May 14th date, however, seems to be the most probable one.

[3] Vasyl' Stefanyk, *Povne zibrannya tvoriv v tr'okh tomakh* (Kiev, 1949-1954), II, 10. Henceforth this edition will be referred to as *Povne zibrannya tvoriv*.

[4] *Ibid.*, p. 14.

[5] *Ibid.*, p. 18.

[6] See letter of Stefanyk to W. Moraczewski dated February 17, 1896, in *Povne zibrannya tvoriv*, III, 54.

[7] V. M. Lesyn, *Tvorchist' Vasylya Stefanyka* (Kiev, 1965), p. 20.

[8] Yuriy Hamorak, "Vasyl' Stefanyk—Sproba biohrafiyi," introduction to V. Stefanyk, *Tvory* (Regensburg, 1948), p. xv.

[9] Stefanyk *Povne zibrannya tvoriv*, II, 17.

[10] Letter to L. Bachyns'ky, Cracow, December 4, 1895, *Povne zibrannya tvoriv*, III, 27.

[11] A contrary opinion is expressed by B. Lepky (a scholar, writer, friend from those days) in his reminiscences of Stefanyk, *Try portrety*, p. 105, where Lepky writes the following:

Did Stefanyk read much? How it was in Rusiv, I don't know, but during the Cracow days, no. Arne Garborg, Dostoevsky, Knut Hamsun, Ibsen, Przybyszewski, with whom he was friends, and enough.

Judging, however, by Stefanyk's letters, Lepky seems to have underestimated his friend.

[12]Letter to O. Hamorak, Cracow, February 29, 1896, *Povne zibrannya tvoriv*, III, 57.

[13]Letter to O. Hamorak, Cracow, June 1897, *Povne zibrannya tvoriv*, III, 110.

[14]B. Lepky, *Try portrety*, p. 106.

[15]Letter to W. Moraczewski, Cracow, December 15, 1895, *Povne zibrannya tvoriv*, III, 51.

[16]Bohdan Lepky, "Stefanyk u Krakovi," *Novyy chas*, Nos. 14, 15, 16, 1937. Reprinted in Toma Kobzey, *Velykyy riz'bar ukrayins'kykh selyans'kykh dush*, p. 134.

[17]Letter to L. Bachyns'ky, Cracow, April 29, 1896. *Povne zibrannya tvoriv*, III, 64.

[18]In a letter to O. Kobylyans'ka, Cracow, February 13, 1899, Stefanyk wrote that he disliked the city because of its constant bustle, because there is no time to talk, because there are too many churches and taverns, because in the city they have hospitals, and finally claimed that only the prostitutes walk like people and suffer for it. See *Povne zibrannya tvoriv*, III, 169.

[19]Letter to L. Bachyns'ky, Cracow, June 14, 1894, *Povne zibrannya tvoriv*, III, 32.

[20]V. Lesyn, *Tvorchist' Vasylya Stefanyka*, p. 36. Interesting in this respect is Stefanyk's letter to Sofia Moraczewska in *Povne zibrannya tvoriv*, III, 84.

[21]The story of Stefanyk's "first love" Yevheniya Bachyns'ka is a sad one, which caused Stefanyk great grief and was a trying strain on his relationship with his very good friend and her brother, Lev Bachyns'ky. Apparently Yevheniya and Stefanyk fell in love while he was still in high school. He, however, soon grew out of love, but, unfortunately, she never did and expected him to marry her. To ease the situation Bachyns'ky asked Stefanyk to declare himself. Whereupon Stefanyk wrote the aforementioned letter. Yevheniya died of tuberculosis brought on by a cold in 1897 and at least partially Stefanyk felt himself to blame.

[22]Letter to L. Bachyns'ky, Cracow, May 14, 1896, *Povne zibrannya tvoriv*, III, 68.

[23]Letter to W. Moraczewski, Cracow, April 22, 1896, *Povne zibrannya tvoriv*, III, 62-63.

[24]See letters to W. Moraczewski No. 100 in *Povne zibrannya tvoriv*, III, 119, and No. 36 in V. Stefanyk, *Tvory* (Kiev, 1964), pp. 374-76.

[25]One scholar has counted as many as forty artistic works in Stefanyk's letters. See M. S. Hrytsyuta, "Vasyl' Stefanyk" in Ye. P. Kyrylyuk and others, eds., *Istoriya ukrayins'koyi literatury u vos'my tomakh* (Kiev, 1968), V, 236-37.

[26]A similar conclusion is reached by Yu. Hamorak, "Vasyl' Stefanyk—Sproba biohrafiyi," p. xix.

[27]Fedir Pohrebennyk, "Debyut Vasylya Stefanyka," *Radyans'ke literaturoznavstvo*, No. 1 (1967), p. 58.

28See the letter from Osyp Makovey to Stefanyk, L'viv, March 9, 1898, published for the first time by M. Hrytsyuta in *Literaturna Ukrayina*, November 27, 1964; and Stefanyk's answer in *Povne zibrannya tvoriv*, II, 72-74.

29A writer of long stories and novels depicting haughty heroines and lonely heroes bound by an aristocracy of the spirit and in search of higher beauty.

30Letter to V. Stefanyk, March 24, 1899, in O. Kobylyans'ka, *Tvory* (Kiev, 1963), V, 397.

31"Sertse," *Povne zibrannya tvoriv*, II, 30.

32Ya. Ya. Yarema, "Zv'yazky Vasylya Stefanyka z Stanislavom Pshybyshevs'kym i Vladyslavom Orkanom," *Mizhslov'yans'ki literaturni vzayemyny*, ed. by O. Bilets'ky (Kiev, 1958), No. 3, p. 160.

33Letter to O. Hamorak, Cracow, June 1899, *Povne zibrannya tvoriv*, III, 187.

34See letters Nos. 245, 246, and 250 in *Povne zibrannya tvoriv*, III, 225, 226 and 228.

35In a private interview on May 25, 1966, in his home in Vienna, A. Zhuk, a friend of Stefanyk's from his days in Vienna said that Stefanyk "squeezed out of himself his works with great difficulty." This view is confirmed by V. M. Hladky, "Do pytannya pro psykholohiyu tvorchosti Vasylya Stefanyka," *Ukrayins'ke literaturoznavstvo* (L'viv, 1968), No. 4, pp. 76-69.

36Ivan Franko, "Z ostannikh desyatylit' XIX viku," *Literaturno-naukovyy vistnyk*, Vol. XV, Bk. 9 as quoted in N.Y. Zhuk, ed., *Materialy do vyvchennya istoriyi ukrayins'koyi literatury* (Kiev, 1961), IV, 309.

37Lesya Ukrayinka, "Malorusskie pisateli na Bukovine," *Zhizn'*, Vol. IX, 1900 as reprinted in Lesya Ukrayinka, *Tvory v desyaty tomakh* (Kiev, 1963-1965), VIII, 66-80.

38He had met Lesya Ukrayinka previously in 1901 in Chernivtsi.

39Letter to V. Stefanyk, Chernihiv, February 12, 1909, in Mykhaylo Kotsyubyns'ky, *Tvory v shesty tomakh* (Kiev, 1962), VI, 87.

40Letter to O. Makovey, January 13, 1899, in O. Kobylyans'ka, *Tvory*, V, 390.

41M. Dan'ko, "Kray skorby," *Ukrayins'kaya zhizn'*, No. 1 (1915), p. 65.

42V. M. Lesyn, *Pislyavoyenna tvorchist' Vasylya Stefanyka: konspekt lektsiy spetskursu* (Chernivtsi, 1965), p. 3.

43For more information on the political situation in Western Ukraine and on the Radical Party in particular see: E. Vytanovych, "The Western Ukrainian Lands Under Austria and Hungary, 1722-1918," V. Kubijovych, ed., *Ukraine: a Concise Encyclopaedia* (Toronto, 1963), I, 697-707.

44Yuriy Hamorak, "Vasyl' Stefanyk—Sproba biohrafiyi," p. ix.

45For the articles themselves see *Povne zibrannya tvoriv*, II, 51-83. For a discussion of Stefanyk as a publicist see S. Kryzhanivs'ky,

"Publitsystyka Vasylya Stefanyka," in V. Stefanyk, *Publitsystyka* (Kiev, 1953), pp. 3-14.

[46] V. M. Lesyn, *Tvorchist' Vasylya Stefanyka*, p. 25.

[47] Stefanyk, "Autobiohrafiya," *Povne zibrannya tvoriv*, II, 17-18.

[48] Pavlo Murashko, "Druhyy naybil'shyy pys'mennyk Zakhidnoyi Ukrayiny," *Duklya*, No. 2 (1967), p. 57.

[49] V. Doroshenko, "Vasyl' Stefanyk," *Zhyttya i znannya*, X, No. 1 (1937), p. 2. For historical background to the Act of Unification see S. Vytvytsky and S. Baran, "The Period of the Directory," in Kubijovych, *Ukraine: a Concise Encyclopaedia*, pp. 754-81.

[50] Letter to I. Lyzanivs'ky, Rusiv, October 9, 1923, in Stefanyk, *Tvory* (1964), p. 464 serves as a good example.

[51] Marko Cheremshyna, Les' Martovych, and Stefanyk are often referred to as the Pokuttya Group of Writers (*Pokuts'ka Hrupa*) since they all were contemporaries from the region of Pokuttya in Western Ukraine and all three wrote "peasant" stories. Cheremshyna and Stefanyk dealt with similar themes though Cheremshyna's narrative method was much more lyrical and stylized often à *la* folk laments. Although the two had met in gymnasium they did not become friends until Cheremshyna established his practice in Snyatyn in 1912.

[52] Marko Cheremshyna, a letter to Andriy Muzychka, Snyatyn, January 22, 1926, in M. Cheremshyna, *Tvory* (Kiev, 1960), p. 401.

[53] Hamorak, "Vasyl' Stefanyk–Sproba biohrafiyi," p. xxxvi.

[54] Letter to the editors of *Svit*, Rusiv, March 7, 1927, Stefanyk, *Tvory* (1964), p. 474.

[55] Hamorak, "Vasyl' Stefanyk–Sproba biohrafiyi," p. xxxvii.

[56] Kobzey, *Velykyy riz'bar ukrayins'kykh selyans'kykh dush*, p. 76.

[57] Since there often is a discrepancy even in the presentation of the novellas in the various editions, and since it is virtually impossible to check the various printings with the original drafts, in this study the novellas are quoted as they appear in the 1949-54 edition. To get some idea about the various discrepancies among editions of Stefanyk's works, especially in regard to orthography, see O. O. Bilyavs'ka, "Pryntsypy naukovoho vydannya tvoriv V. Stefanyka," *Pytannya tekstolohiyi* (Kiev, 1968), No. I, pp. 243-301.

CHAPTER II

CRITICAL APPROACHES TO STEFANYK

It is the fortune, or perhaps misfortune, of writers who wrote sparingly, that the study and criticism of their works by far exceeds in quantity the works themselves. This is also true of Stefanyk. From 1899, when a small review appeared in the newspaper *Dilo*, to the present, Stefanyk has been studied, interpreted, discussed and criticized. And yet, as I. Myronets' pointed out in 1929, L. Hranychka[1] repeated in 1937, and B. Kravtsiv reasserted in 1969,[2] there is yet to be produced a good critical appraisal of Stefanyk's work. In a short review of the 1929 edition of Stefanyk's novellas, I. Myronets' gave an accurate, even if general, account of critical literature on Stefanyk to date. He asserted that:

> With few exceptions, speaking generally, this critical literature suffers from a simplified understanding of Stefanyk's works. For the most part, critics try to find in these works a direct and true reflection of concrete reality, of the concrete peasant of Galicia at the end of the 19th and the beginning of the 20th century.[3]

Hranychka, on the other hand, amplified his assertion by discussing individually the major critical works on Stefanyk up to that time. From this discussion it becomes evident that there are basically four approaches to the appraisal of Stefanyk. Writing a decade before Hranychka, Ivchenko had already discerned three of these:

> Some saw in him [Stefanyk] the bard of the wretched dark village, where social-economic problems in sharp conflicts were of first importance. Others, denying this, said that generally human problems pertaining to all strata of humanity, to all eras were treated in Stefanyk's works. Still others saw in him a great accomplished master of style who

managed to combine in his achievements national
peculiarities with the best European models.[4]

To these three, socio-economic, universal, and formalistic,
Hranychka added a fourth, the nationalistic. In the thirty years
that have elapsed since Hranychka's article, perhaps one more
approach can be added—the totally biographical—although
critics stressing the other elements also rely, sometimes quite
heavily, on biography and autobiography to support their
contentions.

A study of any great writer will undoubtedly lead to many
different interpretations and evaluations. The difficulty arises
when critics, in their zeal, insist on the infallibility and
omniscience of their interpretation and, to prove their point,
sometimes go as far as to omit or pervert that which does not fit
or contradicts their theory. It is hoped that the following
analysis of Stefanyk's work will help in discerning the more
salient features of the various critical studies to be discussed in
this chapter and thus lead to a better understanding of Stefanyk
and a truer picture of his works.

By far the most damaging to Stefanyk is the socio-economic "school" of criticism. Dealing as they do with the tragic in
life, Stefanyk's works were readily susceptible to the accusation
of pessimism. Thus, B. Lepky considers Stefanyk a black
pessimist and suggests that *The Blue Book* may be quite freely
called *The Black Book*, "for the pictures [portrayed in it] are so
morose and black."[5] These accusations were in themselves quite
harmless and based on the obvious first impressions from
reading Stefanyk's works. Unfortunately, the critics did not
limit themselves merely to calling Stefanyk a pessimist. They
began to look "deeper," trying to find why he was such a
pessimist, and it is here that they made the first false step. Only
a year later, S. Rusova in her survey of "The Old and New in
Contemporary Ukrainian Literature," labelled Stefanyk "the
poet of the horrible contemporary economic position of the
people of Galicia [Western Ukraine]."[6]

Although, in the same article, Franko immediately pointed
out the error in Rusova's views (see below), other critics
continued to elaborate this thesis to the present day. Although
Antin Krushel'nyts'ky does not go as far as Rusova in his short
study of Stefanyk, he does see the blackness of Stefanyk's
portrayals as a reflection of the "deep sadness of the Ukrainian
peasant, chained to the field for ages . . ."[7] Moreover, he is one
of the first pre-Revolutionary critics to find the depiction of
"class consciousness" on Stefanyk's work. In his discussion of
"Paliy" (The Arsonist) he sees as one of the chief motives the

conflict between the poor and landless peasant majority and the rich landed minority.[8] By saying that Stefanyk's works mirror the deep sadness of the Ukrainian peasant, Krushel'nyts'ky did not state but certainly implied that only a reader who himself is Ukrainian or knows the Ukrainian peasant very well can fully understand and appreciate Stefanyk. If this may be reading too much into Krushel'nyts'ky's statement, it definitely is the view of some critics who saw in Stefanyk a writer deeply concerned with the fate of the Ukrainian peasant. One such, S. Avdiyenko, goes so far as to state that "In order to fully understand the works of Stefanyk one must himself be a peasant and understand and feel the peasant misfortune . . ."[9]

Avdiyenko's title itself reveals a further development along the same lines. For him Stefanyk is the "Singer of a Better Peasant Fate," (*Spivets' krashchoyi selyans'koyi doli*). Nor was Avdiyenko the only one to use such an appellation. As I. Myronets' pointed out:

> The epithet—'The Singer of the Poor Galician Peas-
> antry'—generally accepted among the critics of Ste-
> fanyk's works is in essence a characteristic feature
> which pertains only to the live material on which our
> writer bases his portrayals. To see in this epithet
> anything more than that, to understand it as the basic
> core of Stefanyk's entire creativity is naive realism.
> And yet the majority of articles about Stefanyk
> suffer from precisely this naive realism.[10]

The idea, moreover, that Stefanyk was not only portraying the misfortunes of the peasants in Western Ukraine, but also trying in some way to remedy their plight is not an original one for Avdiyenko. As Hranychka points out in his article, it was probably V. Boyko who, as early as 1919 in an introduction to Stefanyk's stories, erroneously stated the myth that Stefanyk "became a doctor in the village,"[11] thus not only helping the people with his writing, but also physically administering to their ills.

The "class consciousness" line begun by Krushel'nyts'ky was taken up again by V. Doroshenko, who claimed that Stefanyk was the poet of the poor peasantry "between two classes."[12] This appealing formulation was seized upon by Stefanyk's first Soviet critic V. Koryak, who in his introduction to Stefanyk's works (titled "Between two Classes") amplified Doroshenko's views:

> Vasyl' Stefanyk masterfully paints this period of
> transition [from one class to another], this painful

process of the destruction of the patriarchal peasant "standard of living," the class struggle in the village, and the separation of the village proletariat and the pre-proletariat of the city.[13]

Although Koryak's view is neither profound nor, as Hranychka points out,[14] original, it has been repeated and expanded by one Soviet critic after another. S. Kryzhanivs'ky, the second major Soviet Stefanyk scholar, began post-War criticism by claiming that in Stefanyk's works one sees "a true writer of the people, a singer of the grief and poverty of the peasantry of Galicia."[15] Moreover, he continues:

No matter how much Stefanyk loved the artistic principle which forces one to portray actions not from one's own point of view, but through the eyes of the heroes, his objectivism always changed into sympathy for the downtrodden and the impoverished and into hate for the exploiters.[16]

The apparent contradiction in the above statement did not seem to bother Kryzhanivs'ky very much, for it seems that even objectivism in Soviet terms is not free of subjectivism. Though such discrepancies exist in many of the Soviet studies of Stefanyk, they are not as painful to read as those in which critics twist and bend Stefanyk to fit their official view of ideological orthodoxy. Though they are discussing his artistic works, they do not hesitate to use bits of biography, letters, and even publicistic writings to support their contentions. Y. M. Kurylenko admits as much when he writes:

In the light of such political views expressed by the author in publicistic articles, sketches, and letters, his [Stefanyk's] artistic practice becomes even clearer. All the artistic works of Stefanyk are filled with love for the people and hatred for the ruling classes.[17]

The most recent spokesman of the official view of Stefanyk is V. Lesyn who continues in the socio-economic tradition. In explaining the "dark pessimistic" outlook found in Stefanyk's works, Lesyn points to the "tragic life" of the masses at large in the "conditions created by the exploiting feudal-bourgeois society, the horribly oppressive regimes of the Kaiser and the Tsar, and the barbaric private ownership traditions and customs sanctioned by the Church."[18] Having given these broad reasons for Stefanyk's "pessimism," Lesyn, in another work, maintains that most of the personal tragedies described by Stefanyk were caused by social conditions:

... Stefanyk described the spiritual drama of the pauper, who was chased out of the village by 'economic conditions' and who was forced by these conditions to cross over the threshold of proletarization despite his will to the contrary. And the family and other misfortunes which, in the main, were also caused by social conditions, only assisted in this. And one cannot envision the sufferings of Antin neither in the soul of the *kulak* Kurochka ('Paliy' [The Arsonist]), nor in the soul of the lord of the manor ('May' [May]), nor in the soul of the civil servants ('Takyy panok' [A Petty Squire]). This is a tragedy peculiar to the poor and deeply social.[19]

Although Lesyn is referring only to Antin from "The Blue Book," he is making a general statement about all of Stefanyk's personal tragedies. It is indeed hard to imagine why the same drama cannot be experienced by Kurochka, the lord of the manor, or for that matter anyone at all, provided that they also lost everything they owned and were forced to part with their way of life, not because of some social conditions, but because of a personal ineptitude, bad luck, susceptibility to drink. It is this very fact which makes Antin's experience tragic. One need but recall that in the first sentence Stefanyk describes his character as a man "who always was somehow unlucky."[20] As will be shown in the following chapters, the same type of personal inability to control or better one's fate is at the core of many of Stefanyk's tragedies. Indeed, such is the fate of man in general and hence Stefanyk's ability to portray a universal through the description of particulars. Social and economic conditions have nothing to do with this and serve, at best, as more or less distant backgrounds for his novellas.

Actually, the secondary role that social and economic conditions play in the novellas of Stefanyk was pointed out as early as 1929, but this information has been consistently ignored by the proponents of the socio-economic approach to his works. It was I. Myronets' who maintained that although Stefanyk uses as material the West Ukrainian village, together with the poverty-stricken Galician peasant," ... both the former and the latter only delineate certain separate components of his style ..."[21] A few years later (1931), M. Kozoris wrote an article on the social moments in the works of Stefanyk and stated that:

Looking at all of the works of Stefanyk from the viewpoint of their social orientation, one can divide them roughly into three groups: in the first group must be considered such works in which the social moments are not noted at all or are noted very weakly, and in which the psychological moments prevail. (. . . about 15 works) . . . The second group, the largest, consists of those works which have only a general social background, emphasized sometimes more and sometimes less, and at whose base lie in general the miseries of the Galician village without any clear class distinctions . . . And finally the third, the smallest group, consists of those works, in which the author presents, on top of the general social background, clear lines of class struggles ('The Arsonist,' 'Sud' [The Judgement]. 'Zasidannye' [A Meeting], 'Lan' [Potato Field]. [Only four!])[22]

One can even question how much class differentiation really exists in the four novellas mentioned. It is true that in "The Arsonist" the protagonists belong to two different economic classes, but certainly one must realize that the point of the novella is not to show the struggle between Fedir and Kurochka as representatives of their classes, but as the title itself implies, to show the consuming and destructive arsonist fever of Fedir, a man who by fanning this fever, first of all, was nursing his injured pride. In "The Judgement" one does see the poor as a group attacking the rich as a group, but again the main emphasis is not on showing two groups, two classes struggling with each other, but rather (here too the title provides the key) on the macabre judgement of the poor by the poor, the guilty few by the innocent mob, avenging their jealousy of the former's guilt. In "A Meeting" also, though there is more of a study of two classes, here more than in any of the others, it is not a split on social terms but a conflict of generations between the village bailiff and the young Petro Antoniv. As for "Potato Field," a little vignette not quite a page long which describes the shocking death of an infant while its mother sleeps, tired out from working in the potato field—how this illustrates Stefanyk's concern with class struggle is quite difficult to explain. The same thought must have occurred also to Kozoris for, toward the end of his article, he admits that "the literary works of Stefanyk beside their high formal artistry, are distinguished by very few clear proletarian moments."[23]

The whole socio-economic approach to the works of Stefanyk is at best a superficial appraisal and at its worst a tendentious misreading of his works to suit the political tastes of certain critics. As this line of criticism developed, it presented Stefanyk first as a pessimist, then as a peasant sympathiser, peasant lover, and finally as a conscious delineator, and, therefore, an instigator of peasant struggles against the oppressive socio-economic conditions. Although this approach to Stefanyk was attacked by those who emphasized his formal and artistic achievements, as well as by those who saw in his works dramatic tragedies of the human soul on a universal scale, it was most vehemently attacked by another group of critics who in many ways were as tendentious and as guilty of misrepresentation as those whom they attacked. This group may be referred to as nationalistic, and embraces those critics who stressed the national moments in Stefanyk's works.

Their main objection to the socio-economic line of criticism was that it did not stress the fact that Stefanyk was not just writing about any peasants, but about *Ukrainian* peasants. As the socio-economists were primarily concerned with Stefanyk's early work where they found most of his "class conscious" novellas, so the nationalists turned their attention primarily to the second post-war period of Stefanyk's work, where they saw the author consciously presenting not only the economic struggle of the Ukrainian peasant but his national struggle and his burning desire for his own land, conceived in broader terms than his own plot of soil.

Dmytro Dontsov, the most influential and popular ideologist of the Organization of Ukrainian Nationalists (OUN), wrote about Stefanyk as the "poet of the hard soul."[24] In his article, Dontsov points out all those places in Stefanyk where the peasants are tough, hard and unbending. Emphasizing the scorn with which peasants in "Zlodiy" (The Thief) refer to the weak Maksym, Dontsov sees as the real heroes of Stefanyk's works those other two peasants, Mykhaylo and Georgiy, who do not hesitate to kill the thief; the peasant from "Mezha" (The Boundary) who even before God is not sorry for having killed to protect his land; and others who exhibit this firm determination to stand up for what they believe to be right. Dontsov bases his eloquent, but not always convincing, arguments on the fact that Stefanyk, himself of peasant stock, knew the primordial law of the land which demands hard work and unwavering love and loyalty. Stefanyk's peasant, according to Dontsov, served the "god of Must," and Stefanyk, by writing about this peasant, cultivated the notion of the hard soul which knows what it must do, sacrifices aside, to attain its end. Carried away by his own ideology, Dontsov sees Stefanyk as the proclaimer of a "new race"[25] and claims that "The Boundary" contains the essence of Stefanyk's ideology:

In the last work ["The Boundary"] of the poet are

collected, condensed into one, as never before, both his symbolism and his basic idea. There is both the woman who weeps—the symbol of the transient, corporal, which endeavors to stifle the voice of his [Stefanyk's] truth—and God, who punishes for a self-willed measure of justice—the symbol of the abstract truth, also hostile to his [Stefanyk's] truth—the earth. Appearing elsewhere separately, here they are joined in one thus strengthening the effect of the work . . . Finally, here in the arguments with the wife and God are united the personal and the collective 'sin.' A knife to the one who covets his land, bullets and cannons to those who come to take away the land from him and others. The hero of the story is the very same hero as in "Doroha" [The Road], only he has gone into the offensive and his affair is now everyone's affair. His land is already a different land! The 'Land' [Earth] of Stefanyk is no longer 'village,' nor 'potato field' nor 'hill,' it is a great symbol . . . It is no longer a piece of land but the universe worthy of great sacrifice and dedication; it is that land for which '(once) brave Rusychi died on the banks of the swift Kayala' . . .[26]

The final reference to *Slovo o polku Ihorevi* (The Tale of Ihor's Campaign), a 12th century epic of Kievan Rus' is not a haphazard slip of Dontsov's eloquence but part of the nationalists' subjective reinterpretation of literature stressing the long tradition of Ukrainian heroism. Dontsov would have his readers believe that Stefanyk is a direct descendant and a continuator of this tradition. These ideas served well to emphasize the struggle of the Ukrainian nationalists for control of Ukraine, but they certainly did not truly reflect either Stefanyk's peasants or Stefanyk's own political, not to mention artistic, views.

Although it is quite true that some of Stefanyk's peasants exhibit this stubborn determination, it is in no way presented as an ideologically laudable characteristic, as Dontsov implies. Although some of Stefanyk's post war works, notably "Mariya," are permeated with a deep national pathos, these are not the best by far nor the most characteristic of Stefanyk's post-war work. Yet Dontsov's highly subjective interpretation of Stefanyk did have some followers. O. Hrytsay wrote that Stefanyk's man "becomes the grandiose expression of the people and the international law of the right to one's land."[27] L. Hranychka, who supported Dontsov's views and criticized all those which came from the socio-economic (and Soviet) group, maintained in his own appraisal of Stefanyk that the *"idea of 'the land,' the idea of 'Ukraine'—are in Stefanyk the basic philosophy of all his literary personages."*[28]

Since the socio-economic view of Stefanyk was embraced by the Soviet scholars and critics of Stefanyk, the nationalist view became almost the official view of all scholars of Stefanyk outside of Soviet Ukraine. It has survived to the present day and one can notice its influence in the most recent non-Soviet work on Stefanyk, Toma Kobzey's *Velykyy riz'bar ukrayins'kykh selyans'kykh dush.*[29] Even the title to this work is already indicative of Kobzey's stand. Whereas any Soviet Ukrainian work on Stefanyk would or could contain the appellation *"riz'bar selyans'kykh dush"* (a sculptor of peasant souls), Kobzey inserts the adjective *"ukrayins'kykh"* to make sure that the point is not missed that these peasants are Ukrainian. On the whole, Kobzey tries to portray Stefanyk as a fighter for peasant rights, but with a nationalist conscience. The Soviet scholars do the same, but emphasize his proletarian conscience. Thus they concentrate on the first half of Stefanyk's work and Kobzey stresses the second post-war period. Both quote sources to support their contentions, primarily letters and other non-artistic material. Some letters and facts appear in Kobzey that never appear in Soviet studies and vice-versa.[30]

Although most studies of Stefanyk rely to some degree on his biography, there are two works which are devoted almost exclusively to this aspect of Stefanyk. The first to appear was an introduction to the first edition of Stefanyk's works among the Ukrainian émigrés after the Second World War.[31] Written by Stefanyk's youngest son and the editor of the edition, Yuriy Hamorak, the forty-odd-page "Attempt at a Biography" approaches the subject of the author's life primarily through his artistic works. As Yu. Hamorak maintains, "The best biography of Stefanyk is his work."[32] Under the term work, Hamorak understands not only the novellas but also Stefanyk's correspondence, and his autobiography, as well as those novellas which he, Hamorak, designates as autobiographical.[33]

This is an interesting biography in that it sincerely tries to pick out only those biographical facts which have some sort of relevance to Stefanyk's creative work; it is invaluable in that it gives accounts of Stefanyk's later life and his relations with the Soviet Ukraine, information which is never presented without bias in Soviet studies.

The other major biographical work is the Soviet version written by Vasyl' Kostashchuk under the title *Volodar dum selyans'kykh* (The Sovereign of Peasant Thoughts, L'viv, 1959).

42

It is a detailed, at times too detailed, account of Stefanyk's life beginning with a genealogy of his family and ending with his death, and unquestionably a useful work for all interested in Stefanyk but one which should be supplemented by some facts which do not and cannot appear in a Soviet edition.

Both the socio-economists and the nationalists have a tendency to view Stefanyk as a writer who continues the traditions of nineteenth-century populist-realism. Both play down the influence of modernism by relegating it to the most obvious examples in the early poems in prose and in the two autobiographical novellas "My Word" and "The Road." Although it would be erroneous to maintain that Stefanyk was a modernist in the sense of some of his Polish colleagues like Przybyszewski, Stefanyk's associations with members of "Young Poland" and his knowledge of current literature left an indelible mark on him and his works.

A separate study could be undertaken which could show that much of what makes Stefanyk different and new in Ukrainian literature can be attributed to the influences of modernism.[34] These influences are apparent in his concise lyrical prose, in the merging of content and form, in the predilection for the omissions of descriptions and explanations, in the notes of pessimism, as well as in the interest for the psychological peripeteiae of the soul. Even the preponderance of death in the novellas can be seen as an affinity with such modernists as Maeterlinck whom Stefanyk greatly admired.[35] Moreover it would not be unreasonable to suggest that the peasant's distrust of the city was intensified in the young Stefanyk not only by his life in Cracow but also by the reading of modernist authors who envisioned the city as a huge destructive monster. Finally, the refusal to merge his art with a desire to serve social reform is something which distinguishes Stefanyk from his predecessors, the populist-realists, and draws him into the ranks of modernists, some of whom also gave up the pen when they felt that their services were needed more in social and political work (for example: Ostap Luts'ky, the organizer of the West Ukrainian modernists, *molodomuztsi*, also stopped writing when he became involved with politics).[36]

Unfortunately, as B. Rubchak points out,[37] there is yet to be written a serious study about the influences of modernism on Stefanyk, Cheremshyna, Ukrayinka, Kotsyubyns'ky and other writers who span the period of transition in Ukrainian literature between realism and modernism. It is curious, however, that despite Stefanyk's stay in Cracow and his friendship with members of "The Young Poland" group of modernists his philosophical outlook was affected by Polish modernism only superficially. One need but to read the penetrating analysis by Wyka of the *Weltanschaung* of the Polish modernists[38] to realize that Stefanyk's basic wholesomeness of a Ukrainian peasant was indeed very slightly, if at all, influenced by the predominantly urban "decadence" of the Polish modernists. (This explains, for example, Stefanyk's disapproval of the life led by his friend Przybyszewski.[39]) The influence of modernism on Stefanyk is not therefore so much an influence on his philosophy of life as it is on his artistic method. In this respect the influence of modernism on Stefanyk has been noticed, since there are at least some references to Stefanyk's artistic achievements and therefore indirectly to the influence of modernism on his work.

Since one cannot help but notice Stefanyk's extremely short form of narration and his use of the dialect, most critics of Stefanyk have devoted some part of their analysis to Stefanyk's formal or artistic achievements. Therefore the third approach to Stefanyk's works is not so much a separate school of criticism as it is a parallel one. Save for a few articles and a dissertation on Stefanyk's language, as well as a few articles devoted to a structural analysis of his work, in most critical works the formalistic elements of Stefanyk's novellas are given superficial descriptive treatment. Some of the more salient points of the various presentations of Stefanyk's technique will be presented in Chapters III and IV. Of interest here are the moments when critics have tried to explain the unique quality of Stefanyk's art by comparing him with other writers.

Some of these comparisons were of such a personal nature that they have never been repeated by others and have remained sometimes clever and sometimes incomprehensible insights of a given critic. Other comparisons have been persistently repeated, supported by some critics and denied by others. Still others were contrastive and served, not to point out resemblances between Stefanyk and another author, but to delineate and separate from other authors unique features in Stefanyk. Such is the well-quoted statement of Marko Cheremshyna in which he contrasts almost aphoristically several of the major writers of Ukrainian short prose:

> Marko Vovchok was a story teller, Franko was an observer-researcher, Martovych—a satirist-photographer . . . Kotsyubyns'ky—a painter, and Stefanyk is a poet of peasant anguish.[40]

Cheremshyna's formulation is indeed an excellent one and captures the formal differences between the writers he mentioned and Stefanyk. If one were to add the word "dramatic" and thus make Cheremshyna's statement read "and Stefanyk is a *dramatic* poet of peasant anguish" one would then have a one-line analysis of the laconic, highly emotional, short dialogue style of Stefanyk's prose, which differs greatly from the simple stories of Vovchok, from the studies and researched observations of the realist Franko, from the photographic cartoons of Martovych, and from the lyrical impressions of Kotsyubyns'ky.

Not many critics of Stefanyk have been as successful in their comparison of Stefanyk with another author as Cheremshyna. Thus, for example, B. Lepky saw a similarity between Stefanyk and Gorky in that both authors "paint life with great verity" and that both use speech "as the universal means by which they speak, carve, paint and play."[41] With all due respect to B. Lepky, this very statement can be made equally about almost any two authors and therefore is of minimal, if any, value.

Similarly one reviewer maintained that Stefanyk is both "similar to and different from Chekhov in "Muzhiki" [The Peasants]: Chekhov has control over himself, Stefanyk holds himself back; Chekhov rules over his subject, Stefanyk is all in its power."[42] How this reviewer reconciles his statement with the dispassionate tone of Stefanyk's tragedies, with the fact that Stefanyk never allows himself to be drawn into the emotional dramas of his novellas, what finally he means by the fact that Stefanyk is all "in the power" of his subject—all this is quite difficult to understand.

A good example of a comparison at one and the same time clever and incomprehensible is the likening of Stefanyk to Peter Altenberg. Today one would not even know of this were it not for the fact that the comparison greatly angered Gorky who spoke of this to Mykhaylo Kotsyubyns'ky with whom he spent some time on Capri. Kotsyubyns'ky, in a letter to Stefanyk, wrote:

> We, Gorky and I, often talk about you here, for he [Gorky] is a great admirer of yours. He was angered by the fact that in some article you were compared to P. Altenberg.[43]

Were it not for this letter this comparison would be unknown, for no one knows who made the comparison and in which article. The inscrutability of this comparison may explain why no work on Stefanyk has ever made a further study of this. Altenberg (1859-1919), a writer who is all but forgotten now, was known in his day for short sketches in which he tried to capture momentary impressions of the world around him. In an afterword to one of his collections, Alfred Polgar writes:

Altenbergs schönste Skizzen, die, in denen er nicht
von seinem transportablen Berg Sinai herab predigt,
sind in einer wundervoll graziösen Ausspartechnik
verfasst: das Nichtniedergeschriebene ist ihr eigent-
lichster, von dem Geschriebenen nur herausschattier-
ter Inhalt. In den Zeilen ist Ruhe, zwischen ihnen
tobt das Drama.[44]

Stefanyk often achieved his drama also by not stating everything, by creating a tension between "overt" and "implicit"
reality. It therefore becomes clear that, at least in the matter of
Ausspartechnik (Omission Technique), there is some similarity
between Stefanyk and Altenberg.[45] It is hoped that when the
unknown critic compared the two authors he had in mind this
technique and the brevity of the narrative form (Altenberg even
surpassed Stefanyk in this; some of his sketches are no longer
than a paragraph), for here the similarity ends. There is virtually
no similarity in content or in purpose. Whereas Altenberg wrote
mostly notes, first person observations of a perceptive and at
times cynical observer, on the hypocrisies of life, Stefanyk
himself remained silent and allowed his heroes to bare their
souls and reveal the anguish that lay within. Omitting some
similarity in technique and the brevity of form, the two authors
are as different as can be.

A similar "esoteric" comparison was more recently made
by the Soviet Ukrainian critic Ivan Dzyuba who indirectly
compared Stefanyk to Ernest Hemingway. In an interview
conducted by the Ukrainian paper *Nove zhyttya* (Preshov,
Czechoslovakia), Dzyuba maintained that among other things
he was working on a book on Stefanyk, who, in his opinion,
was "the greatest Ukrainian prose writer and one of the greatest
in world literature of the twentieth century. He [Stefanyk],"
Dzyuba continued:

is a predecessor of several phenomena of modern
prose. Unfortunately, in Ukrainian literature almost
no one went along the path opened by Stefanyk, and
now, after decades, we search under the influence of
Hemingway and others for that for which previously
Stefanyk should have been the stimulus.[46]

Although Dzyuba does not really compare Stefanyk to
Hemingway, he does draw an indirect parallel between the two
authors, suggesting that Stefanyk had preceded Hemingway in
that which Hemingway is credited with contributing to the
development of modern prose. Perhaps Dzyuba intended to
clarify this intriguing statement in his book on Stefanyk.

46

Unfortunately, he has not yet written the book and this suggestion could have led to various theories as to its significance were it not for the fact that a close friend of Dzyuba somewhat clarified what the latter meant. Ivan Kochur, in a personal letter to Miss Skorupsky of New York, wrote:

> Your question *a propos* Stefanyk and Hemingway. The author [Dzyuba] did not have in mind some sort of more accurate comparison of these two writers, and I don't think that he could cite any convincing parallels which would show the affinity between them; it is a question of only certain traits of the narrative manner, of a certain 'modernness' of literary technique! If one were to compare Stefanyk with any traditional classic of Ukrainian literature, as, for example, Nechuy-Levyts'ky or Myrny, then he [Stefanyk] will appear very 'European' and acqually quite modern. Therefore what is propagated in the article is the thought that young Ukrainian writers simultaneously with a fashion for such writers as Hemingway should also turn to Stefanyk, . . . who is worthy of being considered on a par with writers of world renown. That is all there is in this juxtaposition of these two names. The idea is undoubtedly useful, but quite removed from the precision of literary scholarship.[47]

Kochur's last comment is difficult to refute. The comparison of Stefanyk and Hemingway is indeed "far removed from the precision of literary scholarship." At best, this comparison, as well as the one with Altenberg, can serve to indicate that the critic perceived a general similarity between two authors. A closer examination reveals, however, that there are many more dissimilar elements than similar. Often such comparisons, sometimes nothing more than a confusing name-dropping by the critic, can be quite harmful for they tend to generalize and, by equating one author with another, lead to easy misconceptions.

Stefanyk seemed to have the misfortune of being constantly likened to other authors. Some of these comparisons, especially those in which Stefanyk is compared to some of his Ukrainian predecessors or even contemporaries, show how greatly his contribution to the development of Ukrainian literature was misunderstood. One of the most disturbing was made by Stefanyk's first publisher, Stepan Smal'-Stots'ky. In the introduction to the first edition of *The Blue Book*, Smal'-Stots'ky indicated that Stefanyk resembled the Bukovinian poet-writer Yuriy Fed'kovych (1834-1888) in "his ability to indicate, by a few words—strokes, the clear contours of an image, the education of a character, show their soul, and give the whole work a mood ..."[48] The same was echoed by a contemporary writer-friend of Stefanyk, Ol'ha Kobylyans'ka, who in a letter to Stefanyk predicted that he would "become the Galician Fed'kovych, if he did not abandon his pen ..."[49] It is indeed hard to understand the basis for this comparison, outside of some similarities in the fact that both authors used their native locale and elements of their own dialect in their writings. Lesya Ukrayinka, another contemporary writer (1871-1913), revealed a far superior critical perception when she maintained that, outside of outward methods, Stefanyk is quite different from Fed'kovych in both mood and perception. Furthermore, she maintained that, whereas Fed'kovych showed primarily the ethnographic side of the folk life in descriptive romantic plots, Stefanyk concentrated on the inner elements of this life.[50]

So far all these comparisons were made only to explain the nature of Stefanyk's creativity by comparing it with others which were more known. With the comparison of Stefanyk to Les' Martovych, his school friend, as well as to Marko Cheremshyna, another school friend, the comparisons grow into a search for influences. Thus S. Yefremov was the first to note that there existed a sort of school of Pokuttyan writers (all three, Stefanyk, Martovych, and Cheremshyna, come from the district of Pokuttya in Western Ukraine), with Stefanyk as the leading and most influential writer of the group.[51] Yefremov's notion of a school turned out to be a very superficial appraisal of the three authors in question and was soon denied, first by Mykola Zerov and then by H. Hrebenyuk. Zerov admitted that, though their literary paths were at first close,

> they soon separated into various directions, as is dictated to them by three mutually different perceptions of the world and artistic temperaments. Therefore, let us not call Stefanyk, Martovych, Cheremshyna a 'school,' for in the conception of a school there enters an idea of one primary artist and several of his artistic subvoices; but let us not be afraid of talking about a separate group of writers, for all three of the mentioned masters are tied by personal friendship, uniformity of origin and a given unity of ideological atmosphere spread throughout their works.[52]

Hrebenyuk went even farther than Zerov and showed in

his study of the three authors the basic artistic differences which separated the three friends. After showing that the difference between Stefanyk and Cheremshyna lies primarily in that the latter incorporates into his writings the rhythm and style of folk-laments,[53] and after showing that Martovych, by the very fact that he tends toward a more broad narrative method, belongs more to the novelists (*povistyariv*) and therefore is on a somewhat lower plane than the former two,[54] Hrebenyuk admitted that although their themes come from the same source, namely the village, there is no question of any school. He summarized the artistic peculiarities of the three by comparing and contrasting their manner of narration:

> [Stefanyk]—*dialogue, quiet-unconcerned story telling, tragedy, contrasts* . . . Cheremshyna—*quiet retelling of a historian* (chronicle), *immersion into aestheticism, technique of funeral laments and 'dumy'* [folk epic songs], *maintenance of rhythm*, for Martovych characteristic is *humor*, which sometimes turns into satire, and a *predilection toward the long tale* [povist'].[55]

Another comparison often made is one involving Stefanyk and Franko. This comparison was invited by Franko himself and was studied in detail by Nenadkevych in the article "Iz studiy nad stylem Frankovoyi i Stefanykovoyi novely" (From the Studies of Style of Franko's and Stefanyk's Novella). Some of Nenadkevych's findings are discussed below in Chapter III, and, as Franko predicted, reveal the great difference between the two authors. Nevertheless, it will be worthwhile to quote Nenadkevych more fully here. His conclusions not only show the difference between the artistic manner of Stefanyk and Franko but also show how Stefanyk differed from his immediate predecessors in Ukrainian literature, the realists. In point form, Nenadkevych summarizes the major differences:

I. Deliberations about the "organization of the soul" of the author of "The Peasant Commission" [Franko's *'Khlops'ka komisiya'*] in connection with the stylistic-compositional features of the novella, shall be the following:
    1. It is a characteristic of the author to be interested in the concrete, in the social forms and manners, in the human deeds, as such, in their social context and importance. It is characteristic for him to see the world through a 'prism of his own authoral feeling,'

or through the prism of a sole character chosen by the author; all the activities, social milieu, manners are described from this point of view. *It is characteristic for him to have a precise exposition, and a full novellistic composition*, the portrayal of details in the manners and the outer appearance of the heroes, etc.

2. In connection with this a greater value is placed on every person (separate hero), as a member of a social collective than as a separate individual.

3. Clarity and simplicity in the understanding of the psychological mechanism, a certain simplification of the psychology of the heroes, a certain straight-lined portrayal and treatment of psychological experiences. The complexity and contradictory nature of the psyche, the incomprehensibility of its subconscious processes, are not taken into account. From this, it follows, that *contrast* (between the characters of the heroes, situations, scenes) appears as the most characteristic method of composition.

4. In connection with the preceding, there is a greater schematism in the division of heroes into groups in relation to a moral evaluation of them. The moral evaluation is clearly stated and merges with the social evaluation. Hence the basic *social motivation for the denouement.*

5. . . .

II. Completely different is the "organization of the soul," perception of the world, in the author of "The Thief," as it appears in the stylistic-compositional features of the work.

1. An interest for the inner feelings, for psychology *per se*, in all its complexity, contradiction, and entanglement; the author's attention is captured not by the simple and clear in human experiences but by the dark and elemental, the "voice of the forefathers" in the consciousness of the contemporary person.

2. Not the actions themselves are at the center

of attention but the psychological processes that lead to these actions. With this deeper approach to the psychology of motivation, the action looses the characteristics of a straight-lined clear action. The moral evaluation is no longer easy and the assigning of social meaning to the behavior becomes more difficult. Hence—the total absence of any moral evaluations, the absence of the *motivation for the denouement* (moral or social).

3. The last point is connected with the fact that social interrelations, social preconditioning of human behavior falls into the background: the human being interests the author first of all not as a member of a collective unit but as an individual personality with fine shades of experiences, with capricious turns in the behaviour line, with secret blind forces that murmur someplace on the bottom of consciousness and in the abysses of the subconscious.

4. There is a lessened interest in outer conditions, in manners; it appears inasmuch as these elements of the artistically recreated world are reflected in the psyche of every hero, how they are comprehended by his consciousness, and how much they help to illuminate his experiences . . .

5. The author's dominant interest in psychology, in the complex and interesting experience, has its characteristic counterpart in the stylistic-compositional features of the novella. First of all is its [the novella's] compression, shortness, fragmentariness, "without a beginning and without an end." Not a complete and refinished story, not an integral picture of life that has its definite place in the life of the society, but a fragment, a moment snatched from life, interesting and valuable from the psychological point of view, for the presentation of a psychological experiment independent from its social meaning. In order to show the delicate complexity and entanglement of psychological experiences the artistic devices are finer. Having rid itself of the moral-social teleology, the psychological novella does not

require contrast as a compositional method
.... Instead its natural property is the technique of *gradation* (between heroes, among
the various moods of a hero, in the development, complication, and in the entanglement
of psychological experiences; among the situations, scenes, and ... [?]) It [this technique
of gradation] organically grows in the soil of
atomistic differentiation in the psychological
analysis which is the very essence of Stefanyk's novella.[56]

This rather long quotation is justified not only by the fact,
as stated above, that it shows how Stefanyk differed from his
immediate predecessors, the Ukrainian realists, but also by the
fact that it can serve as a good point of departure for the
discussion of such writers as Gleb Uspensky and Władyslaw
Orkan.

Stefanyk himself is guilty for having some critics claim
that Uspensky (1843-1902) had a profound influence on him as
a writer. As early as 1896 in a letter to his friend Moraczewski,
Stefanyk wrote, "During vacations I have left in Storozhyntsi
[my copy of] Uspensky. I'd like to have it for I derive great joy
from it; please send this book to me somehow."[57] Later in his
autobiography he wrote the following:

In the fourth grade, jointly we bought two huge
volumes of the writings of Gleb Uspensky in Russian
.... for two years I did not part with them and, even
though it was very hard at first to understand the
jargon of his "Rasteryaevaya Street" [Stefanyk is
referring to the series of sketches united under the
title "Nravy rasteryaevoy ulitsy"], I read it all and he
had the greatest influence on me in the gymnasium.[58]

Critics, and especially Soviet Stefanyk scholars, have seized
upon these statements and in almost every work the "great
influence" of Uspensky on Stefanyk is noted.[59] Yet if one were
to use the Nenadkevych analysis of the two styles, Uspensky
would fit into the first and Stefanyk into the second. One
wonders how Cheremshyna could maintain that "Uspensky had
the greatest influence on his creativity,"[60] or how Kryzhaniv-
sky can talk of sketches in "the spirit of Gleb Uspensky."[61]
The fact that Uspensky appealed to Stefanyk in gymnasium is
certainly not enough to claim that he had a great influence on
Stefanyk's creative efforts.[62] Nonetheless Ya. Yarema who had

made a study of both writers insists that

> The indisputable merit of Uspensky lies in the fact
> that Stefanyk, despite certain doubts, became a peas-
> ant writer [!!!] and a realist. In the works of Uspen-
> sky, Stefanyk came across for the first time an author
> who, in portraying the manners and mores of the
> village, did not idealize it and did not adorn, did not
> fall into the traditional sentimentality so character-
> istic of many of his contemporary populist writers.[63]

Yarema, in reading Stefanyk, seemed to have missed only
one minor point, and that is that nowhere is Stefanyk interested
in portraying the manners and mores of the village, idealized or
not; nor, for that matter, was he really interested in portraying
peasants in any particular way other than as people who, as all
people in the process of life, undergo various tragedies which
reverberate in their psyche. Stefanyk was interested in these
reverberations and not in becoming a peasant writer.

A more perceptive critic, M. Rudnyts'ky, also, however,
seemed to feel that Stefanyk owed something to the influence
of Uspensky:

> . . . Uspensky has a brutal, almost biological force,
> which differs from the force of our [Ukrainian] writ-
> ers of manners in the same way that the pain of a
> wronged person differs from the clenched fist of a
> rebellious pariah. After the talks of the Cracow
> modernists about the "freedom of the artist," per-
> haps Stefanyk would never had dared to use all those
> "strong" words which for such a long time struck us
> in his stories . . . had he not known Uspensky.[64]

One can only agree with Hranychka, who in answer to this
statement wondered why Stefanyk had to rely on Uspensky for
his strong words when he heard these same strong words from
such an influential source as his own father.[65] Rudnyts'ky,
however, was cautious enough to qualify his statement with a
"perhaps" and to follow it immediately with praise of Stefanyk
for *not* "following Uspensky in the expanded narrative and in
the expanded dialogues, which are so characteristic for peasant
literature . . ."[66] By the same token, Rudnyts'ky's second statement can be used also as an argument against Yarema's contention that Stefanyk learned to be a "peasant writer" under the
influence of Uspensky. Stefanyk's peasants don't even talk like
most peasants do in literature and, for that matter, in real life;
they, unlike Uspensky's characters, are stingy with words. What
they have to say comes from within and that is not always

easily put into words.

Even if one were to note some similarities between Stefanyk and Uspensky, the husband's role in "Leseva familiya" (Les' Family) is similar to the episode in "Rasteryaevaya Street" where a man steals from his wife and takes it all to the tavern for drink, then hides from her[67] – even if such similarities exist, it is hard to justify the statement that Uspensky influenced Stefanyk. If he did then he did so no more than Franko, for an examination will reveal that there are also episodes common to Franko and Stefanyk. The already noted similarity between the "Peasant Commission" and "The Thief" is a case in point. Yet the differences in narrative method and the "organization of the soul," to use Nenadkevych's term, are so great that they preclude any discussion of any meaningful influences of Franko upon Stefanyk. Since the same differences exist between Stefanyk and Uspensky, any influence of the latter upon Stefanyk is hardly justifiable if any criterion of literary scholarship is to be maintained.

Similarly, it is hard to justify seeing any influence from the Polish writer Władysław Orkan (Franciszek Smreczyński, 1875-1930) on Stefanyk. Such uncritical statements as Yarema's that "probably under the influence of direct relations with Orkan, he [Stefanyk] was captivated by the idea of trying his strength also in other genres [i.e., drama] . . ."[68] remain nothing more than conjectures. More to the point is H. Verves, who points out that although certain similarities exist between the two writers especially in that both rely on dialogue and monologue as the method of narration and curiously have similar titles for their novellas,[69] they differ primarily in author involvement:

> Unlike Stefanyk, who does not interfere with the course of events, does not moralize, does not add his own statements and comments, but leaves the right to draw conclusions with his readers, Orkan, in the novella "So It Was Fated" [*Tak sudylos'*] and in other works of the first collection, actively interferes in the tone of the narration, makes remarks and throws in his own statements of a didactic character, brings in special episodes in order to move the reader.[70]

What Verves fails to mention is that this difference is a basic one, one which differentiates Stefanyk not only from Orkan but from almost all other writers with whom he has been compared. Where sometimes themes may be similar, the manner of presentation is always quite different. In respect to Orkan,

54

one can talk more in terms of mutual writer-friends who undoubtedly had some influence on each other but in no case more than the mutual influences of Stefanyk and his other writer-friends, Martovych and Cheremshyna.

Having examined most of the contended influences on Stefanyk and comparisons of Stefanyk with other writers, one cannot help but agree with Hranychka who maintains that none of these can be supported[71] or, for that matter, with Bohdan Lepky's rather emotional emphasis on Stefanyk's originality:

> Neither Turgenev's "Sportsman's Sketches," nor Chekhov's "The Peasants," nor even the stories of peasant life by the genial short story writer Guy de Maupassant can be compared with "Kamyanny Khrest" [The Stone Cross] or with "Klenovi lystky" [The Maple Leaves]. Stefanyk's stories are something quite separate, dependent on no one or anything; these are works in a full understanding of this great word .... As an artist of prose, Stefanyk is for me the artist above all artists, the absolute artist.[72]

What has been evident in all these juxtapositions of Stefanyk with another author is that, though such comparisons serve sometimes to illuminate a facet of Stefanyk's creativity, and therefore are helpful, they are by no means always supportable and are not necessarily limited only to authors Stefanyk knew or admitted to admiring. Sometimes the comparisons are made solely on the grounds that Stefanyk reminds a critic of an author with whose works the critic is familiar. Such comparisons as that between Stefanyk and Altenberg could have been made also by substituting for Altenberg Giovanni Verga (1840-1922) whose tales of the lives of Sicilian peasants are somewhat reminiscent of Stefanyk (especially in certain motifs, i.e., too many children, high cost of doctoring and therefore a preference for death, importance of animals for the peasant, etc.). Although Verga also keeps his descriptions at a minimal level and often reverts to the dramatic dialogue as a means of narration, he never manages the concision and brevity of form which is found in Stefanyk. Moreover, the similarities between the two end when it comes to the essential reason for portraying the peasant life which each knew so well. While Stefanyk's prime interest is in capturing the anguish of an individual's experiences of life, Verga is more concerned with revealing the individual in the more primitive peasant form, for here "the mechanism of the passions that determine human activity is less complicated and can therefore be observed with greater precision."[73] Basically it is, on the one hand, Stefanyk's interest to see how a blow received from the vicissitudes of life reverberated in the victim's soul, and on the other hand, Verga's interest to observe how this blow serves as a motivation for the victim to aspire for material, social, or other protection from a future blow.

One could continue such comparisons indefinitely. For example, one could also compare Stefanyk to a contemporary Mexican writer of short stories dealing with peasant lives, Juan Rulfo (1918–). He resembles Stefanyk in his use of dialect, in his employment of dialogue and monologue as a vehicle of narration, and finally, as a recent study of his stories indicates, in that he, like Stefanyk, "delves into the fundamentals of the life of the humble people whose existence is a drama of unending despair."[74]

There is really no question of influences here. There is simply the matter of analogues which serve to emphasize the fact that relegating Stefanyk to a "peasant writer" solely interested in portraying the life of Ukrainian peasants in a specific historical and temporal frame would be tantamount to maintaining that Verga's prime interest lay in portraying the specific problems of the Sicilian peasant, or that Rulfo's main aim lay in describing the unique conditions of the Mexican peasant. If this were true, all three would appear in the category of social commentary and not literature. What really unites these three authors is that each is able to utilize artistically very specific local material in his study of man in general. If these authors are to be considered as true creators of literature, their peasant milieu can only be the material and never the end product of their creations. As M. Rudnyts'ky expressed it:

> The life of peasants and their psychology will remain
> an inexhaustible source for literature . . . but all those
> characteristic features of surroundings, which we call
> "manners" [*pobut*] can not be the aim in a work, but
> only a means.[75]

There have consistently been scholars of Stefanyk who have seen in his works more than just clever studies of peasant lives. This last group of critics who have been termed the "universalists" were few and far between. As with the other groups of critics discussed in this chapter, these can also find support for their approach to Stefanyk in his own comments about his work. In a letter to Moraczewski about his translation of "The Blue Book" into Polish, Stefanyk expressed great pleasure with the translation and stated that it (the novella) "is such a little tragedy of all the peasants in the world."[76]

One of the first to realize Stefanyk's universality was Ivan

Franko. In his rebuttal of Rusova's article (see above), Franko perceived the most important element of Stefanyk's novellas:

No, these tragedies and dramas which Stefanyk paints do not have much in common with economic misery; these are tragedies of the soul, conflicts and dramas which can *mutatis mutandis* reappear in the soul of every man. And it is precisely in this that their great suggestive force lies; from this they derive their staggering influence on the soul of the reader.[77]

As it was so often the case with Franko, he did not follow through on his brilliant critical insight, and did not support his perceptive appraisal of Stefanyk with a concrete and broader study of Stefanyk's work. His statement, however, was re-echoed several years later by O. Hrushevsky, who maintained that in the better stories the tragedy described by Stefanyk becomes universal (*"zahal'no-lyuds'kym"*) and it is because of this that they "leave behind such deep sadness with which they envelop the human soul."[78] But again he did not develop this any further.

Similarly W. Moraczewski, in his tribute to Stefanyk after the latter's death, also stressed the universality of Stefanyk's novellas. According to him, the life which Stefanyk portrayed in his works was "not a life of work, or a life of misery, or a life of injury, but that it was simply the life of every one of us, the life of man, felt and recreated by a poet. In the life of Rusiv gathered the life of all humanity, not only the life of peasants."[79]

Since Moraczewski, as also Franko, Hrushevsky, and a few others who have mentioned the universal aspect of Stefanyk's novellas, did not amplify their comment; since these comments were more declarations than conclusions to appropriate studies of Stefanyk's works, it was felt that a study of Stefanyk was necessary which would prove that these insights into the nature of Stefanyk's creative work were indeed correct. It is hoped that the following chapters will fulfill this role.

FOOTNOTES

[1] L. Hranychka, "V. Stefanyk u literaturniy krytytsi," *Vistnyk*, Vol. V, Bk. 2 (1937), p. 124.

[2] Bohdan Kravtsiv, "Yuriy Stefanyk-biohraf 'Poeta tverdoyi dushi,'" *Svoboda*, February 15, 1969, p. 4.

[3] I. Myronets', Review of V. Stefanyk, *Tvory*, p. 157.

[4] M. Ivchenko, "Tvorchist' Vasylya Stefanyka," *Ukrayina*, Bks. 2-3, p. 184.

[5] B. Lepky, *Vasyl' Stefanyk. Literaturnyy narys*. L'viv, 1903, p. 4, as quoted by L. Hranychka, "V. Stefanyk u literaturniy krytytsi," p. 125.

[6] S. Rusova, "Stare y nove v suchasniy ukrayins'kiy literaturi," translated and ed. by I. Franko, *Literaturno-Naukovyy Vistnyk*, XXV (1904), 76.

[7] Antin Krushel'nyts'ky, "Vasyl' Stefanyk" in *Ukrayins'ka novelya, Vybir narysiv i novel'* (Kolomyya, 1910), p. ix.

[8] *Ibid.*, p. vii. In a later study, Krushel'nyts'ky vehemently states that Stefanyk not only notices class differentiation in the village but that he emphasizes these class inequalities on every page. See Antin Krushel'-nyts'ky, "Bo pany tebe ne pryymut,'" *Novi shlyakhy*, No. 6, 1931, pp. 273-80, as reprinted in Fedir Pohrebennyk, ed., *Vasly' Stefanyk u krytytsi ta spohadakh* (Kiev, 1970), p. 113-19.

[9] Semen Avdiyenko, "Spivets' krashchoyi selyans'koyi doli," in *Doroha*, an addition to *Hromads'kyy holos*, No. 17, 1931, commemorating the 60th anniversary of Stefanyk's birth, as reprinted in T. Kobzey, *Velykyy riz'bar ukrayins'kykh selyans'kykh dush*, p. 243.

[10] Myronets', Review of V. Stefanyk, *Tvory*, p. 158.

[11] V. Boyko, Introduction to V. Stefanyk, *Opovidannya* (Kiev, 1919), p. iii, as quoted by L. Hranychka, "V. Stefanyk u literaturniy krytytsi," p. 127.

[12] V. Doroshenko, *Vasyl' Stefanyk (Z nahody 50-littya urodyn)* (L'viv, 1921), p. 22, as quoted by Hranychka, "V. Stefanyk u literaturniy krytytsi," p. 128. Original was not available.

[13] V. Koryak, "Mizh dvoma klasamy," introduction to V. Stefanyk, *Tvory* (2d ed.; Kharkiv, 1927), p. 24.

[14] Hranychka, "V. Stefanyk u literaturniy krytytsi," p. 128.

[15] S. Kryzhanivs'ky, *Vasyl' Stefanyk* (Kiev, 1946), p. 26.

[16] *Ibid.*, p. 23.

17Y. M. Kurylenko, "Spivets' znedolenoho halyts'koho selyanstva," *Literatura v shkoli*, No. 2, 1951, p. 30. See also the most recently published article by S. Kryzhanivs'ky, "Iz literaturnoyi spadshchyny Vasylya Stefanyka," in F. Pohrebennyk, *Vasyl' Stefanyk u krytytsi ta spohadakh*, pp. 236-53. Kryzhanivs'ky uses the unpublished and unfinished works of Stefanyk to prove Stefanyk's preoccupation with social themes. It never occurs to Kryzhanivs'ky that it is quite possible these works were left unfinished and were not published precisely because they lacked in artistic merit what they may have gained in socio-political propaganda.

18V. Lesyn, *Vasyl' Stefanyk i ukrayins'ka proza kintsya XIX st.* (Chernivtsi, 1965), p. 31.

19V. Lesyn, *Tvorchist' Vasylya Stefanyka* (L'viv, 1965), pp. 158-59.

20V. Stefanyk, *Povne zibrannya tvoriv*, I, 13.

21Myronets', Review of V. Stefanyk, *Tvory*, p. 159.

22M. Kozoris, "Sotsiyal'ni momenty v tvorchosti V. Stefanyka," *Zakhidna Ukrayina*, Nos. 4-5 (1931), pp. 144-45.

23*Ibid.*, p. 172.

24D. Dontsov, "Poet tverdoyi dushi," *Literaturno-naukovyy Vistnyk*, Vol. XXVI, Bk. 2 (1927), pp. 142-54.

25*Ibid.*, p. 150.

26*Ibid.*, p. 151.

27O. Hrytsay, "Stefanykova lyudyna," *Natsional'na dumka*, No. 4 (1927), p. 5, as quoted by L. Hranychka, "Stefanykovyy svit," *Vistnyk*, Vol. V, Bks. 3-4, p. 223.

28*Ibid.*, p. 269. His stress.

29Published in the Shevchenko Scientific Society Ukrainian Studies Series, Vol. XXI, Toronto, 1966.

30It is interesting to compare this work with a similar one just published by Soviet scholars, namely F. Pohrebennyk, ed., *Vasyl' Stefanyk u krytytsi ta spohadakh* (Kiev, 1970). Although both books embrace the same topic and consist of reprints of critical and memorial articles about Stefanyk, with a few exceptions (e.g., Franko), the authors in one are not to be found in the other, and some (e.g., Myronets') in neither.

31Yu. Hamorak [Yuriy Stefanyk], "Vasyl' Stefanyk. Sproba biohrafiyi," introduction to V. Stefanyk, *Tvory*, ed. by Yu. Hamorak (2d ed.; Regensburg, 1948), pp. ii-xliii.

32*Ibid.*, p. ii.

33*Ibid.*

34For a lucid discussion of the development of modernism in Ukrainian literature see Bohdan Rubchak, "Probnyy let," an introduction to Yuriy Luts'ky, ed., *Ostap Luts'ky—Molodomuzets'* (New York, 1968), pp. 9-43.

35*Ibid.*, p. 19.

36*Ibid.*, p. 28.

37*Ibid.*, pp. 30-31.

38 See Kazimierz Wyka, *Modernizm polski* (Cracow, 1968).

39 See for example Stanisław Heļsztynski, *Przybyszewski* (Cracow, 1958), p. 244 where Stefanyk in a letter to a friend criticizes Przybyszewski for keeping the company of drunkards and decadents.

40 Marko Cheremshyna, "Stefanykovi muzhyky," in *Tvory* (Kiev, 1960), p. 302.

41 B. Lepky, "Vasyl' Stefanyk," *Ruslan*, Nos. 112-18, 1903, as quoted by F. Pohrebennyk, "Maksym Hor'ky i Vasyl' Stefanyk," *Radyans'ke literaturoznavstvo*, No. 3, 1968, p. 41.

42 M. G., a Review of V. Stefanyk *Rasskazy* (Perevod s ukrainskogo V. Kozinenko, St. Petersburg, 1907), *Vestnik Evropy*, Bk. 7, 1907, p. 371.

43 Letter to Vasyl' Stefanyk, Capri, June 29, 1909, in M. Kotsyubyns'ky, *Tvory v shesty tomakh*, VI, 122.

44 Alfred Polgar, "Peter Altenberg," In Peter Altenberg, *Der Nachlass* (Berlin, 1925), pp. 151-52.

45 One should mention a letter of O. Makovey to Stefanyk (see Ch. III), in which Makovey accuses Stefanyk of writing in a way similar to a painter not painting the object itself but around it.

46 Ivan Dzyuba, in an interview for the Preshov newspaper *Nove zhyttya* of January 14, 1967, as reprinted by *Ukrainian News* (Edmonton), No. 9, March 2, 1967.

47 Ivan Kochur in a letter to Marta Skorupsky, Kiev, October 18, 1969. The letter is the personal property of Miss Skorupsky, who graciously sent a photocopy to the author of this work.

48 Stepan Smal'-Stots'ky, "Moyi spomyny pro Stefanyka," *Novyy chas*, No. 50, 1937, as reprinted in T. Kobzey, *Velykyy riz'bar ukrayins'kykh selyans'kykh dush*, p. 176.

49 Ol'ha Kobylyans'ka, letter to Vasyl' Stefanyk, November 23, 1898, in *Tvory*, V (Kiev, 1963), 372.

50 Lesya Ukrayinka, "Malorusskie pisateli na Bukovine," in *Tvory v desyaty tomakh*, VIII (Kiev, 1965), 311.

51 Mykola Zerov, "Marko Cheremshyna i halyts'ka proza," in his *Vid Kulisha do Vynnychenka* (Kiev, 1929), p. 145.

52 *Ibid.*, p. 146.

53 H. Hrebenyuk, "Pokuts'ka hrupa pys'mennykiv," *Chervonyy shlyakh*, No. 4, 1929, p. 110.

54 *Ibid.*, p. 124.

55 *Ibid.*, p. 126. Emphasis is Hrebenyuk's.

56 Ye. O. Nenadkevych, "Iz studiy nad stylem Frankovoyi i Stefanykovoyi novely," *Zapysky Volyns'koho Instytuta Narodnoyi Osvity im. Ivana Franka*, 1927, Bk. 2, pp. 100-1.

57 V. Stefanyk in a letter to W. Moraczewski, April 2, 1896, in V. Stefanyk, *Povne zibrannya tvoriv*, III, 61.

58 V. Stefanyk, "Avtobiohrafiya," *Povne zibrannya tvoriv*, II, 14.

59 What Soviet scholars never quote is another statement made by Stefanyk and reported by B. Lepky, *Try portrety*, p. 90:

"I like to read him [Uspensky] too, but not too much. Knut Hamsun is much more pleasant . . ."

[60]Marko Cheremshyna in a letter to A. Muzychka, January 22, 1926, in M. Cheremshyna, *Tvory*, p. 401.

[61]S. Kryzhanivs'ky, *Vasyl' Stefanyk*, p. 20.

[62]L. Hranychka, "Stefanykove slovo," *Vistnyk*, Vol. V, Bk. 5, 1937, p. 363.

[63]Ya. Yarema, "Vasyl' Stefanyk i Hlib Uspens'ky," *Radyans'ke literaturoznavstvo*, No. 17, 1954, p. 117.

[64]M. Rudnyts'ky, "Vasyl' Stefanyk," in *Vid Myrnoho do Khvyl'ovoho* (L'viv, 1936), pp. 243-44.

[65]L. Hranychka, "Stefanykove slovo," pp. 364-65.

[66]M. Rudnyts'ky, "Vasyl' Stefanyk," p. 244.

[67]See G. Uspensky, *Sobranie sochineniy v devyati tomakh* (Moscow, 1955), I, 47-49.

[68]Ya. Yarema, "Zv'yazky Vasylya Stefanyka z Stanislavom Pshybyshevs'kym i Vladyslavom Orkanom," *Mizhslov'yans'ki literaturni vzayemyny*, ed. by O. Bilets'ky and others (Kiev, 1958), No. 3, p. 165.

[69]H. D. Verves, *Vladyslav Orkan i ukrayins'ka literatura* (Kiev, 1962), pp. 142 and 145. On the subject of titles Verves makes this interesting observation on p. 145:

As a matter of fact, how close the Polish writer is to the Ukrainian one can be judged also on the basis of the similarity in the titles of their novellas. Compare: *"Na godne święta," "Wilia," "Krótki sen," "Pogrzeb"* — *"Svyatyy vechir," "Son," "Pokhoron,"* and others.

[70]*Ibid.*, p. 143.

[71]L. Hranychka, "Stefanykove slovo," p. 364.

[72]Bohdan Lepky, *Nezabutni* (Berlin, 1922), pp. 80-81.

[73]G. Verga, *I Malavoglia*, Milano, 1953, (Preface), pp. 9-11, as quoted and translated by Olga Ragusa in Verga's *Milanese Tales* (New York, 1964), p. 102.

[74]Donald Keith Gordon, "The Short Stories of Juan Rulfo," (an unpublished Ph.D. dissertation, University of Toronto, Toronto, 1969), p. 2.

[75]M. Rudnyts'ky, *Vid Myrnoho do Khvyl'ovoho*, p. 89.

[76]V. Stefanyk in a letter to W. Moraczewski, June 1898, in *Povne zibrannya tvoriv*, III, 142.

[77]Ivan Franko, comments to his translation of S. Rusova, "Stare y nove v suchasniy ukrayins'kiy literaturi," *LNV*, XXV (1904), 83.

[78]Oleksandr Hrushevs'ky, "Suchasne ukrayins'ke pys'menstvo v yoho typovykh predstavnykakh," *LNV*, Vol. XLIII, Bk. 7, 1908, p. 30.

[79]W. Moraczewski, "Wasyl Stefanyk," *Sygnaly*, No. 25, 1937 as quoted by Ya. Yarema, without giving the original page number, in "Vasyl' Stefanyk i Vatslav Morachevs'ky," *Mizhslav'yans'ki literaturni vzayemyny*, (Kiev, 1963), No. 3, p. 84.

CHAPTER III

DEFINITION OF GENRE

Novella in General

By 1897, when Stefanyk's first novellas appeared in print, modern Ukrainian prose had been developing for almost seventy years. This process was a rapid one, running swiftly through the various literary trends. At times the pace was so swift that several literary movements merged in the writings of one author. Thus Kvitka-Osnovyanenko (1778-1843) embraced in his writings both the burlesque traditions of classicism and the moralistic as well as didactic elements of sentimentalism. Similarly, Marko Vovchok (Mariya Vilins'ka-Markovych, 1834-1907) combined in her style romanticism and realism by mixing a realistic portrayal of actual social problems with a wealth of ethnographic romanticism, especially when using a narrator. Ethnographic romanticism, naturalistic minutiae, realistic themes and populistic propaganda characterize the next stage of Ukrainian prose in the two masters of Ukrainian Realism, Ivan Nechuy-Levyts'ky (1838-1918) and Panas Myrny (Atanasiy Rudchenko, 1849-1920).

The best and the worst of pre-modernist Ukrainian prose can be seen in the works of Ivan Franko (1856-1916). The foremost writer in the second half of the nineteenth century, Franko turned to a wide range of themes and employed various genres. From his early works in a romantic vein, Franko progressed to novels dealing with the oil proletariat of Western Ukraine and treated these themes in a realistic manner, with naturalistic depictions of various forms of degeneration. At the same time Franko managed, in some of his short stories devoted to the life of small schoolchildren, to capture an atmosphere of warmth and innocence. The wealth of genre—story, etude, sketch, historical novel, drama—and his treatment of themes from the social, political and psychological point of view were marred only by the curse of most of nineteenth century Ukrainian prose—Romantic ethnographism. The inability to exclude the nonessential detail in long naturalistic descriptions of mores hindered Franko's prose no less than it did the prose of his predecessors. Although in his later life, already under the influence of modernism, Franko turned toward impressionism and the psychological treatment of subjects, he never abandoned his realistic narrative technique. This can be said of pre-modernist Ukrainian prose in general. Although it developed thematically both in the approach and variety of theme, and although it developed in the sphere of genre, embracing various prose types, it progressed very slightly in respect to form. Experimentation with and the extension of the narrative form is the fruit of modernism.

Modernism in Ukrainian literature first appeared in poetry. Such modernist groups as *Moloda Muza* (Young Muse) in Western Ukraine and *Ukrayins'ka Khata* (Ukrainian House) in Eastern Ukraine embraced poets who were conscious of the new trends in Western literature, who refused to make art subservient to any cause other than that of art itself. In their poetry they abandoned realistic expression for the symbolic, allowing a polysemous interpretation of poetic images and expressions.

Following in the footsteps of poetry, modernist prose became much more conscious of form. The long and often chaotic narratives of the realists gave way to very short stories based usually on some sharp impression. Prose writers, no longer concerned with a naturalistic photocopy of reality, turned their attention to capturing the brief and subtle impressions perceived by them or their heroes. Traditionally Mykhaylo Kotsyubyns'ky is considered the transitional figure between realist and modernist Ukrainian prose. Although he began writing under the influence of Nechuy-Levyts'ky and Myrny, he soon forsook the realistic narrative for impressionistic prose. Stefanyk appeared in print, however, before Kotsyubyns'ky's changeover which came in the early years of the twentieth century. It is no wonder then that Stefanyk's short, precise, highly impressionistic novellas made such a strong and immediate impact. Although the psychological novella was first attempted by O. Kobylyans'ka,[1] Stefanyk was so different that he had no predecessors in Ukrainian prose. As one critic notes:

> . . . his [Stefanyk's] works differed from all literature of the time. . . . Instead of the wide panoramas of Myrny, Nechuy-Levyts'ky and Franko himself where, in the foreground, appear broad national types, their experiences, struggles, painted in precise conditions of outward life, in Stefanyk, in comparison to them, there is a colossal economy of all verbal material, a concentration of attention. When in the former

authors, forgetting the form, we paid most attention to the content, then in Stefanyk the formal achievements themselves were such an important feature, that unawares, we notice this and value it on a par with content.

This is not so because the form is masterfully executed, as a new cultural achievement, but because in this form, *per se*, appears the outlook of the author. Here to some degree even the form itself becomes the content of the work.[2]

In respect to form, Stefanyk is a child of his time. The influence of his university days in Cracow where he made friends with members of the avant garde "Young Poland," his wide reading in contemporary West European literature, as attested by his letters and even translations of some of the works he read—the influence of all this is indisputable when Stefanyk's development as a writer is investigated. His short prose poems, his early "novellas" in letters, all show that from the very beginning he worked for brevity and conciseness.

The exact nature of his prose is hard to define. Although Stefanyk's works are customarily referred to as novellas, he used this term only once, in his third collection, *The Road*. His first collection, *The Blue Book*, he subtitled "pictures" (*Obrazky*), perhaps under the influence of the editors of *LNV* who published three of his pieces in 1897 under the title "Photographs from Life" (*Fotohrafiyi z zhyttya*). The works in the second collection, *The Stone Cross*, were termed "Studies and Pictures" (*Studiyi y obrazky*); the forth, *My Word*, a reprint of the first two collections, used the all-embracing "Stories" (*Opovidannya*); the last, *The Earth*, he labeled "Sketches and Stories" (*Narysy y opovidannya*).

From this it can be seen that there was a discrepancy in Stefanyk's own mind about what genre described his works best. It is curious to note that he did not hesitate to designate the same works by two different terms, as he did in *My Word* which contained the "Pictures and Studies" of the first two collections. Length could not have served as a criterion for his nomenclature, for with the exception of five "longer" pieces (from six to twelve pages) the average length of a story was about two and a half pages.

Nevertheless a definition of Stefanyk's form is absolutely necessary for the understanding of his work. As Ivchenko has pointed out in the remarks already cited, Stefanyk's form often becomes the content. The problem lies, not so much in describing the type of prose Stefanyk wrote, as in fitting this type into the confines of existing genres. The term novella cannot be accepted without clarification. This in itself is a formidable task—larger than the scope of this work. The novella, as H. Remak has pointed out, is a history full of "unexpected twists, . . . irony and paradox."[3] Rafael Koskimies fully illustrates this statement in his "Die Theorie der Novelle" by pointing out how one theoretical rule based on a classic example of the genre does not apply to another equally classic example. This he maintains is true in respect to most of the major points ever made about the novella as a genre: is it based on an anecdote or on a bit of unusual news; is it dramatic or epic; does it begin with an author's narration or *in medias res.* Basically he sees the novella as a split genre embracing the classical novella of Boccaccio, closely related to the French *conte*, and the modern novella of Chekhov, closer to the short story.[4]

The problem is complicated by the fact that in each national literature the novella assumed certain particular national features. Moreover the term itself does not have an identical meaning in all languages. Thus in "English speaking areas 'novella' usually means . . . no more than a short novel . . .,"[5] whereas in German, the *Novelle* is a specific genre of the short story. In Ukrainian literature, the term *novelya*, though retaining some of the definitions of the original Italian *novella* and the German *Novelle*, is opposed to the short story, *opovidannya*, and the short novel, *povist'*. In order to attain some sort of clarity as to what is meant by the term novella in Ukrainian literature as well as to show how Stefanyk used this genre, the definition of the Ukrainian novella has to be delineated in respect to the classical novella, the German *Novelle*, and the modern short story.

In his study of the genre, Ihor Kachurovs'ky traces the origin of the novella back to ancient Egypt where it existed in the form of fables.[6] According to him, it appeared in Europe as written anecdotes in the age of Charlemagne, but received its legitimacy as a genre only in the fourteenth century in the *Decameron* of Boccaccio who used the Italian term *novella* (news) to describe his tales.[7] Although Kachurovs'ky never really defines the novella except as a short piece of prose closely related to the anecdote, he maintains that it "appears in the literature of various times and of various peoples under various names: *Milesian tale, facetiae, fableau, Schwank,* and *short story.*"[8] All of these are united by one common feature—brevity—and all, with the exception of the erotic Milesian tales and the short story, are humorous or satiric. Thus indirectly Kachurovs'ky delineates the genre of novella as a piece of prose with anecdotal brevity and possibly, but not necessarily, humor.

Although Kachurovs'ky considers the short story a variant of the novella, which perhaps is correct in respect to English literature where the term "short story" is applied to various types of short prose, in Ukrainian literature there is a difference between the "story" (*opovidannya*), sometimes not necessarily short, and the "novella" (*novelya*) which must be. The difference primarily lies not only in the quantity but also in the manner of narration. Whereas in the *opovidannya* several episodes about several people are portrayed with large descriptive elements in a causal as well as temporal sequence, in the *novelya* only one episode is portrayed without the exposition of past or future happenings.[9]

It is important to note that, as F. M. Bilets'ky points out, "in West Eruopean literatures—English, French—'novella' meant a short story. . . . And that which in the West was considered a novella, in Russian and Ukrainian literatures was called a story (*opovidannya*)."[10] This confusion of terms is clearly seen in B. Tomashevsky's treatment of the genre of novella, which he calls in Russian *rasskaz* and defines as a short piece of prose with a non-dramatic but narrative method of presentation of some drama in life, framed by a narrator, hero or place, often cyclical, with or without a distinct fabula but with a hard and sudden ending to cut the thread of narration.[11] What Tomashevsky defines is in reality a hybrid genre, a mixture of the novella and the story (*opovidannya*) as these terms are understood in Ukrainian literature. Nonetheless one Ukrainian theoretician, namely Kachurovs'ky, was so confused by the differences between the novella and the short story that he claimed there really was no such thing as the novella in Ukrainian literature with the exception of a few by Franko, Kotsyubyns'ky, and Vynnychenko.[12] About Stefanyk he made the curious and erroneous observation that:

> We often speak about the novellas of Stefanyk, but this is a plain case of misunderstanding. Perhaps there are a few novellas among Stefanyk's works (for example "Basaraby" [The Basarabs]), but, on the whole, his genre is a plotless miniature which for the most part reminds one of stylized notes of some dialectological expedition.[13]

This assertion shows that Kachurovs'ky not only did not differentiate between the *novelya* and the *opovidannya* in Ukrainian literature, but that his idea of a novella was based only on one very specific type of short story—(he considered Pushkin's *Tales of Belkin* the highest example of the novella genre)—not necessarily a *short* story in the Western sense at that. For the definitions of a short story as given by O'Faolain and Esenwein are much closer to the Ukrainian novella than to the definition of the novella implied by Kachurovs'ky or stated by Tomashevsky.

According to O'Faolain, a good short story is one where the story or anecdote is least essential, where the author vanishes behind the conversation of his characters, where characterization is brought to a minimum, where the sentence and not the paragraph provides the main unit of construction, and where the whole composition serves to make a subtle comment on human nature.[14] In a similar manner, Esenwein defines the short story as

> . . . a brief, imaginative narrative, unfolding a single predominating incident and a single chief character, it contains a plot, the details of which are so compressed, and the whole treatment so organized, as to produce a single impression.[15]

The similarity between these definitions of the short story and the definitions of the novella by Denysyuk and Fashchenko is indeed striking. For Denysyuk, the novella is the "shortest form of prose, a work with an asymmetric composition, which underlines one event, conflict, scene, slice of life, embraced by one experience."[16] Moreover, this "slice of life" is such that it "expresses a genuine sense of life."[17] Fashchenko even makes the point more explicit by stating that the "novella is an epic narrative work in which there occurs a compositionally compact discovery of the whole world in one moment, in a small circle of relations which form one epicentre of mood and thought . . ."[18] He also points out that the "fullest point of view of the character is achieved in the monologue form"[19] and that the more the point of view is switched from the character to the author the closer the work is to a larger work prose, a story (*opovidannya*) or a novel (*roman*).[20]

Three of the above definitions are united by this aspect of the universal: O'Faolain's "subtle comment on human nature," Denysyuk's "slice of life," and Fashchenko's "discovery of the whole world in one moment" all say one and the same thing. In short, a novella (or a short story as defined here) is a short form of prose narrating one episode in the life of man, but an episode which reveals the whole life of the man or of mankind in general.

Since Stefanyk knew and read German and even translated two novellas by Thoma, he must have been aware of the German use of the novella genre. It is interesting to note, therefore, that E. K. Bennett in his *A History of the German Novelle* describes the genre in terms similar to those above, but adds several features which definitely help to establish Stefanyk's genre as that of the novella. Bennett stresses the fact that the novella deals with the event and its effect rather than simply with the action itself. "It restricts itself to a single event (or situation or conflict), laying the stress primarily upon the event and showing the effect of this event upon a person or group of persons."[21] Moreover, it

> should deal with some definite and striking subject which marks it clearly and distinguishes it from every other Novelle. This striking element in the subject matter is frequently connected with a concrete inner symbolical significance. The effect of the impact of the event upon the person or group of persons is to reveal qualities which were latent and may have been unsuspectedly present in them, the event being used as the acid which separates and reveals the various qualities in the person or persons under investigation.[22]

What Bennett describes here is in reality the workings of the psychological novella, the writing of which was Stefanyk's prime concern. In her classification of types of short stories, Olga Scherer-Virski calls this type a "story of character" as opposed to a short story "of action" and "of setting."[23]

Bennett's definition of the *Novelle* can be amplified by some features of the modern German novelle as seen by Remak and of the modern novella in general as seen by Koskimies. Remak stated that:

> The (particularly German) novella must continue to guard against moralizing (except in the frame), theorizing, melodramatic wallowing in sentiment, and lyric expansionism, against wordiness, excess of learnedness and psychological unplausibilities . . .[24]

Koskimies showed that in modern times (since the end of the last century) certain features of the classical novella were changed. He considered Chekhov the founder of the new novella and claimed that the main change brought by Chekhov was in the use of everyday occurrences for subject matter and in the absence of a sudden or strong ending:

> Aber die Meisternovellisten jener Zeit, von Kielland und Strindberg bis zu Tschechov, erwecken oft den Eindruck, dass sie nur ein Stück von passender Grösse

aus dem gewöhnlichen, wirklichen Leben herausschneiden, sozusagen eine Altägliche Episode ohne Steigerung und Senkung, ohne Höhepunkt und Katastrophe erzählen .... Wir haben auch besonderen Grund, uns daran zu erinnern, dass einige der berühmtesten Novellen von Tschechov eighentlich keinen Höhepunkt und besonders kein Ende haben; das Leben geht ebenso unklar und ebenso natürlich weiter wie vorher ...[25]

Koskimies also attributed to the influence of impressionism the extreme brevity of the novella of which Peter Altenberg was a great master.[26] The fact that Stefanyk was compared to Altenberg (see Chapter II), the fact that he too did not choose the unusual but the everyday events, the fact that he avoided the sharp ending, moralizing, theorizing, verbosity, and "lyric expansionism"—all of this places him as a practitioner of the modern novella.

Bennett makes one more very interesting point about the German novella by claiming that "there" is a definite resemblance between the Novelle and the drama in construction, the Novelle by its very succinctness having a certain dramatic quality of tension and swiftness of catastrophe."[27] Here Bennett is completely opposed to the assertions of Tomashevsky who stressed the narrative element above the dramatic. Both Bennett and Tomashevsky can be somewhat reconciled if one accepts the typification of the short story adopted by Scherer-Virski, who subdivides her "short story of character" into two groups:

... dynamic or dramatic stories of character—those that catch a significant moment in the formation [or development] of a character—and static stories of character—those that draw the development or history of a characteristic trait.[28]

Scherer-Virski's description of the "dynamic or dramatic story of character" almost perfectly describes the majority of Stefanyk's novellas:

... a character is presented in a dramatic situation. It may, and frequently does, represent the turning point in a man's life, a point at which all the given values of a character are crystallized into their finished form. Such stories rarely use biographical references about their character, for such digressions would detract from the dramatic suspense created by the crisis.[29]

In her work, however, Scherer-Virski does not differentiate between the short story and the novella and treats both as variants of the same genre. Yet it is possible to see in her two-fold division another aspect distinguishing the novella from the short story, the novella being the more dramatic of the two. The difference between the novella and the story, or tale as he calls it, was best summed up by the German poet Wilhelm Hauff who claimed that:

> ... a tale could easily be renarrated, merely by allowing the memory to follow the natural course of events recorded, whereas a Novelle could be renarrated from memory only by very careful thought, because the order of events was not the natural one, but had been altered for the sake of effect.[30]

—thus actually restating Bilets'ky's assertions that the *opovidannya* differs from the *novelya* because of its treatment of events in a causal and temporal sequence.

When all of Bennett's assertions are brought together, there emerges a definition of the novella as a short work in prose dealing with a single event, the unfolding of which is concise and dramatic. It presents the effects of that event on the person or persons concerned, the order of exposition being neither strictly causal nor strictly temporal, but such as will assure the most striking impression upon the reader. With the addition of O'Faolain's, Denysyuk's and Fashchenko's concept of the event as revealing something universal about life through the particular, the definition of the novella as a genre becomes complete.

The fact that Stefanyk indeed wrote novellas becomes self-evident when this composite definition is juxtaposed to his prose. There are five characteristic features of Stefanyk's novella: it is extremely short; it is dramatic; it concentrates on one moment in the life of a character; it reveals the personality of the character and simultaneously a facet of Man himself; it is rhythmic.

Features of Stefanyk's Novella

Brevity is perhaps the most important feature, for from its confines emerge all of the others. In the words of Tomashevsky:

> The indication of size—basic in the classifictaion of narrative works—is by far of more importance than this may seem at first glance. It depends on the size of the work how the author will deal with the narrative material, how he will arrange his plot, how he will bring in to it his themes.[31]

The small size of Stefanyk's literary corpus makes it possible to examine each one of his fifty-nine stories separately. This, however, is unnecessary in respect to length, for as all critics attest and any one who picks up a volume of Stefanyk notices immediately, his novellas are extremely short, ranging anywhere from one to three pages. The only exceptions to this are five novellas which verge on the point of being short stories. Stefanyk's first longer piece appears in the second collection, the title story, "Kaminnyy khrest" (The Stone Cross), which Stefanyk subtitled a "Studiya" (Study).

Although "The Stone Cross" still deals with only one episode in a life of a character, it differs from the shorter novellas by an increase in author's narration and an added description of the previous life of the character in the first part of the seven-part novella. The other six scenes all deal with the leave-taking of Ivan and his wife. The whole story is constructed like a ritualistic wake with Stefanyk focusing on various aspects of the leave-taking in each separate scene: scene two sets the locale and the circumstances; scene three provides reasons for the separation and a symbolic parting between husband and wife; scene four focuses on the parting between Ivan and his friends as well as with his stone cross; scene five concentrates on the merry-making during a "wake"; scene six is devoted to the final good-byes; and the mini-scene seven focuses on the stone cross—the grave left by the still-living but spiritially dead Ivan and wife.

The second longer piece "Paliy" (The Arsonist), appears in the third collection of novellas and consists of elements of a drama which Stefanyk always wanted to write, but never really did.[32] This work is closest to the *short story* of all the works which Stefanyk wrote. It is not only the longest (thirteen pages), but also has two characters and is multi-episodal. It is also marked by increased author's narration and character depiction. The story contains seven scenes and nineteen episodes from the life of the protagonist Fedir. Yet some elements of the novella are present in that the episodes are not arranged in chronological or causal order. In scene one, Stefanyk relates two episodes from the life of Fedir: his meeting with the antagonist Kurochka and his dream in which the idea of arson, which unites the whole short story, is introduced. Scene two has as many as ten episodes, all relating to Fedir's background, presented as flashbacks in the protagonist's mind, and leading up to the decline of Fedir's strength while serving at the manor. Scene three contains only one episode, describing Fedir's life just before the episodes in scene one. The two episodes of scene four take up after Fedir's dream in scene one and describe his

71

life as a menial swineherd at Kurochka's place. In scene five, the first episode shifts to Fedir's family life and the second continues where the second episode in the scene before ended. Scene six again is composed of two episodes, both dealing with elections in the village, and ends with the episode in which Kurochka hits Fedir in the face, insulting him and leading to the act of arson which is the subject of the single episode in the last scene.

Although highly praised by Soviet critics, primarily for the social protest which they saw in the act of arson, "The Arsonist" is, in comparison with other novellas of Stefanyk, poorly and rather chaotically constructed. It seems as if Stefanyk could not maintain his high dramatic tension when the confines of the work were expanded. The one redeeming merit of the story lies in the handling of the all-embracing idea of arson which grows steadily through the story, from the foreshadowing in the dream to the final act which is a scene of superb impressionistic imagery.

The third of Stefanyk's longer stories is also from the same collection as "The Arsonist." "Klenovi lystky," (The Maple Leaves) made up of four scenes and five episodes, is curiously constructed in that it is split in half by scene three which can stand as a novella in its own right[33] without, however, upsetting the strict temporal sequence to which Stefanyk adheres in this story. "The Maple Leaves" illustrates very well that Stefanyk was not really at ease in the longer form. The length seems to have stood in the way of a sharp focus; although the picture is there, it is somewhat blurred. This becomes more than evident when the final version of the story is compared with an extant first draft consisting of only two and a half pages of six mini-scenes. Whereas the final draft indulges in some rather heavy padding, especially on the social level (although the inserted novella in no way detracts from the point of the story but rather underlines an aspect of it), the first draft's precision and clarity in showing the little tragedy in the life of a recently increased family about to lose its mother makes that version superior by far and a more typical Stefanyk novella.

Without a first draft, however, it is hard to imagine how Stefanyk could have treated the theme of the next long story in a more concentrated form. "Basaraby" (The Basarabs), also from the third collection, is a study of the malady of suicide as it afflicts a family from generation to generation. Although Kachurovs'ky considered this one of Stefanyk's few true novellas (see above p. 66), it is in reality a classic example of the tale as Hauff understood it. The sequence of events is temporal and such that it can be easily retold; though it consists of four scenes, there are only two episodes and a surprise ending. Here Stefanyk's atypical length is quite justified since it is devoted to the description of a peculiar spiritual malady hardly describable in few words.

The final longer work appeared in Stefanyk's last collection. Although "Mariya" (Mariya) is seven and a half pages long, it is in reality an oversized novella. It consists of one scene and one episode in the life of one character. The length is due to the fact that almost half of the novella is devoted to a flashback of the protagonist during which prior events are revealed, events which have to be known in order to understand the reaction of the protagonist to the episode in the novella.[34]

These five works are all exceptions to the rule and represent Stefanyk as he is not. The majority of the remaining stories are extremely short (from one to four pages), mono-scenic, and mono-episodic. Another exception in respect to length is the novella "Zlodiy" (The Thief). Although it is six and a half pages long, it so well represents the other four features of a Stefanyk novella that an analysis of its structure in detail will serve as a model for all of Stefanyk's novellas.

The fact that "The Thief" illustrates the essence of Stefanyk's manner was recognized already by Franko who described the elements of the new style, of which, for him, Stefanyk was the best representative:

> Please compare this wonderful story ["The Thief"] with my "Khlops'ka komisiya" [A Peasant Commission] —a story . . . written from the lips of a victim of the same conflict which is portrayed by Stefanyk. A comparison of those two stories can, in my estimation, give the best understanding of the new manner, of the new way of seeing the world through the prism of feeling and heart—not the author's but of the heroes painted by him.[35]

When such a comparative study was finally made by Ye. Nenadkevych, it not only vindicated Franko's assertion; it provided the most detailed definition of Stefanyk's psychological novella.[36] Although Nenadkevych's definition is primarily concerned with contextual elements of the novella, elements which make the novella a psychological one, there is one point in his definition which provides an important clue also to the structural elements of the novella. In describing Stefanyk's psychological method of observation, Nenadkevych points to the technique of "objective impressionism" by means of which the author reveals the impressions of his characters as they see them, while he himself is hidden behind the scenes as in a drama.[37] Thus Nenadkevych points to the second structural feature of Stefanyk's novellas, to their dramatic construction.

That Stefanyk's novellas are dramatic is by now a truism. A perusal of any work on Stefanyk will reveal statements like these:

> Stefanyk's stories are like acts that take place in the soul of man . . .[38]

> Not to narrate about something, but directly to paint it through the language, thoughts of a person, to present a person's feelings through an act, like in a drama—these are new slogans in literary theory practiced by Stefanyk.[39]

> Stefanyk had developed for himself some separate form for his stories, a form closest to the spoken actionless 'dramas' of Maeterlinck.[40]

Not only critics, but also a foremost Ukrainian actor and director, Volodymyr Blavats'ky, saw the inherent dramatic qualities in Stefanyk's novellas and prepared for the stage in 1933 a collection of six novellas: "Vona zemlya" (She—The Earth), "Syny" (The Sons), "Mariya," "The Thief," "Pobozhna" (The Pious Woman), and "Morituri." The performance of this "play" called "Zemlya" (The Earth) was extremely successful, even in the eyes of Stefanyk himself.[41]

It is no accident that one of the novellas chosen for this "play" was "The Thief," for it is perhaps one of the most dramatic novellas in Stefanyk—a veritable one-act play. Yet the dramatic qualities of Stefanyk's novellas are not necessarily due to any action occurring in them. In fact, most of them are quite static; "The Thief" is more active than most and even here the action is but momentary. It quickly solidifies, like hot wax poured into cold water, and then the real drama begins. The wax, like the action, remains liquid for only a second and then hardens into various configurations, the study of which provides the drama. In "The Thief," for example, the drama unfolds only after the initial fight between the thief and the *gazda*. Only then the dramatic tension grows. The antagonists are frozen, as if hypnotized by the approaching and unavoidable act of retribution. The next action, the coming of the neighbors, provides a momentary relief from tension, but when the characters again settle into immobility around the table and commence heavy drinking, the tension grows with each drink and each word until the final explosive moment when the two *gazdas* pounce on the thief.

Stefanyk, then, bases himself not on activity, but on the

74

essence of drama, on dialogue. By means of direct speech he builds the tension, reveals the personalities of his characters, hints at their motives, and portrays the upheavals, the eruptions of their souls. As narrator, he limits himself to short remarks akin to stage direction in a play. Not always are there several characters on the scene as in "The Thief." Very often Stefanyk's novellas contain only one character and all the drama and tension then occurs in a monologue which provides an *agon* where the contestants are opposing factions of one soul. Both in dialogue and monologue, the sentence and not the paragraph provides, as O'Faolain pointed out, the main unit of construction—for people speak more often in sentences than in paragraphs. Even in monologues, Stefanyk often breaks up a novella consisting of one monologue, into many little sentences punctuated either by the author's short remarks (describing physical actions or changes in the expression of the speaker: such as "he ground his teeth," "he wept" and the like) or by the character's own pauses during which he recollects himself or just catches his breath. This is well illustrated in the beginning of "The Thief" where only the *gazda* speaks. His monologue is broken into seven parts, sometimes by an author's remark, sometimes just by the fact that the person spoken to is different, as in the break between the second and third parts of his initial monologue, the second addressed to his wife and the third to the thief.

Another method of dramatization was pointed out by H. Hrebenyuk who made a word count of Stefanyk's novellas and came up with interesting, but not surprising, statistics. Stefanyk's prose has a predominance of verbs:

> Stefanyk uses very many verbs, especially where there is a lot of action (on the average 32, sometimes reaching 40 or more per page). This one bit of statistical information alone shows how tense is the potentiality of action in the works.[42]

In "The Thief" the first page of the novella (in the Ukrainian version) has forty-seven verbs out of 105 words and page five has as many as seventy-three out of 311 words. Yet these statistics must be approached cautiously and their real significance is still questionable. They would be much more meaningful if compared to a verb count in an average piece of Ukrainian prose and to a verb count in the Ukrainian language in general. It must be remembered that, unlike English, Ukrainian is very much a verbal language with more verbs than nouns.[43]

The dramatic quality of Stefanyk's novellas is also enhanced by the fact that Stefanyk begins most of them *in medias res.* This gives the effect of a rising curtain. Suddenly the reader is brought upon the scene; there is no descriptive introduction of setting or characters (they introduce themselves through their speech, as in drama), and no introduction to the problem or drama unfolding; (it unfolds itself, again through the discourse of the characters or character). "The Thief" provides a good example. As the imaginary curtain rises the reader sees "two huge, strong, men, with ripped shirts and bloodied faces, in the middle of the room." Nothing is said about who they are, what they are doing there, why they are bloodied and why their shirts are ripped. All this becomes apparent as they speak. Even the names of the characters are revealed as in a play; the reader discovers that the *gazda's* name is Georhiy only when his neighbors come and one of them addresses him. The thief's name is never mentioned, for it is unknown to the characters and therefore to the reader.

It is interesting that this important feature of Stefanyk's method of construction was one of the things for which he was criticized when his stories first appeared. When Stefanyk sent three of his novellas for publication in the *LNV*, he received a letter from the editors in which Osyp Makovey wrote:

> In the photograph "Z mista yduchy" (Coming from Town)—you are so miserly in respect to words that you write only: The First (speaks), The Second (again speaks). One can agree that they speak, but since this is a "photograph" and not two photographers, then it might be worthwhile to describe, in a few words at least, these speakers.
>
> The sketch "Hour" [he's referring to the novella "Vechirnya hodyna" (Evening Hour)] I liked even though here too I see this stinginess with words: the reader has to figure out so much. It comes out just as if a painter left a place for a man in his painting and left it up to the viewers to figure out that there should be a man in that place and that the man is a student of the university from peasant origins .... You read and you think to yourself: who is it? Some peasant, or gentry, or someone else? Only later it comes out that this is a peasant's son, who went to school. So! If that's the case then one has to read again from the beginning ... The impression is spoiled.[44]

Makovey, so unaccustomed to Stefanyk's new method, had missed the point entirely. Stefanyk, as he himself pointed out in his reply,[45] was not interested in painting detailed descriptions of the characters speaking. He knew that they, as the characters in plays, would paint themselves when they spoke. Fortunately, Makovey's advice did not alter Stefanyk's style at all. Whether he knew the old maxim that "Speech is a mirror of the soul; as a man speaks, so he is" or not, he certainly adhered to it. As M. S. Hrytsyuta pointed out, "Monologue as well as dialogue, in various forms and variations became Stefanyk's beloved stylistic method,"[46] and it must be added, one of the most important elements in the dramatization of his novellas. For it must be remembered that Stefanyk wrote psychological novellas and his main interest was not in the drama of events but in the drama of the soul.

To obtain the best possible focus on this inner world, Stefanyk concentrated on one moment in the life of the character. This *Augenblick* vision of a character's life, the third feature of Stefanyk's technique, is closely linked with the first two, with the brevity of exposition and with the dramatization of presentation. Stefanyk chose the kind of moment in life which would present the soul charged with emotion. The physical motivations for such states of being Stefanyk found either in some tragedy which had just occurred or was about to occur, in some physical struggle, or even in alcohol which loosens the inhibitions and bares the soul. In "The Thief" the single moment is the capture of the thief. The physical motivation for the highly charged emotional state, in addition to alcohol, is the realization by the characters of the approaching act of unlawful judgement. Stefanyk's concentration falls on the reactions to this knowledge both of the *gazdas*, the judges, and the thief, the judged. In this respect even the title of Stefanyk's novella is appropriately chosen. Nenadkevych, in his study, pointed out:

> The title puts the stress on the individual-psychological direction of the novella. In the centre of interest lies not the self-judgement, as a concrete act and a social phenomenon, but the psychic reaction of the heroes—each in his own way—to the idea of lynch-law applied to the thief. The role of the thief is wholly psychological: his behavior is the catalyst which reveals the various moods of the other heroes.[47]

Thus, the thief's capture is the moment (Bennett's "acid"—see above, p. 68), the *Augenblick*, in the life of the *gazdas* and their reaction to this moment provides the substance of the novella, made into a psychological drama by the short, terse and intense presentation of feelings, heightened by the author's total detachment.

Other titles also provide clues to the moment on which

Stefanyk is concentrating. "The Blue Book" concentrates on the moment when a character has lost everything and received a *blue service book*; his reaction to this and all it entails provides the substance of the novella. In "Novyna" (News) the moment of filicide is minutely examined and, as the first sentence of the novella informs the reader, this moment at completion becomes the *news.* "Sama samis'ka" (All Alone) presents the moment of total *loneliness* just before death. Most but not all of Stefanyk's titles function this way. Some, like "Lan" (A Potato Field), or "May" (May), serve more as symbols or contrasts. In "A Potato Field" the field not only eats up other little fields but also the little child who dies there while his mother is busy working in it. In "May" the hero's worries pale when contrasted with the languid mood of May, and he dreamily resolves them and succumbs to sleep.

By choosing this one moment in the life of a character and by examining the reactions of the character to this moment, Stefanyk reveals the character's personality. This fourth feature of his novellas has two parts: the revelation of the character's personality, and, by the same token, the revelation of something much more universal, a feature of Man in general. The most important method in this feature of construction is the use of language.

It is commonly stated that Stefanyk wrote in the dialect of Pokuttya, the region of Western Ukraine from which he came. This is not quite correct. Stefanyk wrote in contemporary literary Ukrainian and used a stylized version of the Pokuttya dialect as the *argot* of his characters. Although several studies have been made of Stefanyk's language,[48] M. F. Stanivs'ky's views seem to express well the contention that the language used by Stefanyk is dual:

> . . . the language of Stefanyk's novellas forms a structural unity, constructed from elements of the Pokuttya dialect and elements of literary Ukrainian (both West and East Ukrainian). These elements "Intertwine in a varying percentile relationship both in the author's language and in the discourse of the characters but during this it is noticed that the first elements are almost consistently used in the language of the Pokuttyan characters to which Stefanyk opposes the language of the author which, with few exceptions, coincides with the literary language. Furthermore, the language of the Pokuttyan characters does not copy with photographic accuracy the Pokuttyan dialect. The components of the language of Ste-

fanyk's novellas are literary forms and dialecticisms stylistically preconditioned depending on the artistic objectives of that which is portrayed.[49]

In short, what Stefanyk was doing was revealing the character's personality through his traits of speech. Actually, this technique is very similar to *skaz*, which, as Victor Erlich points out, "allows ample scope for sub-literary verbal materials—the relative formal incoherence and 'sloppiness' typical of spoken language, the 'slangy,' substandard expressions, the dialectal peculiarities, inane misuses of language characteristic of the uneducated or semi-educated speakers."[50] Even more important than this definition of the workings of *skaz* is its function as a "mode of characterization," in which the "idiosyncratic verbal mannerisms often reveal his [the character's] personality traits."[51]

Not only does the use of *skaz* enable Stefanyk to reveal character, but the mixture of the *skaz* and the author's own standard language, or even the lack of the author altogether, provides a necessary dramatic tension between two realities. In other words, to quote Erlich once more:

> The narrative manner becomes thus a technique of indirection—a kind of compositional synecdoche. A tension is effected between two views of reality—the "overt"—and clearly inadequate view, offered by the speaker . . . and the implicit one, presumably that of the author and of the "ideal" reader.[52]

In "The Thief" this tension comes about from the lack of any moral judgement whatsoever from the author. The two sides to the issue are presented from the point of view of the characters. Each is right in his own way; no one is damned; no one accused. Yet the "implicit" reality calls forth from the reader several "buts" when it comes to the question of lynch law. In many of the other novellas the peasant characters have their own stoical explanations of the tragedy which falls on them and all of these become much more poignant because they are opposed in the reader's mind to the implicit reasons shared silently between author and reader. In this respect the novella "The Maple Leaves," in its final form, is a failure. Stefanyk ruins it by the addition of various reasons (social conditions, exploitation by the gentry, etc.) for Ivan's plight. This outward complaint, this "it is all their fault," destroys the necessary tension between the "overt" and "implicit" realities. Everything becomes overt.

Although from what has been said, the use of dialect seems full of merit and indispensable to the structure of Stefanyk's novella, most scholars dealing with the works of Stefanyk, his critics, and his editors, as well as Stefanyk himself, have had serious doubts about the necessity or usefulness of dialect. Stefanyk's own attitude to this question was rather ambivalent. In his incipient years as an author he seemed to favor dialect very strongly. In 1899, in a letter to his future wife, O. Hamorak, he complained about the translations of his novellas into Polish by W. Moraczewski:

> . . . I became convinced from the translations in Życie that one, it seems, can't translate my novellas into any language. It comes out poorly.[53]

This feeling that something was lost when his novellas were translated, Stefanyk carried over also to the idea of having his works rewritten in literary Ukrainian. He felt that "in the course of correcting the text [putting it into literary Ukrainian], something evaporated from it—that fragrance of my own native tongue, which has in it both the briny peasant sweat and the fragrances of wormwood and wild thyme . . ."[54]

Writers from Eastern Ukraine, admirers, and editors-to-be, however, incessantly bombarded Stefanyk with requests to clean up his jargon, to make the novellas more accessible to the Ukrainian reader at large. A good example is a letter from Borys Hrinchenko in which he asks for permission to include two of Stefanyk's novellas in an almanac he was preparing and then makes a plea for the purity of language:

> But here the language stands in the way. Your language is very local. Because of this it gives a story an original color and in general I like it very much. But the wide reading public here will at times not understand it at all . . .

> Therefore would you permit me to make some changes in the language?

> 1. Would you permit me to write words without adhering to all the phonetic local characteristics, but to write them the way they are written in our literary language, that is:
> not *ch'isaty* but *chesaty* [to comb]
> not *vistariv* but *vystariv* [grew old]
> not *papirch'yk* but *papirchyk* [piece of paper], and so forth?

> 2. Would you permit the changing of some words: for example, *bakhur* [brat] (47), for here *bakhur* is a profligate man (can one not write *khlopets'* [little boy] instead?)

80

You will say that this will dull somewhat the original colors, make the style pale. It is hard to argue against this. But instead you will reach a wider audience . . .55

Although such arguments as Hrinchenko's were not extremely convincing (any reader with intelligence can figure out that *ch'isaty* and *chesaty* mean the same and lexical differences can always be footnoted), toward the later part of his life Stefanyk began to change his mind. In 1922, in a letter to V. Simovych, Stefanyk makes a plea for the standardization of his language:

Even though you are begging off, I really entreat you, if you have the time, to Ukrainianize my jargon, if not now, then later.56

A few years later he admits to I. Lyzanivs'ky that in his old age his jargon irritates him somewhat.57 And in his speech in 1926 at his jubilee he cautions other writers to avoid the use of jargon in their works.58

Simovych, however, had great difficulty in purifying Stefanyk's language without the loss of artistic merit.59 Lyzanivs'ky's Ukrainianized edition of Stefanyk's work in 1927 was bitterly attacked for its "perversion" of Stefanyk's language,60 and the battle between the adherents of a "literary" Stefanyk and the "dialectal" one has been raging ever since. It must be admitted that something is certainly lost from the flavor of a Stefanyk novella when it is rendered in pure literary Ukrainian. Even more is lost, of course, when the work is translated into another language. But to maintain that without the dialect Stefanyk loses all of his artistic merit is a little too strong. This would relegate Stefanyk's art to Kachurovs'ky's description of the novellas as "stylized notes of some dialectological expedition."61 More to the point are the views of Ivan Ohiyenko, a scholar of the Ukrainian language and an advocate of a "literary" Stefanyk, who maintained:

. . . that the matter is not in the language but in the magnitude of the literary talent can be seen from the writings of other writers who wrote in a dialectal language, for example the works of Marko Cheremshyna. V. Stefanyk towers over Cheremshyna with his literary talent, even though the use of the literary language is the same in both of them.62

Nevertheless, the use of a dialect, a stylized dialect at that (incorporating individualized peculiarities of character), was quite necessary for the *skaz* manner of characterization used by

Stefanyk. This individualized language also added a note of endearment, of human frailty and foible. It is in a way a humorous note which acts like laughter through tears, emphasizing the tragic hopelessness of the uneducated and simple peasant in his daily plight, in his struggle with a world in which he is merely a pawn. Words like *dokhtir* (*doktor* = doctor), *uptyka* (*apteka* = pharmacy), provide sadly comic relief, a heightened catharsis, bringing a wry smile and a tear into the reader's eye at one and the same time.

Yet, Ohiyenko is also correct that it is more a matter of literary talent than of language. Although there are a few stories in Stefanyk which are humorous ("The Pious Woman" for example), where the humor to a great degree comes not only from the situation but also from the language used by the characters, and although in every story the dialect provides personalized characterization and the note of human frailty, the majority of the novellas can carry the great power, the great emotional charge, which Stefanyk's novellas generate, even when they are transformed into literary Ukrainian or translated into another language. Moreover, it seems that the universality of Stefanyk's characters, a universality which partially comes across in the psychological motivations and situations provided by the author, is heightened even more when the language is standardized. The reader can much more readily visualize the situation in terms of "there but for the grace of God," if the characters speak in a language to which he is accustomed.

It must be realized that the problem is at best scholarly, if not pedantic. It cannot be finally solved. The fact remains that Stefanyk used a dialect in his writings and, though he minimized its use in the later stories, he never abandoned it despite his exhortations to the contrary. The fact also remains that Stefanyk used the dialect as part of structure and as such it becomes an essential element of his novella. The use of the monologue and dialogue in dialect, interspersed with author's remarks in a more literary language; the short exchanges, the fact that the sentence is the basic unit of writing—all this leads to the fifth and final feature of a Stefanyk novella, its rhythmic quality. A separate chapter, however, is needed for an adequate discussion of this last but, in respect to structure, most important feature of a Stefanyk novella.

FOOTNOTES

[1] V. M. Lesyn, *Vasyl' Stefanyk i ukrayins'ka proza kintsya XIX st.* (Chernivtsi, 1965), p. 12.

[2] M. Ivchenko, "Tvorchist' Vasylya Stefanyka," *Ukrayina*, Bks. 2-3 (1926), p. 184.

[3] Henry H. H. Remak, "Novella," in Wolfgang Bernard Fleischmann, ed., *Encyclopedia of World Literature in the 20th Century* (New York, 1969), II, 466.

[4] Rafael Koskimies, "Die Theorie der Novelle," *Orbis Litterarum*, XIV (1959), 65-88.

[5] Remak, "Novella," p. 466.

[6] Ihor Kachurovs'ky, *Novela yak zhanr* (Buenos Aires, 1958), p. 20.

[7] *Ibid.*, pp. 6-8.

[8] *Ibid.*, p. 24.

[9] F. M. Bilets'ky, *Opovidanny, novela, narys* (Kiev, 1966), pp. 9 and 25.

[10] *Ibid.*, p. 25.

[11] B. Tomashevsky, *Teoriya literatury: poetika* (Moscow, 1931), pp. 191-97.

[12] Kachurovs'ky, *Novela yak zhanr*, p. 29. Volodymyr Vynnychenko (1880-1951) is a writer of short stories as well as novels in which he examined the morality of the *fin de siècle* intelligentsia and advocated a new morality of being honest with oneself, that is, having one's thought, will and feelings in total harmony. By this one can justify all sorts of degradations of human dignity and arrive at total amorality.

[13] *Ibid.*, p. 29.

[14] Sean O'Faolain, *The Short Story* (New York, 1964), pp. 169-223. The fact that O'Faolain's theories on the short story are applicable also to the novella was realized by other theoreticians of the novella. See, for example, Rafael Koskimies, "Die Theorie der Novelle," where he disputes certain of O'Faolain's points.

[15] J. Berg Esenwein, *Writing the Short Story: A Practical Handbook on the Rise, Structure, Writing, and Sale of the Modern Short Story* (New York, 1909), p. 30 as reprinted in Eugene Current-Garcia and Walton R. Patric, *What is the Short Story?* (Chicago, 1961), p. 56.

[16] Ivan Denysyuk, "Problemy suchasnoyi novely," *Radyans'ke literaturoznavstvo*, No. 8 (1966), p. 6.

17 *Ibid.*

18 V. V. Fashchenko, "Novelistychna kompozytsiya," *Ukrayins'ka mova i literatura v shkoli*, No. 7 (1968), p. 18.

19 *Ibid.*, p. 20.

20 *Ibid.*, p. 21.

21 E. K. Bennett, *A History of the German Novelle* (Cambridge, 1965), p. 18.

22 *Ibid.*, p. 19.

23 Olga Scherer-Virski, *The Modern Polish Short Story* (The Hague, 1955), pp. 27-30.

24 Remak, "Novella," p. 468.

25 Koskimies, "Die Theorie der Novelle," pp. 85-86.

26 *Ibid.*, p. 86.

27 Bennett, *A History of the German Novelle*, p. 12.

28 Scherer-Virski, *The Modern Polish Short Story*, p. 31.

29 *Ibid.*

30 Arnold Hirsch, *Der Gattungsbegriffe 'Novelle'* (Germanische Studien, Heft 64), p. 37, as quoted by E. K. Bennett, *History of the German Novelle*, p. 147.

31 B. Tomashevsky, *Teoriya literatury, Poetika*, p. 191.

32 See Stefanyk, Letter to W. Moraczewski, Cracow, June 1900, in *Povne zibrannya tvoriv*, III, 217. Stefanyk writes:

> The novella "The Arsonist" is written live from a similar drama which I wanted to send to a competition, but which I destroyed.
>
> I In the house of Kurochka
> II In the tavern outside of town
> III In the manor barn
> IV In the house of the Arsonist
>
> Such was the distribution of acts. The third act was the best, but I did not like the drama as a whole. I did not give up the idea of writing this play, but later when I am a little more peaceful.

33 D. Koziy, "Spynys' khvylyno! Ty prekrasna!" *Lysty do pryyateliv*, Nos. 171-73, Bks. 7-9 (1967), p. 27 does not call this scene a separate novella, but hints at this in his discussion of the way Stefanyk captured a single moment in its absolute immobile purity.

34 Usually Stefanyk is not concerned with the biography of a character. As M. S. Hrytsyuta points out: "If he takes from it [the biography] certain facts, it is only those facts which have a direct relationship to that which is portrayed." See M. S. Hrytsyuta, "Vasyl' Stefanyk," p. 246. One may also recall Scherer-Virski's statements that biographical references detract from the dramatic suspense. (See above, p. 69.)

35 I. Franko, Afterword to his translation of S. Rusova's article "Stare y nove v suchasniy ukrayins'kiy literaturi," *LNV*, XXV (1906), 82-83.

[36]Ye. O. Nenadkevych, "Iz studiy nad stylem Frankovoyi i Stefanykovoyi novely," *Zapysky Volyns'koho instytutu narodnoyi osvity im. Ivana Franka*, (Zhytomyr, 1927) Bk. 2, pp. 81-109; see especially the definition above on pp. 49 to 52.

[37]*Ibid.*, p. 101.

[38]M. Yevshan, "Vasyl' Stefanyk," *Pid praporom mystetstva* (Kiev, 1910), Bk. I, p. 106.

[39]A. B. Muzychka, (no source given) as quoted by Mykola Zerov, "Marko Cheremshyna i halyts'ka proza," *Vid Kulisha do Vynnychenka* (Kiev, 1929), p. 159.

[40]D. Lukiyanovych, "Nova faza tvorchosty Vasylya Stefanyka," *LNV*, Vol. LXXXIX, Bk. 2 (1926), p. 179.

[41]See Volodymyr Blavats'ky, "Stefanyk u teatri—storinka z istoriyi teatru 'Zahrava,' *Kul'turno-mystets'kyy kalendar Al'manakh Ukrayins'-koho slova na 1947* (Regensburg, 1947), pp. 66-67; and Volodymyr Blavats'ky, "Moyi zustrichi z Stefanykom," in Toma Kobzey, *Velykyy riz'bar ukrayins'kykh selayns'kykh dush*, pp. 185-91; as well as V. Stefanyk, "Pid vrazhinnyam vystavy 'Zemli,'" *Novyy chas*, No. 15 (1937), reprinted in *Povne zibrannya tvoriv*, II, 83-85.

[42]H. Hrebenyuk, "Pokuts'ka hrupa pys'mennykiv," *Chervonyy shlyakh*, No. 4 (1929), p. 116.

[43]Nonetheless a quick comparison between Stefanyk's "The Thief" and Franko's "The Peasant Commission" shows that for the first 105 words Franko uses only 19 verbs and for 311 words only 54. See: I. Franko, *Tvory* (New York, 1956), II, 383-84.

[44]Osyp Makovey, Letter to V. Stefanyk, L'viv, March 9, 1898, published by M. Hrytsyuta, *Literaturna Ukrayina*, November 27, 1964.

[45]See Stefanyk, *Povne zibrannya tvoriv*, II, 72-74.

[46]M. S. Hrytsyuta, "Vasyl' Stefanyk," p. 234.

[47]Nenadkevych, "Iz studiyi nad stylem Frankovoyi i Stefanykovoyi novely," p. 101.

[48]For a phonetical analysis of Stefanyk's language see: Julian Genyk-Berezovs'kyj, "Die Sprache V. S. Stefanyks," (unpublished Ph.D. dissertation), Karl-Franzens University, Graz (Austria), 1947. For a controversy on the approach to Stefanyk's language see: O. O. Bilyavs'ka, "Pryntsypy naukovoho vydannya tvoriv V. Stefanyka," pp. 258-59. For a short description of typical dialecticism see V. Lesyn, *Vasyl' Stefanyk i ukrayins'ka proza kintsya XIX st.*, pp. 81-82.

[49]M. F. Stanivs'ky, "Tvorchist' Vasylya Stefanyka; Tezy dopovidey," as quoted by O. O. Bilyavs'ka, "Pryntsypy naukovoho vydannya tvoriv V. Stefanyka," p. 259. Similar views are expressed by Ivan Kovalyk, "Do kharakterystyky movy V. Stefanyka," *Ridna mova*, No. 4 (1937), pp. 160-64, where he writes: "This language dualism of Stefanyk . . . is not a chance thing, it is a preconceived fact, a system . . ." Also by V. Lesyn, *Vasyl' Stefanyk i ukrayins'ka proza kintsya XIX st.*, p. 65 and also in all other works by the same author where he talks of language he stresses the

duality of Stefanyk's language.

[50] Victor Erlich, "Notes on the Uses of Monologue in Artistic Prose," *International Journal of Slavic Linguistics and Poetics*, Nos. 1-2 (1959), p. 225.

[51] *Ibid.*

[52] *Ibid.*, p. 226.

[53] Letter to O. Hamorak, 1899, as printed in *Novyy chas*, No. 44, March 1, 1937, as reprinted by T. Kobzey, *Velykyy riz'bar Ukrayins'kykh selyans'kykh dush*, p. 224.

[54] V. Stefanyk (no source given) as quoted by M. Rudnyts'ky, *Pys'mennyky zblyz'ka* (L'viv, 1958), p. 129.

[55] Borys Hrinchenko, Letter to V. Stefanyk, Chernihiv, October 16, 1899, as published in *Literaturna Ukrayina*, January 28, 1964.

[56] Letter to V. Simovych, Rusiv, May 16, 1922, *Tvory* (1964), p. 462.

[57] Letter to I. Lyzanivs'ky, Rusiv, March 17, 1924, *ibid.*, p. 466.

[58] M. Rudnyts'ky, "Yoho slovo. Vasyl' Stefanyk pro sebe," *Dilo* Vol. 45, No. 6 (10,974), January 7, 1927, p. 4.

[59] See note in *Tvory* (1964), pp. 530-31.

[60] See Yu. O. [Yuriy Okunevs'ky-Morachewski], "Review of V. Stefanyk, *Tvory*, ed. I. Lyzanivs'ky (Kharkiv, 1927)," *LNV*, Bks. VII-VIII (1928), pp. 355-59.

[61] See note 13 above.

[62] Ivan Ohiyenko, "Hovirka chy literaturna mova?" *Ridna mova*, No. 3 (1937), p. 122.

CHAPTER IV

STRUCTURE OF STEFANYK'S NOVELLA

The fifth feature of a Stefanyk novella is its rhythmic quality. Although there is a cadence and a rhythm in every prose and even in speech itself, readers of Stefanyk notice immediately that in Stefanyk's novellas this rhythm is very pronounced and specific. V. Lesyn pointed out that this is the case with all authors of psychological prose, for "they paid considerable attention to the formation of an original rhythm of prose, since it also has an effect on the mood of the reader."[1] M. Ivchenko went even further and maintained that "the first and most important peculiarity of form, on which the whole is based, is rhythm."[2]

In discussing this point, Ivchenko, however, limited himself only to the most obvious element of rhythm, that of cadence, and quite rightly maintained that Stefanyk's prose has a pounding staccato rhythm. He did not fully explore how Stefanyk achieves this, as he calls it, "energetic" rhythm, nor did he really indicate how the whole work is based on this "most important peculiarity of form." Yet it can be shown that indeed the form, the structure of Stefanyk's novella is based on its rhythm. For this, however, rhythm has to be viewed in broader terms than mere cadence. One does not argue with Ivchenko's assertion that Stefanyk derives his "energetic" rhythm from a specific sentence structure, but one disagrees with the idea that these short, abrupt sentences, often grammatically incomplete, are the only components from which the staccato rhythm is derived. Though important and perhaps most readily noticeable, they are, nonetheless, but part of a larger whole.

The rhythm of a Stefanyk novella, rhythm viewed in its totality, rhythm as the basic element of structure, as the "soul" of composition, consists of five functions: the function of time, the function of narration, of syntax, of vocabulary, and of tropes. A study of the workings of these functions in a given novella leads to the description of its rhythm and at the same time shows how the author structured his novella to achieve this rhythm and why.

Perhaps the best way this can be accomplished is by a thorough dissection of one of Stefanyk's novellas. Since each novella necessarily has its own peculiarities, it is important to chose for this dissection one which structurally best typifies a good Stefanyk novella. Stefanyk, unlike most writers, did not develop gradually from one collection of novellas to another. He appeared as an accomplished writer already with his first published work. Although there are still novellas in his later life which are just as good as his first ones, they are never better. It seemed appropriate, therefore, for this analysis of structure to choose one of his first novellas, namely "The Blue Book."

One of the first things the reader notices about "The Blue Book" is that it, like most of Stefanyk's novellas, is extremely short (not quite two pages). As mentioned in the preceeding chapter, brevity is one of the primary features of a Stefanyk novella. Since rhythm is the basis of construction, the brevity of a novella is dependent on one of the functions of rhythm, namely on the function of time. By the function of time in general one means the forward movement of time in a given work of prose. H. E. Bates postulates that "the forward movement of time is the pulse and nerve of the novel, but in the short story time need not move, except by an infintesimal fraction."[3] From this it would appear that in a short story, in a novella, there need not be a movement of time and therefore no rhythm of time since rhythm presupposes movement. That, however, is not the case.

The study of the function of time as an aspect of rhythm in a novella reveals that indeed there is a movement, a rhythm of time, and that dependent on it are all of the other rhythms. The very length of the novella is dependent on it. Thus for example, as Scherer-Virski points out:

> If a story is constructed upon the principle of a small amount of objective time, this time, which must fill the story, passes slowly and has to be treated intensively and in detail. A temporal back-stage makes itself felt; the short time which actually passes is assisted by the *time which may have passed or the time which will or would pass in the future.* In this way psychological time is blown up to tremendous structural proportions. It ceases to be a static frame and becomes a rather dynamic force that moves the story itself. Something possessing the unity of a whole is required to happen in this short time; noth-

ing may happen outside of it. The story thus becomes either a turning point in a character or in a life, or the dream of a whole life, or the significant moments preceding death, or a great discovery, a vision, a decision, the dramatic meeting of two forces, of the consummation of a conflict between two forces or within one force.[4]

Thus, whereas the short objective time delineates the length of the novella and determines the type of an episode described, the relationship between the moment, the time now, and the time which passed or will pass provides the novella with a definite rhythm.

The above can be readily shown in "The Blue Book." To illustrate, however, Stefanyk's use of the function of time as well as the other functions of rhythm it is necessary to cite the novella in its entirety:

The Blue Book[5]

That Antin, the one hollering over there on the common, was always somehow unfortunate. He always lost everything and never gained anything. He'd buy a cow and it would die; he'd buy a pig and it would develop swine measles. Every time like this.

But when his wife died, and his two sons followed her, Antin was no longer himself. He drank, and drank, and drank; he drank away his piece of land, his garden, and finally sold his house. He sold the house and got from the bailiff a blue book for servants, and he's supposed to go and hire himself someplace.

There, drunk, he's sitting and reciting out loud for the whole village to hear to whom he sold the land, to whom the garden, and to whom the house.

"I sold it, that's all. It's not mine and that's it. Not mi-i-ne. Oh, if only my granddad would rise from his grave. Yes sir, four oxen smooth as snails, twenty-four acres of land, houses all over the village. He had everything. And his grandson—look."

He kept showing the blue book to the village.

"I'm drinking and I'll keep on drinking. I'm drinking out of my own money and it's nobody's business, no one has any right to it. And he says to me: so you've pissed away your land. He stamps the book and he scolds me. In my time, I've seen better bailiffs than that."

"May you croak as easy as it is easy for me here."

"I'm leaving the house, leaving it completely; I kissed the threshold and I'm going. It's not mine and that's all. Beat me away like a stray dog. You're welcome—go ahead. It was mine and now it's not. I'm coming outside and the forest whispers, speaks in words: return, Antin, to your house, return, return."

Antin is pounding his chest with his fists and the sound carries all over the village.

"Such a longing came upon me, you know, such a longing. I'm going back into the house. I sat and sat and then I'm leaving; it's not mine, what am I to say, if it's not mine . . ."

"Hope my enemies have such a time dying as I had leaving my own house."

"I'm coming outside and it's as if a spell came upon me. There's green moss on the roof; it needs thatching. It's all over; finished; a stone into water. No, I'm not the one, my dear, who's going to thatch you. Even a stone, if it were really a stone, would burst from grief!"

After this word, Antin is pounding the earth as if it were a stone.

"I sat at the base of the house [a bank of clay or earth around a peasant's hut, used for sitting]. The wife, rest her soul, whitewashed it and I brought clay in the wheelbarrow. I want to get up and the base won't let me; I'm trying to make a step and it won't let go. And I'm so sorry, so sorry. I'm ready to die . . . I'm sitting there and moaning, I'm moaning as if someone were skinning me alive. People are staring at this contrition."

"Look, there by the gate the priest bid the wife farewell. The whole village cried. She was, he says, a proper wife, industrious . . ."

"Go ahead, turn in your graves, you wretches, for I'm no good. I drank away everything right down to the skin. I even drank away the material you left, do you hear, Maria, and you, Vasyl'ko and you too, Yurchyk; now your dad will wear hemp shirts and go about bringing water for the Jews . . ."

Now Antin is pointing to the bailiff's house.

"But the bailiff's wife, she's a good woman. She brought me some bread for the road, so that the

90

bailiff wouldn't see. May the God Almighty do well for your children, wherever they go. May God give all of you better than he gave me . . ."

"What right do I have to sit on someone's base? I'm going. As soon as I made a step, the windows began to cry. They started weeping like little children. The forest keeps whispering to them and they send tear after tear . . . The house started to weep for me. It wept like a child after its mother."

"I wiped the windows with the bottom of my coat, so that they wouldn't weep for me, for it's silly; and away I went, completely."

"Oh, it's as easy as to chew rocks. The world is dark ahead of me . . ."

Antin is making a sweeping motion with his hand around himself.

"I still have some money here and, yessir, I'll drink. I'll drink with our people. I'll let it all go with them. Let them remember the time I was leaving the village."

"Look, here in my pocket I have my blue book. This is my house, and my field, and my garden. I'm going with it to the end of the world. The book is from the Kaiser; I have an open door wherever I go. Wherever. Among the lords, among the Jews, among all faiths."

From the above it can be seen that the objective time is indeed very short, not more than an hour, hence the extremely short length of the novella. Readily discernible as well is the fact, as pointed out by Scherer-Virski, that the objective time is "assisted by the time which may have passed or the time which will pass in the future." Also as pointed out by Scherer-Virski, such a blowing-up of the psychological time makes the subject of the novella a study of the effect on a character caused by a turning point in his life: the passing of Antin from a proprietor of his own to a servant. All this is the result of the function of time in general. What cannot be seen as readily and what must be pointed out is the result of the function of time in particular with reference to rhythm.

A perusal of "The Blue Book" will show that there is a definite rhythm of time derived from the interactions of the tenses. "The Blue Book" is one of six novellas[6] written in the present tense, that is, the author-narrator acts as a reporter for something being seen by him and the reader at the time of narration. Thus the novella begins with the narrator pointing to "that Antin, the one hollering there on the common." This sets the objective time limit of the novella; that is, the novella will describe this Antin or will reveal what it is that he is shouting or doing. Immediately the narrator shifts to the past tense to support the objective time with the previous history of Antin. This arresting of the progression of the objective time (which, one must remember, will move at an infinitesimal pace) lasts for two brief paragraphs which form the *Vorgeschichte* of the novella. In the following paragraph the narrator returns again to the present objective time ("There, drunk, he's sitting and reciting . . .) after which the reader himself is allowed to hear what Antin is reciting. From this moment on to the end of the novella, the narrator periodically interrupts the monologue of the hero with statements which describe what the hero is doing during the span of his monologue. Besides describing the actions of the hero, these interruptions by the narrator serve a two-fold rhythmical function: one, they punctuate the minuscule passing of objective time, thus providing the novella with a certain syncopation; and two, they enable the narrator to return the reader's attention from the time-past and time-future, into which he is taken by the monologue of the hero, to the time-present. This oscillation back and forth again provides a certain undulating rhythm which is necessary to emphasize the psychological undulations of the hero's soul.

It must be noted that in all of these interruptions by the narrator the present tense is used—in all except the first one: "He kept showing the blue book to the village." "Kept showing" *pokazuvav* is in the past tense imperfective aspect which implies a habitual action, suggesting that whereas all the other activities of the hero (pounding his chest, pounding the earth, pointing to the bailiff's house, making a sweeping motion with his hand) are done only once, the showing of the blue book was done repeatedly. This does not, however, explain effectively why the verb is in the past tense. There are only two possible explanations: that Stefanyk forgot himself and made an error, or that he did this on purpose for the sake of the emphasis produced by this jarring shift in tense.

The first explanation is highly unlikely when one considers that all these interruptions were additions to the second version of the novella. The first printed version which appeared in "Pratsya" did not have any of these remarks. It is highly unlikely, therefore, that Stefanyk upon editing his novella for second publication in his first collection while making these additions would have carelessly written one in the past tense and all the others in the present. The explanation must lie elsewhere. And indeed, when one carefully rereads the novella, one will see that this first interruption comes after a monologue which in reality, though coming from the mouth of the hero, is still a part of the *Vorgeschichte* of the narrator. In this monologue the hero relates once again that he has sold everything and then goes back into the past to recall how rich his grandfather had been and to contrast his grandfather's oxen and houses with his sole possession—the blue book. To make this contrast more effective what one requires here is not just a description of the hero's actions but a greater pause, a greater arresting of objective time. By placing the verb in the past tense, the narrator virtually prolongs, stretches, this moment to the point where from the vantage point of the present time it seems to be in the past.[7]

A specific rhythm is also derived from the alternation of tenses in the monologue of the hero. It soon becomes apparent that although the hero is narrating something which happened to him before the objective time of the novella (before he is seen drunk on the common), he relates most of his experiences in the present progressive tense. This not only gives the impression that the hero is reliving his parting with the house, as he is narrating, but also shows that it is extremely difficult for him to accept this tragic moment as something which has already happened and is therefore in the past. Only after he relives the incident and reaches an emotional climax as he addresses his deceased wife and children, does he begin to view the whole thing in the irrevocable past. The former "I'm leaving" becomes the final "and away I went, completely."

Moreover, there is still another rhythm of tenses in his monologue. In each segment of the monologue there is always at least one shift of tense: "I'm drinking (objective time now) to the historic present "And he says to me" to the past "I've seen better bailiffs . . ." One can see a similar alternation in each segment of his monologue except for the closing one which is totally in the present tense. The hero is back in the objective time and now quite aware of his present reality: "I have my blue book . . . I have an open door wherever I go. Wherever. Among the lords, among the Jews, among all faiths."

Equally important to the function of time, and closely related to it, is the function of narration. The function of narration as an element of rhythm determines the way in which the author arranges his narrative material. The rhythm is derived from the alternations between descriptions, dialogues, monologues, pauses, and interruptions in narration. In Stefanyk's novellas descriptive narrative is at a bare minimum: a short *Vorgeschichte* followed by even sparser authorial comments. But although the narrative is usually wholly dialogue or monologue it never flows smoothly but proceeds in little spurts, periodically punctuated by the author's narration. This narration can be as condensed as one word, as seen, for example, in the novella "Svyatyy vechir" (Christmas Eve) where the monologue of the heroine is punctuated by one word from the author: *pyla* ([she] drank). This is done for five consecutive times followed by three authorial remarks which progressively grow longer as the drunken frenzy of the heroine increases: *napylasya* ([she] had a drink) to *vypyla reshtu* ([she] drank the remainder) to finally *hatyla holovoyu v stiny, yak skazhena* ([she] was pounding her head against the wall, as if mad).

In "The Blue Book," however, these authorial interruptions serve, as pointed out above, not only to punctuate narration but also to keep the reader aware of the objective time. This is a peculiarity of the six novellas narrated in the present tense. In the other novellas these interruptions serve primarily the rhythmic function of punctuating the flow of narration.

The pulsing, or spurting of narration is achieved not only by the alternations between direct narrative and direct speech but also by the fact that even in the direct speech there are pauses and turns. Each such pause or turn Stefanyk indicates physically by starting a new paragraph even though the speaker is still the same. This technique has been previously illustrated in respect to "The Thief." In "The Blue Book" it can be seen best in the three, three, three, and then four breaks in the monologue of Antin, starting with the passage "I'm drinking" and ending with "The world is dark ahead of me . . ." In the first trio as well as in the second, Antin breaks off the first section of his monologue to invoke a curse, first on the bailiff ("May you croak . . .) and then on his enemies in general ("Hope my enemies have such a time . . ."). In the third trio the interruption is in the form of a flash-back to the day of his wife's funeral. This flash-back not only interrupts the narration but sets up the third segment of this monologue in which Antin reaches the height of his anguish: the address to his wife ("proper and industrious") and to his two sons stating that he's no good and that finally he will "go about bringing water to the Jews . . ." From this moment on the emotional pitch of the novella is on the decline. The following quatrain of monologue begins with a recollection of the bailiff's wife and an invocation to God to give her and her children all of the best—thus effectively setting up a contrast with the first monologue segment of the first trio where Antin recalls the bailiff himself and then wishes him a hard death. The second segment of monologue in this quatrain is a lyrical interlude by which the hero's anguish is somewhat alleviated by the realization that at least his house cried for him. The third segment of monologue shows the hero reconciling himself with the reality of his situation and cutting short the lyrical mood set up in the segment before ("I wiped the windows . . . so they wouldn't weep for me, *for it's silly.*"). And finally the fourth segment of monologue, the shortest one, is no more than a sigh from the hero who finally accepted the reality of his situation. Finally, after the last interruption of the author, Antin's monologue is split into two segments, each relating to aspects of his present condition—a condition where he can do but two things: drink and go forth with his blue book.

This pulsating rhythm which is derived from these interruptions in the process of narration is further emphasized by the third function of rhythm, the function of syntax, wherein the internal structure of sentences as well as their relation to one another contribute greatly to the rhythm of the whole novella. One can discern four basic features of the internal structure of a Stefanyk sentence: ellipsis, inversion, repetition, and parallelism.

In his study, *The Syntax of Modern Literary Ukrainian*, George Shevelov points to the existence of basically two types of incomplete sentences in literary Ukrainian:

> The incompleteness may be conditioned by the absence of the minimum component of sentence because it is obvious from the context or the circumstances (grammatically incomplete sentences) or by a conscious rejection of a word for the sake of intensifying an emotional tone (emotionally incomplete sentences) . . .[8]

Both types of ellipsis, the grammatical and the emotional, are used very effectively by Stefanyk. The most common form of grammatical ellipsis found in his novellas and evidenced in "The Blue Book" is the omission of the personal pronoun usually in places where its use is totally unnecessary for the meaning of the sentence and its inclusion would detract from the striking rhythm of the sentence. Examples for this type of ellipsis are plentiful; to cite but a few:

> *Pyv, a pyv, a pyv;* ([He] drank, and [he] drank, and [he] drank;)

> *propyv bukatu polya, probyv horod, a teper khatu prodav.* ([he] drank away [his] piece of land, [he] drank away [his] garden, and now [he] sold his house.)

95

vkhodzhu nazad do khaty. ([I'm] going back into the house.)

kupyt' korovy, ta y zdokhne ([he'd] buy a cow, and [it] would die)

This omission of the pronoun is not limited only to the cases where it serves its nominative function and is in a way already incorporated into the ending of the verb. It can also occur in the oblique case function of the pronoun as in the following example where the accusative of the pronoun "I" is omitted:

Byy yak psa vid chuzhoyi khaty! (Beat [me] away as a stray dog!)

Not as frequent but often very pronounced are the instances of emotional ellipsis. One such striking example is:

Kamin' voda (Stone water)

where Stefanyk forms a sentence by just naming two substances both in the nominative case. The reader is expected to supply the rest, i.e., "as a stone into the water is gone forever, so it is with Antin and his house." The context in which this appears enables the reader to supply the meaning correctly. This is quite a striking and extraordinary example used, however, very well by Stefanyk to put across the emotional burden of the hero. In such moments words do not come easily and often the mind just signals forth in images as here: "stone" and "water."

Much more common for Stefanyk is the following type of emotional ellipsis:

Usyuda, I po panakh, i po zhydakh, i po vs'yki viri. (Everywhere. And among the lords, and among the Jews, and among all faiths.)

The omitted part in both sentences preceeds them: *mayu dveri vtvoreni* ([I] have an open door). This willful omission of a whole part of a sentence (because it is understood from the preceding sentence) enables Stefanyk to stress the most important, and, for the purposes of the novella, sarcastic elements of the last two sentences. This type of underlying by omission is also seen in the following elliptic sentence:

Mospane, shtyry voly yak slymuzy, dvatsit' shtyry morgy polya, khaty na tsile selo! (Yessir, four oxen like snails, twenty-four acres of land, houses all over the village!)

The verb *mav* (had) which is omitted is thereby emphasized. The rhythm of this type of construction has been previously noted by V. Hladky in Stefanyk's letters:

> It is this 'elliptic gradation' in the construction of a phrase, and not just 'simple sentences' which forms this generally noted striking rhythm in Stefanyk and likens his sentences to a line of verse, giving them a poetic ring.[9]

Equally important in the syntax function of rhythm is the frequent use of inversion. In Stefanyk's novellas this deviation from normal word order in the sentence ranges from simple transpositions of subject and verb: *Ydu ya* (go I); *Vikhodzhy ya* (Coming out I); *siv ya* (sat I), to a transposition of modifier and noun: *did miy* (granddad my), *knyzhku sluzhbovu* (book servant's), to a transposition of verb and adverbial phrase: *yak iz sela-m vikhodyv* (as from the village I was leaving), to a more complicated splitting and transposition of a verb: *d'yadya me u rantukhovykh sorochkakh khodyty* (should be: *d'ydya khodyty me u rantukhovykh sorochkakh*, father will go about in hemp shirts) where the future particle (in contemporary Ukrainian written as the part of the verb though then still written separately) is left in place but the verb is transposed to the end of the sentence. Stefanyk's artistic use of inversion for a rhythmic effect can be seen very well in the following grouping of sentences:

> *propyv bakatu polya, propyv horod, a teper khatu prodav. Prodav khatu . . .* (drunk away [his] piece of land, drunk away the garden, and now house [he] sold. [he] sold [his] house . . .)

One can readily see the normal pattern of verb-object, which is repeated twice, disrupted by the transposition object-verb (*khatu prodav*). This is done not only to disrupt the rhythm but also to emphasize, by means of this disruption, that the most burning loss is the loss of the house. In the following sentence, Stefanyk again effectively reverts to the normal word order which makes the previous inversion the more noticeable.

The above example illustrates well also another feature of Stefanyk's use of the syntax function of rhythm, namely, repetition. Similar repetitions of verbs can be found all through the novella:

> *kupyt's korovu . . . kupyt' svynuy . . .* (he'd buy a cow . . . he'd buy a pig . . .)
> *posydiv, posydiv . . .* ([he] sat, sat . . .)
> *a pryspa ne puskaye, stupayu—ne puskaye* (and the base does not let go, I step—does not let go)

revu, tak revu (I'm moaning, moaning)

Not only verbs are repeated but other parts of the sentence as well; pronouns in such constructions as *komu prodav pole, komu horod, a komu khatu* (to whom [he] sold the land, to whom the garden, and to whom the house), and *ta y ty Vasyl'ku, ta y ty, Yurchyku* (and you, Vasyl'ko, and you, Yurchuk); nouns in such construction as *kamin'—aby kamin'* (stone—if it were stone); and even whole phrases as *Ne moye ta y reshta* (Not mine and that's all) which is the only phrase repeated twice without any alterations in the whole novella.

Shevelov points out that "repetition of a conjunction with every co-ordinate minimum component of a sentence creates a clear rhythmic pattern, generally with a gradual heightening of tone . . ."[10] This type of repetition can be seen in such series as: *pyv, a pyv, a pyv* (he drank, and drank, and drank), *moya khata, i moye pole, i moyi horody* (my house, and my field, and my gardens), and *I po panakh, i po zhydakh, i po vs'yki viri* (and among the lords, and among the Jews, and among all faiths).

The final feature of the inner structure of a sentence employed by Stefanyk is parallelism. When reading a novella by Stefanyk it becomes quite obvious that he often builds his sentences as a series of phrases. Very often, as in "The Blue Book," there is a very pronounced parallelism to the structure of these series. A one-to-one relationship seems to exist between two equal parts of a sentence which sometimes oppose and sometimes complement each other. The pause which automatically falls between these two components suggests an even undulating rhythm, back-and-forth. Examples of this type of parallelism prevail:

vse yshlo yemu z ruk, // a nicho v ruky (everything fell into his hands // and nothing into [his] hands)

kuput' korovu, // ta y zdokhne, //// kupyt' svynuy, // ta y reshetynu distane. (he'd buy a cow // it would die //// he'd buy a pig // it would get swine measles.)

bulo moye, // a teper chuzhe (it was mine // now it's foreign)

lysh khochu vstaty, // a pryspa ne puskaye, //// stupayu, // ne puskaye. (as soon as I want to get up // the base won't let me //// I make a step // it won't let go)

lysh postupyv-yem sy, // a vinka v plach' (as soon as I stepped away // the windows began to cry)

lis yim napovidaye, // a vony sl'ozu za sl'ozov prosi-
kayut (the forest whispers to them, // and they shed
tear after tear).

Besides this rather obvious parallelism there exists in "The
Blue Book" a greater semantic-structural parallelism of the
whole novella. Each novella has to be treated separately in this
respect since this parallelism is partially based on the "meaning"
of the novella. In "The Blue Book" Stefanyk manages to
emphasize the loss of Antin's possessions and contrasts these
with his new "gains" by an effective parallel opposition. First
Stefanyk sets the pattern: *propyv bukatu polya, propyv horod,*
a teper khatu prodav, then repeats the same: *komu prodav pole,*
komu horod, a komu khatu, follows it with a contrast to the
riches of Antin's granddad: *shtyry voly yak slymuzy, dvatsit'*
shtyry morgy polya, khaty na tsile selo, strengthens the contrast
by linking the three things of his former wealth with the present
possession, the blue book: *otse moya khata, i moye pole, i moyi*
horody (notice, that the order of these things has now been
changed), and finally reveals the ironic "wealth" of Antin at the
present time by pointing to the "three" opportunities he now
has: *i po panakh, i po zhydakh, i po vs'yki viri*. This symmetry
of form, so necessary for a short work of prose like the novella,
greatly enhances the inherent conflict between the cold and
detached presentation of the author (hence the symmetrical
form) and the material presented, the anguished outcry of a
man whose ineptitude has brought his own ruin. In this conflict
between the calm form and the turbulent content one finds a
partial explanation to the striking effect that Stefanyk's novellas produce on the reader.

Helpful in attaining this effect is also the fourth function
of rhythm, the function of vocabulary. The predominant feature of this function when pertaining to Stefanyk is, of course,
his use of dialect. The study of Stefanyk's dialect, however, is a
matter worthy of a separate work. For the purposes of this
study, Stefanyk's use of dialect has been sufficiently treated in
the preceding chapter. Here only certain specific instances will
be pointed out, where it is possible to see that Stefanyk's choice
of certain words was a matter of artistic taste and a sense of
rhythm.

It would be virtually impossible to show whether Stefanyk's use of a certain word was a conscious artistic selection if
one could not compare the finished novella with the manuscript
or at least with a variant which the author changed before
republication. Thus the only way to show Stefanyk's artistic use
of vocabulary is to compare the first published version of "The

Blue Book" with the final version of the novella in respect to changes, additions, and deletions of words and from this comparison see why each alteration was made.

Stefanyk made in all forty-two changes in the first published version of the novella. Only seven, however, can be viewed as strictly changes pertaining to vocabulary. The first such change occurs still in the *Vorgeschichte* of the novella:

First version:
ta y maye ity *do mista* ta tam sobi *yakoyi* slushby shukaty.
(and [he's] supposed to go to town and there look for some sort of serving position)

Final version:
ta y maye yty *des' naymatysya*, sluzhby sobi shukaty.
(and [he's] supposed to go somewhere and hire himself, look for a service position)

Thus the phrase "*do mista*" has been substituted by "*des'*," the indefinite adverb—a superior choice in view of the final paragraph of the novella where Antin claims that he has an open door anywhere he goes. It need not be the town at all. The second change, the insertion of the verb "*naymatysya*" is also an excellent change. For one, it provides Stefanyk with a good means of emphasis. By using "*naymatysya*" and placing it into opposition with the following phrase, "*sluzhby sobi shukaty*," Stefanyk manages through the use of this synonym to emphasize the fate now awaiting Antin. The deletion of "*yakoyi*" shows Stefanyk's preoccupation with concision. Since it is obvious that Antin will look for "some kind of service" (this is inherent in the use of the word "service," unmodified), there is no need to add the totally redundant indefinite pronoun "*yakoyi*." Redundance, after all, weakens the rhythm and the crispness of style. Another change, almost unnoticed at first, is the transposition of "*sobi sluzhby*" to "*sluzhby sobi*." This inversion greatly enhances the rhythm, for following the pause occurring after "*naymatysya*" the stress falls on "*sluzhby*" which could not happen with the weak stressed iambic "*sobi*." Moreover, the placing of "*sluzhby*" initially in the phrase stresses the greater importance of this word in relation to the others.

A second example of the way Stefanyk changed his text consists of an addition. Whereas in the first version Stefanyk had the sentence "*Ne moye, ta y reshta!*" (Not mine, and that's all), in the final version he adds "*Ne mo-o-ye*" (not mi-i-ne). This addition is interesting on two counts. While emphasizing

100

the fact that the house is no longer Antin's it also reflects the drawn-out manner of Antin's drunken speech. It is further interesting in that it is the only word so drawn out in the whole novella, thus underlining the motif behind Antin's sorrow: the house, the field, the garden are all no longer his.

A greater emotional value of the word as well as characterization prompted Stefanyk to make the following change:

First version:
A vin meni kazhe, "*grunt propyv-yes*"
(And he says to me, "you've drunk away your land")

Final version:
A vin meni kazhe: moy, grunt, *prists'yv-yes*
(And he says to me: so, you've pissed away your land)

The reader knows very well that Antin "drank away" his land. The figurative "pissed away," however, is so much more derisive and superbly reflects the scornful attitude of the bailiff.

Another example shows once again Stefanyk's preoccupation with concision and precision of narration:

First version:
Vikhodzhu na dvir, a lis shumyt *ta yak koly by kazav:*
(I'm coming outside and the forest rustles as if it were saying:)

Final version:
Vikhodzhu na dvir, a lis shumyt, *slovamy hovoryt*:
(I'm coming outside and the forest rustles, speaks in words:)

Not only is the phrase "as if it were saying" unwieldy, it is also imprecise. In Stefanyk's impressionistic manner of narration that is reported which the hero sees, feels or hears. In this case his tense imagination perceives the forest talking to him, not just rustling, *as if* it were talking. In the final version the personification is definite: the forest does speak to Antin; the verbs "rustles" and "speaks" are in opposition signifying one and the same act. The former signifies reality as is, the latter signifies reality as perceived by the hero. The use of "as if it were saying" would, however, reveal the hero cognizant of the fact that it only seems to him that the forest speaks.

A similar situation prompted the following change as well:

101

First version:
Lysh khochu vstaty, a to *shchos* ne puskaye, stupayu, ta y ne puskaye.
(As soon as I want to get up, something does not let me, I make a step and it does not let go.)

Final version:
Lysh khochu vstaty, a *pryspa* ne puskaye, stupayu— ne puskaye.
(As soon as I want to get up, the base does not let me, I make a step—it does not let go.)

The indefinite pronoun "something" in the first version suggests a supernatural force. This in itself would not be too bad. The second version, however, is better because it once again shows reality as it is perceived by the hero, and also emphasizes the attachment of Antin to his house. He is so loath to leave it that he sees the house itself as not wanting him to go. Later on the house even weeps for him. Moreover the deletion of "ta y" in the final version and the insertion of "—" in its place makes for a crisper, more rhythmic line and at the same time stresses the fact that the house "does *not* let go." The base, of course, is used synechdochically for house.

Stefanyk revealed great artistic taste and moderation when he made the next change:

First version:
Lis yim napovidaye, a vony lysh *kap, kap!*
(The forest whispers to them, and they only drip, drip!)

Final version:
Lis yim napovidaye, a vony *sl'ozu za sl'ozov prosi-kayut.*
(The forest whispers to them, and they ooze a tear after tear.)

Usually onomatopoeia greatly enriches the sound value of a line. In this case, however, the onomatopoeic "kap, kap" sounds as banal in Ukrainian as "drip, drip" in English. And it would indeed have been unfortunate had Stefanyk not changed this in the final version. This most lyrical and sensitive passage in the whole novella would have been totally ruined in bathos. The use of "sl'ozu za sl'ozov" with its alliterative "z" is further strengthened by the addition of the very specific verb. Stefanyk did not use the normal verb in this particular phrase, the verb "puskayut" (let, shed), but chose to use "prosikayut" (lit. Ukr. *prosyakayut'*) which literally means "to ooze" and, as the verb "ooze" in English, suggests a much more difficult and slow passage of water.

The final change to be discussed here is once more a matter of precision:

First version:
Temnyy s'vit, bo dakelyy navpered mene.
(A dark world, for it lies far ahead of me [literally: I have to go far].)

Final version:
Temnyy svit navpered mene . . .
(The world is dark ahead of me . . .)

Certainly the world is not dark because it is far, as the first version suggests. It is dark because of the hopeless situation in which the hero finds himself.

From the few examples above it can be seen that Stefanyk constructed his novellas very carefully indeed. Due, however, to his habit of discarding a page as soon as there was a mistake and beginning again from the start, there are very few first drafts available. This is unfortunate, for undoubtedly the changes between the manuscript first draft and the final version of the novella would be even more interesting and more revealing than the already later changes which occur between publications. But even these changes show that although Stefanyk's novellas are short enough to have been written in one "creative surge," nothing, almost to the word, was left in them to chance. Everything written was subordinated to the basic rhythm of construction and to the effect which the novella was to produce on the reader.

Part of the effect is derived by Stefanyk's skillful handling of the final function of rhythm, the function of tropes. Stefanyk uses his artistic devices sparingly but effectively, primarily to amplify the emotional value of a given situation. The synecdochial use of base for house, as mentioned above, or a similar use of windows weeping for the house weeping are good examples of this type of amplification of emotion. The same can be seen in Stefanyk's use of personification. In "The Blue Book" there are two personifications: the house with its metonymic variants, the base and the windows, and the forest—both very dear to the hero and therefore seen by him as live personages taking direct part in his woe. On the whole, Stefanyk's images are grounded in the peasant life and the surroundings of his characters. Although this might imply coarseness, very often the opposite is true; the images reflect the lyrical soul of both the characters and the author. The similes generally are quite plain and rooted in the peasant world. Most often it is a comparison between man and animal or some part of nature. In "The Blue Book" such similes appear as: "oxen, [smooth] as snails," "beat [me], like a stray dog," "ground like stone," "as easy as to chew stones." Elsewhere similar similes abound: strong as an ox, tremble like a leaf, soft as the earth, shook his hair like a mane of steel threads, and so forth. Stefanyk does not use many metaphors (in "The Blue Book" there are none), but when he does, it can be in an expanded form as the following example from "The Stone Cross":

> Just as when some underwave dislodges a huge stone from the water and places it on the shore, then that stone sits on the shore heavy and spiritless. The sun chips off pieces of the old sediments and draws on it small phosphorous stars. That stone blinks with dead reflections from the rising and setting of the sun and with its stone eyes it looks at the live water which no longer presses it as it had for ages. The stone looks from the shore at the water as if it were some lost happiness.

> So Ivan looked at the people, as the stone upon water.[11]

This passage provides two more examples of typical personification as it occurs in Stefanyk's works. In the Ukrainian version, moreover, such inversions as "*kam'yanymy ochyma svoyimy*" as well as the alliteration (*khVYlya VYkarbutyt' . . . naMULU i MALYUye . . . MALEn'ki . . . BLYmaye . . . BLYskamy . . . HLYAdyt' . . . HNEte . . . HNItyv*) enhance the rhythm and the poetical quality of the prose.

In "The Blue Book" alliteration is enriched by onomatopoeia in the passage describing the rustle-like whispering of the forest: *liS SHumyt, SLovamy hovoryt: vernySY, Antone, do khaty, vernySY*; or in the passage referring to the weeping of the windows: *LiS yim napovidaye, a vony SL'OZU ZA SL'OZOV proSIkayut.*

It seems that more examples of tropes, although readily available, would serve only in amplifying what has already been said. The same holds true for the whole structural analysis presented in this chapter. Although only one novella has been analyzed, this analysis reveals the general structural features of the majority of Stefanyk's novellas. As in "The Blue Book" so in most of Stefanyk's novellas rhythm is the basic element of construction. Rhythm, however, must be understood not just as the striking pulse, but as a feature of a Stefanyk novella which governs the whole movement of his prose. In this structural capacity, rhythm has five basic traits, the functions of time, narration, syntax, vocabulary, and tropes. The detailed examination of the way in which Stefanyk employs these five functions of rhythm to build one of his novellas shows that he was indeed a meticulous and superb craftsman. His ability to focus on one moment in the life of a character and through this focus, as through a prism, to see the psychological complexities of a man's soul, and then his ability to amplify and project his vision by means of a succinct, controlled, dramatic and poetic prose— all make Stefanyk an unsurpassable master of the psychological novella and a master of the impressionistic manner of narration. His novellas, to paraphrase B. Lepky, are great in their smallness. They are greater than some novels, yet constructed more carefully and sparingly than many poems:

> There are poems from which one can eliminate whole stanzas, but one can neither add nor subtract anything from your [Stefanyk's] prose, nor change around one word for this would be a literary sacrilege.[12]

FOOTNOTES

[1]V. Lesyn, *Vasyl' Stefanyk i ukrayins'ka proza kintsya XIX st.* (Chernivtsi, 1965), p. 18.

[2]M. Ivchenko, "Tvorchist, Vasylya Stefanyka," *Ukrayina*, Bks. 2-3 (1926), p. 185.

[3]H. E. Bates, *The Modern Short Story. A Critical Survey* (London - New York, 1941), p. 19.

[4]Olga Scherer-Virski, *The Modern Polish Short Story* (The Hague, 1955), p. 14. The stress is mine.

[5]V. Stefanyk, *Povne zibrannya tvoriv*, pp. 13-14. The translation is mine. I have tried to stay as close to the original as possible without translating literally.

[6]The other novellas are: "Pokhoron" (The Funeral), "Ozymyna" (Winter Wheat), "Takyy panok" (A Petty Squire), "Pistunka" (A Baby-sitter), and "Mezha" (The Boundary). All other Stefanyk novellas are narrated in the past tense.

[7]A similar emphatic shift of tenses in the narrator's interruptions occurs also in "A Petty Squire" where throughout the novella all the actions of the squire are described in the present tense until the final interruption: "The squire began to cry . . ." This enables Stefanyk to emphasize the sincerity, albeit misguided, of the squire by prolonging this moment until it is viewed as if in the past.

[8]George Y. Shevelov, *The Syntax of Modern Literary Ukrainian* (The Hague, 1963), pp. 157-58.

[9]V. M. Hladky, "Lysty V. Stefanyka do S. Morachevs'koyi," *Ukrayins'ke literaturoznavstvo*, No. 2 (1966), p. 139.

[10]Shevelov, *The Syntax of Modern Literary Ukrainian*, p. 261.

[11]Stefanyk, *Povne zibrannya tvoriv*, I, 65.

[12]B. Lepky, "Koly my shche buly molodymy," *Dilo*, Vol. XLV, No. 6 (10,974), January 7, 1927, p. 3.

CHAPTER V

THE PAIN AT THE HEART OF EXISTENCE

Of all the major Ukrainian writers Stefanyk is by far the least voluminous. Such is the dearth of his output that a study encompassing a detailed analysis of the content in each one of his fifty-nine published novellas could be easily managed in the confines of this chapter. This approach, however, though thorough would not prove very enlightening without some sort of systematization. Although Stefanyk, as a writer of psychological novellas, sought various episodes or incidents in the lives of his heroes, a careful reading of his novellas will show that most of the incidents chosen reveal Stefanyk's major preoccupation with the study of human anguish, of the "pain at the heart of existence." The main unifying element of all of Stefanyk's work is this theme of human anguish which manifests itself in various ways and forms. Usually, however, it is a situation where man finds himself trapped by life, ennui, and death and cannot escape; things are out of his control. The realization of total helplessness, the pain that man endures in such a situation, or even the futile struggle he puts up, are usually the subjects of Stefanyk's novellas.

Other scholars of Stefanyk's works have attempted to delineate his themes, but failed because they confused subject with theme. Thus V. Lesyn in his major work on Stefanyk writes:

> The following thematic groups of Stefanyk's novellas stand out most noticeably: about recruitment [draft], about emigration, about the rapid pauperization of the broad masses, about family tragedies caused by social conditions, about the proletarization of the peasants, and about the first bright indications of class struggle in the village. There is reason to mention separately two novellas where the author appears as a satirist.[1]

Actually what Lesyn describes above are not the themes but the subjects of several of the novellas. And even this is not quite true. There is, strictly speaking, only one story about recruitment, one about emigration. Although there are pauperized peasants there are no novellas about the "rapid pauperization of broad masses." Not all the family tragedies are "caused by social conditions" (e.g., "V korchmi" [In the Tavern] or "Pobozhna" [The Pious Woman]). At most only two stories can be misinterpreted to be about "proletarization of the peasants" and also at most two can be construed to be about "bright indications of class struggle in the village." Even if one were to accept that there are indeed novellas dealing with subjects mentioned by Lesyn, this would embrace not more than ten novellas. What about the other forty-nine?

The sad fact is that Lesyn's assertions are not an isolated case but are typical for the vast majority of Soviet interpretations of Stefanyk and also of all those who have seen in Stefanyk the "great bard of social and economic ills of the West Ukrainian peasant." It cannot be denied that the majority of Stefanyk's characters are indeed very poor and that some of their anguish could be mitigated by improved economic conditions. But by the same token it must be strongly denied that Stefanyk wrote about these conditions. Sometimes poverty provides the stimulus which triggers a reaction in the hero. This reaction would then be the subject of a minute and detailed study, of a novella. Most often, however, poverty remains as the general background, as the setting on which the psychological dramas described by Stefanyk take place. In the second period of his creative life such a setting is provided by war. Both poverty and war serve as the general settings for Stefanyk's novellas. Sometimes they are hardly noticeable; at other times they serve to dehumanize the characters; but most frequently they perform the function of amplifiers which enable Stefanyk to magnify a human condition or situation, the pain or anguish of which would perhaps go unnoticed if the setting were not sharpened by the abnormality of poverty or war.

There are, however, three novellas where the subject is poverty and one where the subject is war. All four are atypical Stefanyk novellas in that they do not deal with anguish of an individual hero or heroes but derive their force from the conflict between the overt and implicit realities. "Vistuny" (The Heralds) is the weakest of the lot. It is about the village poor who go out into the fields to collect stray ears of grain and dry twigs and thus herald the coming of autumn. The habitualness of their action emphasized by the imperfective verbs (the novella is written wholly in the imperfective aspect) creates the impression of resigned automatons. It seems that Stefanyk's main point in this novella was to show the dehumanizing effect of poverty. The overt acquiescence and acceptance by the poor of their wretched lot—they seem almost content in their misery—underlines the implicit horror of their existence.

The second novella where the main issue is the horror of poverty is "Lan" (The Potato Field). It is a very small (one-page) vignette completely in author's narration describing the tragic death of an infant who chokes to death in a potato field while his mother, exhausted from work, sleeps. The death is completely accidental (having fallen face down, he struggles and then suffocates). When the mother wakes up, she is unaware of the fact and thanks God that the child is still "asleep" so that she can catch up on the work which she has slept through. There is no psychological drama in this little scene, but one feels that death here would be more of a blessing than a tragedy. This is at least the overt reality. Implicit is something quite different. How tragic is the situation of man when his lot is such that he cares not whether his children die for he can hardly feed them and himself. Maternal feelings, love, kindness all are thrown under the potato bush and the field which "gobbles up all little fields" also gobbles up human life.

Actually the best thing that a child can do in such circumstances is die. Should it survive infancy, its childhood will be an endless misery leading to an untimely death from hunger and cold. Such is the death of the little boy in "Pokhoron" (The Funeral). Although Stefanyk centers on the funeral procession itself, beneath this grim little scene unfolds the life of a child uncared for and unloved. The father left the family with nothing but an old couch on which the boy died; the mother worked and the boy, as the reader finds out from one of the mourners, was fending for himself like a "chick without a hen." Actually there is no mention of the mother. And one can only surmise that one of the women in the procession was the boy's mother. Yet she never comes to the fore. There is no traditional wailing and one gets the impression that the boy was all alone in the world and that the funeral is the only time that so many people were concerned with him. The irony of it all, however, lies in the fact that even this motley group of young boys and old women who have formed into a funeral procession for him are all strangers who move along in the mist, "Like torn shadows, foreign and unknown to anyone."[2]

The novella concerned with the dehumanizing effect of war is one where Stefanyk uses the naive observations of children who repeat what they hear from adults and do not know the horror which lies behind the words they are mouthing. Stefanyk, of course, realized that humanity can be seen at its naked worst through the eyes of children who have not yet learned to sham. He uses this truism well in the "Pistunka" (A Baby-sitter), a one-page novella in which the little Parasya, the baby-sitter, encourages the other children to play funeral and to lament, for the baby she is taking care of will have to die. She overheard the night before that her father did not want this bastard child (conceived in his absence during the war) and that it would have to be killed. Although the children do not see anything different about this child and cannot understand why it has to die, they soon start the funeral game and contemplate how Parasya's father is going to choke the child. When told by an old woman who overhears their funeral songs that it is a "sin" to lament when no one has died, they answer that it is no sin at all for this "soldier's" child has to die, that it will be choked to death. The old woman crosses herself and the children continue their laments. Nothing more is said by the author and nothing more has to be said. For after all what can be a more logical solution to this unwanted attribute of war?

Three novellas are hardly enough to claim that Stefanyk was the "bard of peasant poverty." The fallacy of this claim becomes even more apparent when one realizes that there are quite a few novellas where neither poverty nor war appear at all. In such novellas as "In the Tavern," "The Pious Woman," "Anhel" (Angel), "Lyst" (Letter), "Portret" (The Portrait), "Skin" (The Agony), "Basarabs," "Ozymyna" (Winter Crop), "The Boundary," "Stratyvsya" (The Suicide), "Mayster" (Master Craftsman),3 poverty and war do not even play the role of settings. At best they are in some of these novellas only very distant backgrounds. But the anguish presented in these novellas is neither heightened by poverty or war nor could it be in any way mitigated by the amelioration of social conditions.

It has been shown in the previous chapters that Stefanyk was too conscious of being an artist to subordinate his art to an ulterior cause. Nevertheless, he did manage to pen a few novellas which fall outside of the main theme of anguish and which are meant to "teach." These novellas are more like works by Stefanyk's friend Les' Martovych and fit well into the nineteenth-century populist "educative" literature. A prime example of this group of novellas is "Pidpys" (The Signature). Though delightful, it is a rather tendentious work in which Stefanyk tries to show the merits of literacy. Fortunately, the novellas in which Stefanyk the artist gives way to Stefanyk the "teacher" are few. Only four in number, they are "The Signature," "Durni baby" (Stupid Women), "Voyenni shkody" (War Casualties) and "Chervonyy veksel'" (The Red Bill of Exchange).

Another group of novellas must be mentioned here because in them the theme of anguish is almost or completely nonexistent. "The Road" and "My Word" are autobiographical poems in prose. "Brattya" (Brothers), although not a poem in prose, is also an autobiographical reminiscence and of very slight literary value. Also quite poor and nondescript is the novella "Did Hryts'" (Grandpa Hryts'). In it an old man tells how it used to be in the good old days and then moralizes for his listeners. The next day he dies. "Rosa" (The Dew) is a weak novella and almost a continuation of "Grandpa Hryts'." It is somewhat split in half, as if Stefanyk changed his mind in mid-stream as to what he wanted to portray. The relation between the first part of the novella where old Lazar reflects on the morning dew and how it eats into the peasant all his life and the second part where Lazar reflects on his children and grandchildren and their recent preoccupation with Ukraine is rather strange, for all the parts have in common is but one character. They might as well have been two short vignettes.

Also in this group are three novellas dealing with nostalgic reminiscences of the good quiet life of the past. "Davnyna" (The Good Old Times), "Morituri," and "U nas vse svyato" (We Always Have a Holiday) are united by the common bond of nostalgia for the tranquil times which have passed. In "The Good Old Times" Stefanyk evokes the spirit of Gogol's *Starosvetskie pomeshchiki* (Old World Landowners) as he tells about the blissful trio, granddad Dmytro, his wife, and the village preceptor, Baz'o. Their life, as recalled by the narrator, was a tranquil one. He was a rich peasant fond of puttering around his hard-earned property; she was a curious and lively woman fond of listening to the "wisdom and readings" of the literate, but drunk preceptor. The village folk recall the good old days which have gone never to return. Thus this little novella ends. There is no grief, no tragedy, and no anguish.

The little bit of anguish which peers through in "Morituri" is lost behind the *pobut* and the slapstick characters. For thirty years they have gathered every Sunday and holiday at the local barber's for a shave and an occasional tooth pulling and some "politicin." The novella is written in little vignettes devoted to various scenes at the barber's. The hard life of the present is contrasted to the good old past, but the impact of hardship is minimized by the humour-evoking *skaz* and the outward (seemingly tendentious) blame of all the ills on Poland and its repressive measures toward Ukraine. The novella is interesting primarily because of its construction, which is based on short dialogue-scenes, and because Stefanyk managed to portray so well the typical barbershop meeting of the oldsters with their earnest dissatisfaction with the youth of the day, and its new morality. The novella ends on a humorous note when one of the members of this "club" fears his wife's wrath because he has indulged in a little bit of drinking.

The weakest of the lot is the novella "We Always Have a Holiday." Stefanyk reverts to the use of a narrator and has an old man telling a group of teachers how it used to be when he was young. The novella is neither well constructed nor interesting except for the mores of village life which it describes.

The last novella in this group where there is no anguish is "Mamyn synok" (Mommy's Boy), in which Stefanyk unfolds a peaceful and happy family centered around little Andriy. The novella is almost completely composed of dialogues among the three members of the family with the father and mother constantly vying for the little son's preference. The pleasant atmosphere which the novella exudes is slightly poisoned toward the end when little Andriy in answer to his father's questions replies that he will go to Canada. Without commenting, Stefanyk implies that it is a sad state of affairs when little "happy" children visualize emigration as something to look forward to.

Before proceeding to the discussion of the majority of Stefanyk's novellas seven more must be singled out. These are sometimes described as socio-political studies and form the core of the argument for critics who consider Stefanyk as primarily a conscious fighter for and protector of the poverty-stricken peasant. The first one of the group "Takyy panok" (A Petty Squire), betrays Stefanyk's sarcastic attitude to the well-intentioned but ineffectual intelligentsia. Stefanyk concentrates on a petty squire in a petty little town. He is a man who loves the peasant and sympathizes with him. He tries to help the peasants whenever he can: he even drinks with them in the local tavern and, when a little less drunk, argues their cause in front of other gentry who laugh at him. He tries desperately to convince the peasants they are equal to if not better than the members of the gentry. Yet the peasants do not and cannot understand him, for both he and they speak on a different wave-length. The peasant, accustomed to the usual disdain and contempt of the gentry, cannot help being suspicious of a squire who reveres him and weeps before him. The peasant draws his own conclusions, as the ending of the novella indicates:

> "This is supposed to be some sort of a good squire."
> "Ye, looks like he's a bit of a drunkard, but he's a good man."
> "There are such squires, who get drunk and then

weep . . ."

"Oh, well, even among them there are these softies," so spoke two peasants going home.[4]

In this novella Stefanyk scoffs at the well-intentioned but ineffectual intelligentsia, the peasant lovers (*khlopomany*), but at the same time does not show too much love for the indifferent peasant who will not believe in or fight for the equality which he deserves.

Since history has also shown the *khlopoman'stvo* (peasant mania) of the late nineteenth century quite unsuccessful in its aim of improving the peasant lot (something more successfully accomplished by the educative programs of *prosvita*), this novella is now a period piece and as such carries little interest. It serves well, however, as an introduction to Stefanyk the "political propagandist" of the Radical Party whose rank and file member he remained all his life.

Also quite dated and devoid of psychological drama is the second story of this group, "Zasidannye" (The Meeting). The manner of presentation is rather conventional. It consists of the author's narration interrupted by bits of dialogue and its plot is more akin to the stories of the nineteenth-century populists than to the usual novellas of Stefanyk. This is especially true of the last part which is devoted to a melodramatic story of an old woman so poor she is forced to steal boards from a church fence. The meeting called to judge her crime gives Stefanyk a chance to reveal the social and political attitudes of the peasants at the time and to outline the rising clash between the older and the younger generation. It is interesting to note that the first title for this novella was "Stari i molodi" (The Old and the Young). Even though Stefanyk, as usual, tries to stay out of the picture, there is little doubt that his sympathies lie with the views of Petro Antoniv, the representative of the younger generation, who argues that the old woman should not be punished, that the church will not become poorer because she took a board of an old fence nor richer if she pays a fine to the chruch as the older councilmen suggest. In line with the anti-clerical views of the Radical Party, Stefanyk does not state but suggests that the older generation is too much concerned with the church, so much so that it is blind to real misfortune.

Compositionally the most interesting novella of the group and even of all of Stefanyk's novellas is "Z mista yduchy" (Coming from Town). The whole novella is composed of a dialogue, with the author limited simply to designating the speakers by "first," "second" and "third." Although Stefanyk was criticized by the editors of *LNV*, to whom he submitted

113

this story, for not describing the speakers (see above, the letter of Makovey to Stefanyk), he nonetheless managed to have the characters reveal themselves in their conversation. The whole conversation centers on a deceased wealthy old man whose ungrateful son squandered all of his father's wealth. It is the ending of the novella, however, which gives away the identities of the speakers. The reader discovers that they are peasants working either for the manor, the Jewish innkeeper, or the priest. The lack of any individual anguish or psychological crisis and the dwelling on the social ills of the time place this story in the socio-political group.

The next two novellas in this group form a sub-group of their own. "Sud" (The Judgement) and "The Arsonist" are united by the fact that in them the poor peasants do not remain passive, but strike back at the rich ones. Yet, although these novellas have endeared themselves to Soviet scholars, who envision a certain class consciousness in Fedir's arson and in the pogrom of the rich peasants by the poor at the wedding in "The Judgement," this aggressiveness of the poor is not the main issue in either of the novellas. Although Soviet scholars claim that here Stefanyk reveals the conscious class struggle, actually Stefanyk's point is a bit more subtle. In "The Arsonist," as shown above, Fedir burns down rich Kurochka not because of any class struggle, but because of a personal insult which he received when Kurochka publicly slapped him in the face. In "The Judgement" the whole issue of class consciousness is actually degraded by Stefanyk for he ends the novella in the macabre judgement of the poor judging the poor. In a scene reminiscent of Kotsyubyns'ky's trial in *Fata Morgana*,[5] the poor, afraid of the punishment of the authorities, hasten to punish the guilty few of their own kind. Both novellas stand as Stefanyk's commentary on the ability and willingness of the pauperized peasants to revolt and Stefanyk makes it quite clear that these peasants had neither.

One of Stefanyk's novellas which also belongs in this socio-political group is the novella "Vovchytsya" (She-Wolf). One of the rare instances of an *Ich-erzählung*, the novella portrays an old woman who gives succor to poor homeless tramps, thieves, unwed mothers and the like. It is a strange novella which can, perhaps, be best understood as an allegory pleading for social as well as political coexistence, for along with the various outcasts of society, her house also provides a refuge for the portraits of "Wilhelm, Franz Josef, Nicholas, Shevchenko, Lenin, and Garibaldi."[6]

The final novella in this group is "Lyst" (The Letter). It comes last in this discussion for no chronological or other

114

reason except for the fact that it well illustrates how Stefanyk, almost despite himself, could not write simply a novella of political propaganda but was drawn to the description of man's despair. Even in such an openly tendentious social story as this one, where a man is in jail due to his political views, Stefanyk manages to focus not on the politics of the situation but on the grief and anguish of a man, be he guilty or not, forcibly torn away from his children and family. That this was Stefanyk's prime concern and not the exploitation of the situation for the advancement of revolt or a political program can readily be seen from the development in the variants to this novella. In the first variant the prisoner, it is very clear, killed his wife and for this he went to jail. The novella concentrates on the anguish of a repentant murderer and on his longing for his orphaned children. In a second variant, Stefanyk decides to dedicate this story to political prisoners and therefore he is forced to drop this line of the story and the wife is said to have died from grief. In the final version, however, still dedicated to peasant political prisoners, Stefanyk cannot help himself and changes this fact—that the wife died from grief—to a more ambiguous statement, hinting but not stating that the man is a wife-killer ("You have orphaned your children," "She has gone into the earth because of me").[7] The greatest part of the letter is devoted to his grief at being walled up in a jail, and at his sorrow and concern for the welfare of his children. Only a slight mention is made that he wanted to help others and, therefore, he is in jail now himself, for political activity among the peasants. This novella is also interesting for its epistolary form, a break from Stefanyk's usual method of presentation in such a case, the monologue. However, it does have a weakness in structure which came about primarily because Stefanyk could not make up his mind as to the main point of the story. The beginning, therefore, is quite weak and the whole novella does not develop into a unified point of interest as do other and better Stefanyk novellas.

The remaining novellas (thirty-five in number) are all united by the fact that in them Stefanyk concentrates on the depiction of human anguish. They can be separated, however, into several groups according to the basic situation which give rise to the anguish in each novella. There are six such basic situations, six varieties of anguish, discernible in the novellas of Stefanyk: man trapped by poverty, man facing an irrevocable loss, man caught in the loneliness of old age, man caught in death, man trying to escape from an inescapable situation, and man forced to choose where no choice is a good one.

Only two novellas are embraced by the first of these

situations, "Osin'" (Autumn) and "Son" (The Dream). Although quite different in content, both are united by the inability of man to extricate himself from the clutches of poverty. In "The Dream" Stefanyk presents a daydream of a field worker who works for one-third of what he gathers. The anguish of this *tretyl'nyk* lies in the realization that the possession of one's own land no matter how hard he works is but a delirious dream. The inescapable wretchedness of poverty and the pain and destruction it inflicts is seen even better in "The Autumn." Stefanyk shows the degeneration of a family where the approaching autumn, cold, lack of means drive a man to a state of frustrated self-destruction. The father ends up beating his children and his wife for no reason at all. No solution avails itself, for even death would be too costly.

As many as eleven novellas are united under the second basic situation where man faces an irrevocable loss. The losses are various and range from the loss of a house, as in "The Blue Book," to the loss of an animal, as in "Shkoda" (Loss); from the loss of a way of life, as in "The Stone Cross," to the loss of self-respect, as in "Master Craftsman"; and finally from a loss of a child, as in "The Suicide," to a loss of a parent, as in "Klenovi lystochky" (The Maple Leaves). In each case Stefanyk studies and presents the anguish that is called forth by the loss.

The pain of Antin in "The Blue Book," the pain of a man forced to give up his house, the symbol of a *gazda*—a master of one's own household, in exchange for a "blue book,"—a pass for worker servants, was masterfully captured by Stefanyk, as illustrated in the preceding chapter. No less poignant, however, is the loss of old Romanykha in "The Loss" (see pp. 143-44) who is forced by fate to part with her cow and thus with her life. Not just a loss of a favorite animal or a pet is at stake (a loss which in itself can be quite painful). The cow is Romanykha's sole means of livelihood; without it she cannot survive. The old woman has tried all remedies, turned for advice to the village "specialist" in matters of cattle, but all is to no avail. Fate has no mercy. The situation is one which Stefanyk often exploited. The sense of the unfairness of the affliction (heightened by the good deeds which the old woman performed) greatly enhances the tragedy of the events. When the death of the cow becomes imminent, old Romanykha covers it with her own sheepskin and desperately tries to keep it alive. Yet the final scene shows her, like some great sinner being punished for infinitely heavy sins, fighting for her own life together with the cow, for the cow in her agony has kicked and torn the old woman to pieces. The image of the dying animal and the old woman bespattered with blood evokes a picture

116

worthy of Goya and yet Stefanyk managed to convey this in no more than three lines. The crisp laconic description contrasts well with the emotional frenzy of the image and provides artistic control over emotion to create a tension which, in turn, is the main source of power for the highly emotional drama.

As the perishing of a cow cost Romanykha her life, so the departing from her land afflicts Mariya with the loss of speech. In writing "Vona–Zemlya" (She–The Earth) Stefanyk vividly illustrated one of his own firm beliefs that the peasant's main blessing is his own piece of land and that without it he is like an autumn leaf blown about by the wind. This novella, however, fits only partially into this group, for toward the end Mariya and Danylo decide to return to their land, despite the war, and she regains her speech.

The damage in the next novella is once again permanent. Although Ivan Didukh in "The Stone Cross" (see pp. 145-54) is not forced to leave his land because of war, and although his life prior to his departure was much harder than that of the wealthy Mariya and Danylo, the loss of his "hill" is tantamount to a spiritual death. The multi-scened wake-like structure of "The Stone Cross" has been discussed previously (see above Ch. III); suffice it to say here that the element of wake in the novella is there because of Stefanyk's feelings about emigration. In many of his letters from Cracow and in an article "Dlya ditey,"[8] (For the Sake of Children) Stefanyk described the plight of the emigrants and suffered greatly the misery which they had to endure. In "For the Sake of Children" he lists the reasons which forced the peasants to emigrate en masse, calls their migration an escape akin to the fleeing from Tartar hordes, and attacks the "patriots" for not doing anything to help these poor people in their plight. But all this was part of Stefanyk's political outlook. How different his concern when it comes to art is seen in his treatment of this subject in "The Stone Cross." Though the railway scenes where the peasants trampled each other in a wild and frantic surge for a seat on a train could have provided Stefanyk with a more emotional and dramatic setting, he chose to study not the process of emigration but the initial step that man has to take before he emigrates—the parting with his home, his land, his relatives, and friends.

This step, as the novella points out, is a very difficult one. As if wishing to emphasize this point, Stefanyk goes out of his way to show that what Ivan Didukh is leaving behind is a life of incessant struggle, symbolized by his "stone cross." All his life, Ivan Didukh has worked at making his little sandy hill give fruit. He harnessed himself together with his horse and carted manure up to the hill and then to save the horse took it to the top

117

himself. The hill finally broke his back. As if destined to fulfill literally God's curse when Adam was chased out of Eden, in the sweat of his brow he tilled his plot of land and did succeed in making it give fruit. Finally broken by the hill, he carried his own stone cross and placed it on top of this personal Golgotha as a sign of some sort of expiation. In short, his life is but a graphic illustration of the reasons peasants gave for emigrating: poor land and little of it, the inability to survive and raise a family no matter how hard one worked. It would seem that Didukh would be more than glad at the chance to leave this life and search for a better one. Yet as the novella unfolds, it becomes clear that quite the opposite is true. No matter how bleak and miserable his life has been, no matter that he has lost his youth, strength and health in trying to sustain himself—this life of sweat, this stone cross he has to bear are still dearer than any promised land across the sea. The children pressure him into leaving for they see no future in this way of life, but for him parting with his wretched hill and all the misery it stands for is tantamount to dying.

The title of the novella is very well chosen, for the "stone cross" not only looms as the symbol of Didukh's difficult life, but also stands as the memorial to it once he departs. It is no wonder, then, that Stefanyk presents Didukh's parting as if it were a wake for the dead; the hill-grave in which all of Didukh's life is entombed and the memorial (the cross) for him are already there. He even asks his friends to say a memorial service for him once a year. The actual leave-taking follows a very definite ritualistic order: first he takes leave of his wife, then of his friends, and then of his "former life" (the cross), all this followed by a frenzied merrymaking and dancing, a scene of grief and anguish bordering on insanity. This whole wake-parting is even more dramatically tragic because the corpse is still only a corpse to be, yet at the same time all realize, Didukh most of all, that as soon as he starts on his way—he will become a spiritual corpse. All that will remain is what remains after everyman—a cross with his name on it. It is with these words that Stefanyk ends the novella.

Didukh's loss of his way of life, even if difficult, results in a spiritual death. The same can be said of the hero in the next novella. "Master Craftsman" depicts the anguish of a man who has lost his self-respect. Even though he tries to find solace in drink, the craftsman cannot help but recall the day of his ruin. He was an excellent craftsman and was offered a chance to build a great church. The thought of this overwhelms and destroys him. Neither drink nor the excuse that a Hutsul (a member of a Carpathian tribe) cursed him alleviate the pain from the realization that from a master craftsman he has become a drunk.

The following six novellas form a sub-group of their own in that in each the loss is either a child or a parent. It seems fitting to begin the discussion of this sub-group with "Vyvodyly z sela" (The Village Send-Off), where the loss is only antici-pated. It is indeed a universal novella in which Stefanyk cap-tures the anguish of parents who are forced to part with their drafted son. Here, more than in any other novella, Stefanyk concentrates on color, making sure that the whole scene re-flects the anticipated tragedy of death. If this novella were staged, it would have to be lit with red stage lights, for this is the predominant color. The clouds are red, there are red stones, copper leaves, crimson light—all foreshadowing the blood which will flow as a result of this parting between a son, just drafted into the army, and his family, friends, and finally the whole village. Stefanyk concentrates on the emotions of the parents and aptly portrays the hysterical mother, unwilling to part with her son not only emotionally but also physically. The father, on the other hand, after one emotional outburst, re-mains calm. It is interesting to note how the setting of poverty emphasizes and magnifies the anguish of the father. For a hard-working peasant, the loss of a son was not so much the loss of a child (although this, of course, also figured in the grief) as the loss of a helping hand; in modern times, the loss of a hard-earned investment. Raising children was not an easy task in such adverse economic conditions, and if they were to die they might as well die early in life. To lose them after they had become a working force was indeed an irrevocable loss. Thus, it is not surprising that the most emotional statement of the father, to which all the other men react strongly is the rhetori-cal question: "... and who will help me hoe the corn?" ... "All the men groaned. The father leaned his head against the wagon and shook like a leaf."9

Although in another novella ("The Suicide"—see below) the father's grief is indeed profound and sincere, in "The Village Send-Off" it is the mother who reacts to the parting most dramatically. After finally letting him out of the house, she laments that she would rather prepare him for the grave than see him go. When they are already on the wagon, she refuses to let him go without her and the villagers have to hold her back forcibly so that the wagon can leave for the station. Finally, when the son has already departed, she sits and wails as if after a funeral. Here Stefanyk uses a real formula from traditional laments: *"Vidky tebe vizyraty de tebe shukaty?"* (From where am I to expect you, where am I to look for you?) The novella ends in an image of lyrical but cold stillness—"The stars twinkled like golden flowers on a smooth iron threshing floor"[10]—providing an excellent contrast with the beginning of the novella where the boiling over of emotions found evidence in the predominance of red.

The anticipated loss in "The Village Send-Off" becomes real in "The Suicide" (see pp. 155-57). Here Stefanyk focuses on the anguish of the father, almost as if he wanted to correct the "economic" considerations in the preceding novella. "The Suicide" painstakingly records the father's doleful trip to the city where his son has committed suicide and then the confrontation with the corpse.

Excellently employing the impressionistic technique of narration, Stefanyk adds greatly to the portrayal of the father's suffering by recreating the effect that the city had on the lonely grieving wretch. The terrible blow dealt to him by the suicide of his son is heightened by the "cave-in" effect that the city has on him. Not only is his own personal world shattered, but it seems to him that the whole world and especially this strange huge city to which he travelled as if to the end of the world is going to cave in and crush him:

> Walls, walls, and among the walls roads, and on the roads there are thousands of lights all strung unto one rope. The light seemed to drown in the darkness and to tremble. Any minute now it will fall and there would be black hell.[11]

Thus, he sees the city when he is left (and Stefanyk emphasizes this fact) all alone, totally helpless. Then it seems to him that "the walls leaned one toward another; the lights gathered together and played in a colorful arc. They closed in on ...[him]...."[12] Totally depressed and downtrodden, he somehow does manage to find out where his son is lying. The novella ends in a tender and moving scene during which the old father dresses the handsome son and tries to wash away the sin of suicide with his own tears. As in any Christian society, suicide is a terrible sin; the grief of the father is compounded, therefore, for he has lost his son both in this world and in the next.

Two other novellas in this group also deal with the anguish of parents who have lost their children. Now the setting for the novellas is war. In "Mariya," Stefanyk focuses on the mother. The novella splits into two parts. In the first, Stefanyk concentrates on the mother's reminiscences of her three sons. They are full of the pain of a grieving mother who lost all she cherished to a cause which she doesn't quite understand. At one time she reacts to this cause with a jealousy of one woman to another.

120

The second part of the novella, though it too contains elements of anguish, is more of an historical piece pertaining to Ukraine's fight for liberation. In this the mother Mariya becomes, at one and the same time, the motherland (for Ukrainians the union of mother, country and the Virgin Mary is quite common) and Stefanyk manages to project in this novella a feeling of national pathos.

The second novella, "Syny" (The Sons) (see pp. 158-62) concentrates on the same situation, the loss of children in the war, but now the central character is the grieving father. "The Sons" is perhaps Stefanyk's most emotionally charged novella. Although Stefanyk deals with a similar situation to the one in "Mariya," "The Sons" is infinitely more powerful, primarily because the human element is placed above national pathos. The novella builds to a crescendo by altering the cursing and groaning of an old father with lyrical interludes during which he recalls his sons. His grief is so strong it verges on blasphemy:

> God, the golden books in churches lie that You had a son, they lie that You had one. They say that You resurrected Your son. And I don't ask You to resurrect my sons; all I'm asking is that You show me the graves so that I may lie next to them. You see the whole world, but You are blind when it comes to my graves . . .[13]

The work he loved, his horses, the soil which he adores, the singing of a lark—all annoy him in his sorrow. He addresses the anonymous lovers of his sons and in an extremely lyrical and gentle passage calls them forth to come and comfort the old man. He recalls how his sons left for war, how their mother had died from grief. Then comes the final crescendo. Turning to the mother of God, he exclaims: "You gave but one son; I gave two."[14]

The howling old man tearing his hair out and cursing everything under the son reminds one of the wounded grief of Lear. Like Lear, the father also at least partially brought upon himself his grief (he had insisted that the youngest son accompany his brother). Stefanyk managed to capture in this novella the immensurable pain of a father who has lost his children and by doing so created one of the most powerful dramas of human anguish.

Anguish seems to grow in intensity when Stefanyk turns to the loss of parents. In "Ditocha pryhoda" (Children's Adventure), "Maple Leaves," and "Shkil'nyk" (The Schoolboy)[15] Stefanyk showed himself to be a master in recreating the psychology of children. One of his favorite and most successful techniques was to use the observations of children and with their innocent comprehension of overt reality to emphasize the tragedy or the horror of the implicit reality. Somehow the fact that they do not realize the gravity of their situation makes the tragedy even more tragic.

The ironically named "Children's Adventure" (see pp. 163-64) illustrates very well the tragedy of the loss of a parent. The novella is the first one of Stefanyk's post-war period and in it the setting of war is very pronounced. In fact it can be viewed not only as a novella about the loss of a mother but also as one condemning the insanity of war which caused this irrevocable loss. The horror of this novella is almost surrealistic. Using children to describe the insanity of war, Stefanyk shows the naive and innocent observations of a child totally unaware of the tragic implications of what is going on around it. The plot, as in all good Stefanyk novellas, is mono-incidental: a mother running away from the line of battle with her two small children gets hit by a stray bullet. Just before she dies she asks the older of the two to take the younger to his uncle. This is where Stefanyk begins carefully to unfold the drama of the situation, concentrating of the stress created by the dichotomy between what is really happening and what the child understands to be happening. Death is something incomprehensible. All the little boy knows is that he has heard of people dying; he has not yet understood the grief of death. The boy's explanations to his little sister of what happened to their mother alternate with a boyish joy at seeing fireworks. At one and the same time, he instinctively feels that he is now responsible, in command, as it were, over his sister and yet he is still the little boy fascinated by the whizzing of bullets and the puffs of smoke. The apex of the drama is reached when the little girl eats a roll which accidentally was drenched in her mother's blood. The boy's reaction to this is so matter of fact that it is frightening. The implicit message is clear: only the illogical mind of a child can make any sense in the horror of death and in the insanity of war. The boy plays his part perfectly. He scolds the little girl for getting herself dirty with blood, threatens to wash her in cold water in the morning and then tries to comfort her by telling her to lie near her mother and that he will lie next to her and so protect her from the wolf (a danger which her mind can comprehend, for the raging battle around them is totally incomprehensible). As the boy himself falls asleep his last thought underlines the insanity of it all: a bullet probably killed his father somewhere at the front, can kill him and his sister and then there will be no one left. He, of course, cannot realize the implication of this "children's adventure," but therefore the reader can even more fully.

As in "Children's Adventure," death in "The Maple Leaves" is seen through the eyes of a child. Although, as already mentioned (see Ch. III) the novella is a multi-scened story split in half by an episode which can stand as a novella by itself, the main point of the whole novella is in a child's comprehension of the difficult situation enveloping him and his confrontation with the death of his mother. Semenko, the eldest boy, is totally incapable of understanding the tragedy that is all around him. His mother is very sick after having had another child; his father cannot afford to stay away from the fields and take care of her. Semenko, as the boy in "Children's Adventure," is left in charge. He tries to be grown up and responsible, yet he is nevertheless still a child and as such can only play at being grown up. Very effectively Stefanyk shows how he bosses his little sisters and how in his naivete he has all of the answers:

> Semenko constantly ran around, and did everything that his mother told him, and time and again pushed his younger sisters and said that girls didn't know anything except how to eat.
> "They're still small, Semenko, when they grow up they will wash your shirts for you."
> "I will hire myself out and there they'll wash my shirts and I don't need them [the sisters]."
> "Don't be too happy about serving, my child, for many a day you will spend in weeping."
> "But look at Dad; he grew up as a servant and there's nothing wrong with him."[16]

He cannot see anything wrong with his father's life, and typically for a child reasons that what was good for his father is certainly good for him. Here again, of course, the overt reality as seen by Semenko is ironically juxtaposed with the implicit reality understood by the reader. With this contrast between two realities, as well as with the constant dichotomy between the child and the role of an adult, forced upon it by fate, Stefanyk builds the tension which leads to the most striking scene in the novella.

This climax comes when Semenko has to fulfill a very important task. The boy who the day before was afraid of a dog when he was carrying lunch to his father in the fields and the boy prematurely saddled with a horrible responsibility merge into a precarious mixture of opposites. Torn between his typically childish lack of comprehension of death and the gravity with which his father approaches the situation, Semenko senses that there is something terribly wrong. He therefore tries to be very serious and helpful, but as a child he does not know what it is all about. Also because he is still a child, he has not yet learned how to mask his feelings; he has not learned what adults call tact. This lack of "tact," this childish frankness, leads him to ask his mother a question, the directness of which serves well to underline the tragic dichotomy between the two realities and simultaneously provides the most spine-chilling moment in the novella:

> Father has rolled a candle and said that when you will be dying I should place it in your hands and light it. But I don't know when to place it . . .[17]

His statement brings tears in his mother's eyes and Semenko recalls how, in the morning, his father also cried and how he struck his head against the door-frame. This mute anguish of his father, indeed the whole fact of the approaching death of his mother, he does not comprehend. The reader, who knows very well the fate of an orphan, does. Hence, Stefanyk underlined the immitigable tragedy of death, the most irrevocable of all losses.

The third basic situation in which Stefanyk observes the anguish of man is when man is caught in a lonely old age. Perhaps at no time is the pain of life more apparent than when man reaches the twilight of his life and finds himself on the inescapable path to death. Much of his life seems then, not only painful in recollection but futile in result, especially when he finds himself abandoned by his children and friends, all alone in a world totally oblivious to his existence. Seven novellas are united by this situation and they can be subdivided further into two groups: those where the reminiscences of life still provide some relief and consolation, and those where the decree of old age has been as severe as to deprive the character even of his own name—he or she is totally forgotten by the world.

In "The Portrait," "Vechirnya hodyna" (The Evening Hour), and "Angel" Stefanyk shows man left only with the bitter-sweet memories of his life. In "The Portrait," a novella which Stefanyk never republished, he concentrates on an old man's memory of his daughter. It forms a beautiful poetical vignette about old age, loneliness, and the love for children who have grown up and left home. "The Evening Hour" also consists of a man's reminiscences. He recalls the most pleasant memories of any man's life, those relating to his early childhood. Reminiscent of Stefanyk himself,[18] the hero muses with bitterness on how he was sent away from his beloved mother and sister to attend school. Now he is alone: mother, father, and sister have all died. All he has to console him is a quatrain of a song his mother used to sing. He can no longer remember the whole song.

Old Tymchykha in "The Angel" finds consolation in recalling the time when her children were still small and needed her and depended on her. Now they do not care whether she lives or dies. Neither does anyone else. People barely greet her. She reflects on the total uselessness of old people and her thoughts drift to her husband who died before her. He certainly was right in telling her that as soon as he died she will no longer be a *gazdynya*. This sad realization is somewhat alleviated by the sight of a picture of an angel. She bought this angel at a fair once when she was still quite young. And now the angel is still as young as always and still smiling. She recalls how she used to decorate him and how he always brightened up her life and her house. The novella ends with her telling the angel that they will part in death, but that he will always brighten the house and always remain cheerfully young reminding everyone of the old woman who bought him. Only so much will remain as a sign that she lived.

Stefanyk sustains a bitter-sweet nostalgic mood in the whole novella. For old Tymchykha, old age is certainly painful for she feels useless and unwanted. Her sole joy in life now is to reminisce about when she was still needed, yet she is reconciled to the fact that she cannot remain forever young and smiling like her angel. She must die. At least he will remain in memory of her.

Even less fortunate in their old age are the heroes of the following novellas: "Sama samis'ka" (All Alone), "Christmas Eve," "Dity" (Children), and "Winter Crop." In all of these the characters have been so abandoned by their loved ones and the whole world that Stefanyk does not even give them names. Nameless old men and women in frightful loneliness await death—such could be the capsule summary of these novellas. The baba (old woman, crone) in "All Alone," (see pp. 165-66) sick and helpless, is left to die. She can no longer recollect anything of her former life; she is too ill for that. Instead, Stefanyk presents the hallucinations which beset her just before she dies.

In "All Alone" Stefanyk develops his usual impressionism a step further and shows a sample of the expressionistic technique. After he has set the scene, he switches to the old woman's hallucinatory impressions. The flies which are buzzing around her now appear as little devils whose main purpose is to harass the old woman and by sitting on her arm in millions prevent her from crossing herself. Her subconscious desire to make amends with God before she dies is thus denied her and her feverish mind calls forth the superstitions of her life as an explanation. She then sees riders charging at her and feels the earth opening up beneath her and that she is falling till some devil catches her. In the struggle she hits her head against the table and dies. In a macabre ending Stefanyk describes how the devils ceased to prance around, but the flies with their wings dipped in the old woman's blood carry it all over the house and also to the plates on the wall with charging riders depicted on them.

The Gogolesque aspect of this expressionistic portrayal should not, however, make one lose the main point of the novella which is made in its title: *all alone*. The misery at being all alone in the moment of death is intensified when it is recalled that the tradition of Ukrainian peasants demanded that a candle be placed in the hands of the dying just before they depart. The subconscious realization of the fact that she is not prepared properly for death leads the old woman to imagine that the devils have taken over her will and prevent her making the sign of the cross. Although the whole pre-death hallucination has a basis in real phenomena, it is nonetheless filled with her fear at not having properly prepared for death. One child, one grandchild with the old woman at this time and her whole fearful experience would not have taken place.

The old woman, Stefanyk points out, is left alone because the children have other things to do; they are busy with the harvest. Here again poverty as the dehumanizing agent plays an important role. Yet this aspect of the children being too busy to bother with the old becomes even more acute when, despite any economic considerations, the children plainly don't care. The case of the nameless protagonist—the old man (*did*) in "The Children" illustrates this very well. Weary from work he stops in the field to rest and in a bitter monologue complains of the mistreatment he receives at the hands of his children.

Though he recalls the time when the lawyer explained to the son how the son was to treat his parents as if they were still masters of the house, quite the opposite has happened. All the bitterness toward ungrateful children as well as the lot of all old and useless people is summed up in this final reproach:

> Croak, you oldsters, for it's a waste to feed you. They drink milk, and they eat cheese, and we, like two miserable pups, look at them. But I gave them the cow, and I gave them the sheep, and I gave them the plow; I gave them everything. Like all people give so gave I. And now they say that you're old, and weak, so eat little. That's how our children treat us.

126

. . . .

And they'll bury us, God be my witness, like a pair of
dogs. They won't even put boots on us . . .[19]

The flying of the cranes south for winter brings the old
man out of his bitter state. He remembers that it is autumn and
that, as in nature, all must follow its natural course. Yet in the
lyrical ending there appears a note of nostalgia for a better life.
If only man could fly away when it became too cold for him to
live and when there was not enough to eat. Despite this it still
would be good to see the cranes flying off another time, yet the
old man feels that either he or his wife will die before the cranes
come back. Life is bitter, cold, and hungry in old age and man
cannot escape, but nonetheless the desire to live is just as strong
as it always was and perhaps even stronger.

How bitter is the pill of old age, Stefanyk illustrates yet in
another novella, "Christmas Eve." Here another nameless old
woman seems, at first, not totally forgotten. Her son visits her
on Christmas Eve and spends a few moments with her, yet the
visit is a sad one. He keeps replying to the old woman's
complaints by wishing that death come quickly to her. Freezing, lousy, she sits and waits for it herself, but it is slow in
coming. Some villagers come to see her after the son leaves and
each brings her some food and asks for prayers for some
deceased member of the family. And again the old woman is
left alone. She is bitterly grateful for the fact that her son did
not forget her and that the people still remember her, yet she is
still extremely lonely. The last part of the novella shows her
utter despair not only at being lonely but at having to suffer the
degradation of old age. Her anguish increased by heavy drinking, borders on lunacy as she castigates herself for becoming a
beggar. At the same time, in a fit of masochism, in a monologue
addressed to her deceased husband, she takes pride in her
wretched state. The novella ends when the old woman, pounding her head against the wall in a drunken mad frenzy reveals
the agony in her soul by clamoring for her husband's punishment for having soiled his name by becoming a "communal
beggar's bag" (*torba hromatska*).

A fit ending to this group of novellas dealing with the
loneliness of old age is provided by "Winter Crop." The griev-
ance of the nameless protagonist, however, is no longer with
uncaring children nor with a forgetful world, but with death
itself. In a highly emotional monologue set against the background of the melodic autumn and contrasted with the green
sprouts of winter wheat, Stefanyk captures a man's frustrated

127

call for death. In a way the novella is both a plea for death by a man who has lived his full and also an argument against premature death. To emphasize this point, Stefanyk shows how the old man gathers all his strength to chase out some hens that have strayed into the winter wheat. It is still young and growing; it is not to be destroyed. In the same way, he argues, death should not kill off young men, but should come and take him. Stressing the eternal youth and beauty of nature, the old man grows calm and, sitting in the green wheat, he is enveloped by the sadness of autumn and besprinkled by falling leaves. The novella ends on this note of pantheistic harmony.

"Winter Crop" provides a good transition to the next group of novellas in which Stefanyk studied man caught by death. Death itself does not always have to produce anguish. As seen above, the anguish of the old woman in "All Alone" is not because of death but because she had no one with her to perform the last necessary rights. There is no anguish also in "Nytka" (The Thread) where death appears calmly and swiftly as an end to a full life. There is no thought of death, only of all the achievements of a happy life. A woman weaves a real thread while her family is asleep. At the same time the "thread" of her thought wanders from her work to her sleeping husband and children. She rejoices in the fact that she can work for them, but at the same time she is tired of the endless sleepless nights. Eternal sleep comes to her as a long-deserved rest offered by the compassionate Mother of God on one of her icons.

Quite different is the death of old Les' in "The Agony" (see pp. 167-68). Stefanyk focuses on the twilight stage when man hangs in abeyance between the conscious and the unconscious. Les' is not afraid of death, but his long sickness has brought much suffering and it is because of this that, in his final moments before death, he is tormented by "another world," the subconscious from which he cannot escape. While he weights his good and bad deeds, his sole support in the conscious world is the flicker of the burning candle. Only by forcing his eyes to remain on the little light, can he maintain himself in the conscious world. At the same time, the flickering flame hypnotizes him and thus his only link with consciousness is also that which makes him break that link. When he falls into the unconscious world, elements of his conscious thought provide the touchstones, the explanations, of his delirious visions. Thus his thoughts wander to the days when he was plowing under a mercilessly hot sun; the black earth seems to consume him and his oxen in flames. When he comes to, he remembers that many a time he thirsted while working his fields. This he knows is written down on the good side in God's book. Then he

128

drifts again and is overpowered by ringing bells, right above his head, till finally they break off and fall, crushing him. Upon regaining consciousness, he remembers that he had promised to buy a bell for the village, but had put it off from year to year and never bought it. This he feels is a strike against him at the Final Judgement. Burning up with fever, he imagines that he is being covered with bushels upon bushels of barley. The real pain in his body seems to be coming from the chafing of the barley; it gets into his mouth, his nose, right into his heart. For a moment he remembers that he owes Martyn barley which the latter has earned and that now this barley is choking him to death. This Stefanyk follows with an extremely interesting and well-accomplished description of the final moment grounded and motivated in Les' thoughts as well as the physical condition of his dying body:

> He wanted to shout to the children so that they would give Martyn the barley owed to him, but the shout could not squeeze out of his throat, and only spread over his body in hot lava. He pushed out his black tongue, pushed his fingers into his mouth to bring out the voice stuck in his throat. But his teeth clamped shut and caught his fingers. His eyelids fell with a thunder.

> The windows open up in the house. A white sheet oozes into the house. It oozes in endlessly. It gives off a brightness as bright as the sun. This sheet swaddles him like a small child, first the feet, then the arms, and the shoulders. Tightly. He feels light. So light. Then it squeezes into his head and tickles his brain; it flows into every joint and fills it with softness. And finally it envelops the throat, tighter and tighter. It flows around the neck in a breeze and swaddles it, swaddles it . . .[20]

In the last two novellas from this group, Stefanyk deals with the anguish of man facing death and unable to expiate his sins. The first of these, "Hrikh" (The Sin), is a last-minute confession by the wife of a self-styled terrorist. The death of innocent people caused by her own and her husband's act of arson hangs heavily on the old woman. Her husband, who died without confessing his role in this crime, has left the sin on her soul. She cannot confess to a priest, but finally manages to unburden her soul to her sister and a few neighbors. Somehow the impact of the novella is broken by the fact that Stefanyk strays into the realm of arson and terrorism. As a result the reader is left in doubt as to the main point of the novella; whether it is about the agony at not being able to confess a sin, or whether it is about the magnitude of the sin itself.

Somewhat better is the novella "The Boundary" in which Stefanyk shows an old man parting with God. In his last breath he insists that his love for his soil, God's daughter, and the work which he put into it, should make God forgive him even though he killed to protect it from someone who wanted to take it away. Should God not forgive, he is willing to go into the "eternal jail," but feels he is right. Unfortunately, here too it seems that Stefanyk diluted his point of concentration. Because the novella was dedicated to Mykola Khvyl'ovy (Fitil'ov, a foremost Soviet Ukrainian writer and publicist of Stefanyk's time who advocated the cultural and political separation of Ukraine from Russia), it takes on a political overtone. Although it becomes an eloquent and an artistic plea for the justification of fighting for one's own land, it loses much by the fact that Stefanyk did not capitalize on the opportunities afforded by man's personal settling of accounts with God.

The four novellas in which Stefanyk examines man trying to escape from an inescapable situation vary in that in each Stefanyk shows man choosing a different avenue of escape, but they are united by the fact that all the avenues are culs-de-sac. Thus the novella "In the Tavern" shows man caught in the clutches of a shrewish wife. His escape seems to be rebellion. He rebels, however, within the safe confines of the local tavern in front of his own friend. With each glass of liquor, his courage grows in a progressive hyperbole until he is ready to chop off his wife's hands for beating him. The horror of having to live with a shrew and the tragic realization that the situation is inescapable and unchangeable no matter how much one shouts and boasts becomes evident as the man approaches his home late at night, his shouts becoming progressively weaker as he nears it. Finally, just before entering, he becomes completely silent.

Similarly in "May" (May), a delightful novella, especially in its lyrical quality, Danylo's vividly imagined conversation with his squire, his "rebellion," results in an escape into dreams. The frustration and tragedy of this simple soul, however, is somewhat obscured by Stefanyk's digression into a long and ironic description of peasants.

Suicide as the avenue of escape from the ennui of life is examined in the third novella of this group. The subject of suicide fascinated Stefanyk, especially since there were times when he wanted to "finish with himself."[21] Moreover, as he admits in his autobiography of 1929, suicide had a long history in his own family.[22] Five members of his closest family committed suicide[23] and the novella "The Basarabs" is, in his own words, a "true family history."[24] In this novella Stefanyk shows in great detail how the sickness of suicide works on the victim's mind, until he can do nothing but give in to this destructive urge.

Toma, one of the rich Basarabs, is stopped just in time from hanging himself. The rest of the novella describes a council of the Basarab family during which Toma tries to explain how it came upon him. With horror, the Basarabs listen and understand for many of them have experienced similar urges: the pounding in the head, the desire to run and not knowing where to go, the sudden elation at seeing a handy branch, or the soothing call of the water. The worst part of it is that not only does it come unexpectedly, but, as Toma says, "it eats at you but it does not tell you why, for if I had killed or set fire to someone, that it knows, but I'm not guilty and it still eats at me."[25] The reasons for this are primordial; in the case of the Basarabs, one of their forefathers committed an unforgivable sin and for this the whole family is punished till the seventh generation. In more general terms, it is a typical situation for Stefanyk. Man is seen trying to escape—but there is no real exit. All escape routes are self-destructive or temporary measures, delusions.

In "The Basarabs" Stefanyk places great emphasis on the eyes, the windows of a man's soul. There is constant reference to the eyes. All of the Basarabs habitually walk around with their eyes downcast, as if they were rivetted to that sin weighing upon the soul. The whole novella can be viewed as an "original sin" explanation for the pain of existence. In this way it is but one more aspect of the same, no matter whether it manifests itself as a suicide, the loss of a needed animal, or the sudden loss of a child, or even filicide. In each case man cannot escape and his struggles are indeed tragic. The point of inevitability is made well in "The Basarabs" where the ending takes an unexpected turn. (This is one of the few Stefanyk novellas with a surprise ending.) No sooner has Toma finished narrating his torturous experiences than another Basarab, Nykola, quietly slips out of the house. No one knows for sure, but the thought that he has gone to commit suicide is present in everyone's mind.

As in "The Basarabs" the escape from self through suicide is, in the final analysis, nothing more than a futile attempt at defeating the anguish imposed by life, so in "The Thief" (see pp. 169-75) is the act of homicide. Stefanyk is not concerned so much with manslaughter itself, as with the whole reason behind it and with the feelings of the men about to kill the thief. He does not judge the morality of the act; he limits himself to an

131

objective presentation of the facts. The *gazda* has caught a thief in the process of robbing his stores. If the thief had succeeded, this would have meant the virtual death of the *gazda*. In a primitive society the law of the Old Testament, a tooth for a tooth and an eye for an eye, still holds and, in many ways, this law is the only one in a world where only the fittest survive. Nonetheless, despite all rationalizations, the *gazdas*, feeling that their way out of the situation is not quite right, approach their primitive retribution with a great many misgivings. One of them cannot go through with it and withdraws, the other two have first to bolster the animal in them with alcohol; only then can they throw themselves upon the thief like a "pack of wolves." Yet their actions lead to a solution which in the final result is no solution at all. If they escape punishment by law, they will forever be punished by their guilt.

Guilt, moreover, can be an infinite source of anguish. It demands expiation. This is well illustrated in "The Sin" (there are two novellas by that title; here the reference is to the one which begins: "Kasiyanykha thinks to herself"). "The Sin" (see pp. 176-77) belongs already to the final group of novellas to be discussed in this thesis. This group is quite closely related to the preceding one. So much so that some of the novellas can fit into both groups. This final group embraces novellas where Stefanyk describes the anguish of man having to choose where no choice is a good one. Thus Kasiyanykha in "The Sin" must chose a way to atone for her sin: a bastard child conceived while her husband was at the front. First she feels that the choice has been made for her. Her long monologue concentrates on all the possible pain she will endure at the hands of her husband. In the morning when he finally sees the child and talks to his wife, it becomes apparent that he is a decent human being and does not intend to punish her at all, but is willing to treat the child as his own. Thereupon, the woman punishes herself. She runs away with her bastard to suffer and to atone for her sin. Stefanyk concentrates on the guilt of the transgressor and shows how it was imperative for the woman to have her husband refuse to carry the guilt with her, how it was imperative for her own peace of mind that he punish her. She was left with two equally bad choices: to stay with her husband and to endure the anguish of an unexpiated sin, or to leave and endure the shame, misery, and hardship of a homeless wanderer constantly reminded of her transgression by her bastard child.

Equally agonizing are the choices facing the wife of Les' in "Leseva familiya" (Les' Family) (see pp. 178-80). She can watch her profligate husband squander all their miserable possessions and have her children and herself starve, or she can try to stop him and commit the gravest of sins. Stefanyk focuses on the moment when the mother and children beat the father on the street for the whole village to see. Turning against one's parents is a horrible crime, but to have the mother egg the children to beat their father in public is the result of utter anguish and despondency. Once the act has been committed, all the characters realize the magnitude of the transgression. Yet the first choice of seeing one's children starve would have been equally horrifying.

Hryts' Letyuchy in "The News" (see pp. 181-83) also faces two choices: watch the children slowly die of hunger, or kill them.

Although many of Stefanyk's characters, downtrodden by poverty, look upon children as an extra burden, and although many of them express the wish that they would rather see their children dead than have them suffer and be a hardship to the rest of the family, none but Hryts' Letyuchy actually takes this choice. Stefanyk is very careful to show that, although Letyuchy does drown his daughter, he is by no means a bad or an unnatural father. Stefanyk paints him as a character who just could not manage after his wife's death. For two years he tries to manage the house and the two little children. Hunger, cold, poverty and the inability to change things for the better all wear him down. Finally he is haunted by the thought of "corpses" every time that he looks at his two emaciated children. Not only can he see no end to his own misery, but he also sees that the life of his children will be one of constant wretchedness. This weighs on his chest so that he can hardly breathe. Finally, he can endure no more and takes his two daughters, carrying the youngest one while leading the oldest one by the hand, and almost runs to the river where he throws the youngest one into the water. Immediately some of the weight disappears. He knows he is guilty of filicide, but he believes that sudden death is much less painful for his children than life-long misery. When he wants to drown the elder daughter, she begs him not to and it is here that Stefanyk points out how much Letyuchy really loves his children. The father agrees, but tells her that her life will be very difficult. He send her on her way to find a serving position and he prepares to go to the city to give himself up for his crime. No sooner has she gone a few steps, when he calls to her and gives her a little stick so that she may protect herself from stray dogs. Just this one little thought, from a father who just moments before had intended to drown his daughter, shows that he cared for his children and loved them very much, that indeed, it was out of love and the inability to endure their suffering that he chose to drown them.

133

Even though the motives are different, the situation is very similar in "Maty" (Mother) (see pp. 184-85). Here an old mother can either suffer the scorn of her townsfolk while watching her daughter lead a life of sin or she can absolve her daughter from the guilt of whoring by death. She forces her daughter to commit suicide. Stefanyk underlines that both choices were unsatisfactory by an interesting twist. All the town-folk avoid the old mother for they heard that her daughter committed suicide at her command. In a rage she lashes out against all of them, who with their derisions about her daughter's whoring drove her to do what she did and who are still unsatisfied and are still chaffing her now for having done what they wanted in the first place.

The choices need not always be so grave. Even in the rather humorous novella, "The Pious Woman" (see pp. 186-88), the husband must either endure the nagging of his wife or shut her up by beating her. He describes the latter, thus introducing a note of grief into this comedy of manners.

The novella which perhaps best summarizes the dilemma of having to make a choice where there is no choice is "Katrusya." In the setting of poverty a child, if healthy, is a blessing and, if sickly, a curse. If the child falls sick and death is imminent, the reaction of the parents is utter despair. They are caught in a vicious dichotomy of feeling. On the one hand, they love the child and have learned to depend on it, on the other the sickness is costly and there does not seem to be any hope in sight. This situation is illustrated very well in "Katrusya."

As Katrusya is slowly burning away in the last stages of consumption, Stefanyk briefly touches on her own youthful desire to live, on her hopes for a better spring, and finally on her bitter realization that she will die. Most of the novella, however, is devoted to the feelings of the parents. First, Stefanyk concentrates on the mother who is utterly forlorn. While Katrusya wavers between consciousness and unconsciousness, the mother pours out her pain in a monologue addressed to her daughter. She bemoans the fact that with the daughter's sickness, all their hopes have been dashed. Nothing seems to help her, not even the potions of the local fortune-teller. Yet the mother has squandered her last cent to buy Katrusya some paper flowers with which to decorate her braids. Stefanyk captures this moment very well as he shows the typical alliance between mother and daughter who hide this "foolishness" from the father.

The father's feelings are much coarser and much more desperate. He, after all, bears the financial responsibility of the family. His daughter's sickness is costing him his last cent.

134

Finally he has to borrow money to make one final attempt at saving her. He takes her to the city to see a doctor, but on the way there all his bitterness and frustration at his hapless situation fall on the poor daughter. Driven into a corner from which he does not see a way out, he blames his daughter, telling her that if she is going to die she might as well die now. Once he's spent the money he borrowed on the doctor and it does not help, then he won't even have any money to bury her. He almost pleads with her, as if it were in her power to change the situation:

> "Tell me, girl, what am I to do with you? You lie there and you lie there, and it's neither life nor death. I keep borrowing money and borrowing more money, and all for nothing. If I only knew where to find your cure, I'd look for it, but as it is what do I know. I hoped you'd go either one way or the other. It would be better for you and for us . . . ."

> Katrusya cried.

> "There's no reason to cry, for this is the honest truth. You will up and die and you won't even think about it. . . . Eh, if I only knew that there will not be any cure for you, then I'd turn right back and go home. Then I'd have at least some money left for the funeral.[26]

Still this is his own daughter and he does love her as best he can. He will try anything to save her and now, when he says all these things to her, not so much to hurt her as to ease his own burdened soul, he realizes that he has hurt her with his callous words. He offers her an apple and "somewhat timidly gave it to her. He had never before given her any sweets."[27] In this one instant, Stefanyk managed so well to portray the anguished soul of a father torn between what he knows is common sense and his own paternal feelings. He knows very well that the doctor will not be able to help. His apple is the best he can do in this situation and is just as "foolish" as the mother's flowers.

The small flicker of hope he had on the way to the city is, of course, snuffed out. The doctor's remedy of fine foods and milk is as good as nothing, for these things are beyond his reach. He realizes that he lost the money and accomplished nothing. The fact is that he knew this all along, but had to take this one chance in a million that the doctor could really cure his daughter. He had to take this chance in the same way and for the same reason that he gave his daughter that apple.

As with the majority of Stefanyk's novellas, there is nothing extraordinary in this situation. It describes a plight common to all poor who are daily forced to make similar choices between a loved one's welfare, comfort, or health and the grim economic consequences. Yet, as this whole chapter illustrates, the issue here is not only poverty. Had Stefanyk been interested in describing the poverty of the peasants of Pokuttya, he would have told us more than just the fact that they are poor. This in itself is sad but no sadder than the statistics that there are so many thousands of people on welfare. Stefanyk's interest lay elsewhere. As the preceding analysis shows, he wanted to capture the universal pain that lies at the heart of existence. Stefanyk wanted to dissect the anguish experienced by man in daily, common situations, whether it be the impossibility of a choice, or of an escape, or the presence of death, or of old age, or the effect of a loss, or even poverty itself. Human anguish, therefore, whatever its cause, is the major theme of Stefanyk's novellas.

FOOTNOTES

1 V. Lesyn, *Tvorchist' Vasylya Stefanyka*, p. 57.

2 Stefanyk, *Povne zibrannya tvoriv*, I, 146. Henceforth, all quotations from this text will be noted only by page numbers.

3 These novellas are individually discussed later in the chapter.

4 I, 170.

5 *Fata Morgana* (1903-1910) is a novel dealing with the peasant's thirst for land. In their struggle they burn down the manor. The novel ends in the macabre scene of the arsonists punishing their leaders so as to avoid the punishment of the approaching militia.

6 I, 232.

7 I, 96.

8 Stefanyk, *Povne zibrannya tvoriv*, II, 75-78.

9 I, 15-16.

10 I, 16.

11 I, 18.

12 *Ibid.*

13 I, 206.

14 I, 207.

15 The novella "The Schoolboy" is one which does not fit into any of the several situations which embrace the majority of the novellas. It is more *a la* novella by Les' Martovych. Stefanyk focuses on a little boy, an orphan, whom all of the people want locked up because he is a "bad" influence. The sad novella ends in wry humor. The schoolboy begs the gendarmes to lock him up and not give him to his aunt who has beaten him because he saw her having an affair. Its whole success hinges on the author's ability to put across the observations of an orphan who knows more than his childish innocence permits him to comprehend.

16 I, 141.

17 I, 143. M. Dan'ko in "Kray skorby," *Ukrayinskaya zhizn'*, 1913, No. 1, p. 63, makes the following remark *a propos* this scene: "The juxtaposition of grave things with trifles usually serves as a source of the humorous, but Stefanyk made it here the source of something deeply tragic."

18 Considering that the novella was written in 1898 and that Stefanyk's beloved sister Mariya died in 1892, this novella can be considered as partially autobiographical.

[19] I, 90.

[20] I, 110-11.

[21] Stefanyk, "Avtobiohrafiya" in *Tvory* (1964), p. 276.

[22] *Ibid.*, p. 276. The same has been confirmed by Stefanyk's youngest son, Yuriy, in a private interview with him in Edmonton, Alberta, June 1967.

[23] *Ibid.*

[24] *Ibid.*

[25] I, 155.

[26] I, 38.

[27] I, 38.

CONCLUSION

The study of Stefanyk's genre, a definite species of the novella, has revealed that the succinct and highly dramatic form of which he was a superb master was best suited to the capturing of single moments in the life of a hero, moments which first of all led to the turbulences of the soul, to an inner *agon*, the denouement of which permitted the author to portray the psychological complexity of his hero. Stefanyk's use of language was also subordinated to this general purpose. Since most of the characterization was achieved through the speech of the character himself, words which were spoken became important not only for their semantic value but also for the shade, the sound, and the elements of *skaz* contained in them. These threw direct light on the character's emotional state of being, on his personality and on his social as well as literate position. The special blend of local Pokuttya dialect with literary Ukrainian created a flavor not easily duplicated and therefore, although the emotional drama can be converted into another language, some of the special power derived from the language is lost during translation.

What serves as a compensation and sustains Stefanyk's appeal outside of the Ukrainian language is the universal nature of his theme. Most of the episodes which serve as catalysts for personal dramas fall into one of the six basic situations into which Stefanyk placed his heroes: trapped by poverty, facing an irrevocable loss, enveloped by the loneliness of old age, approaching death, caught in an inescapable position, and faced with an impossible choice. These situations are certainly universal in nature and applicable to any human being, be he a Ukrainian, a peasant, or neither. The peasants are but concrete symbols—tools which were very well known to Stefanyk, since he was by origin one of them, and which he used to present his observations of the human soul. Though not all of his characters are poor, most are afflicted with the pain which lies at the heart of existence. All of them struggle with the insoluble anguish of life.

Poverty and war provide two broad settings for Stefanyk's

psychological dramas. Sometimes they serve as stimuli for a given drama, but most often they are used by the author as prevailing conditions which erode human dignity and bring to the fore the anguish which otherwise might pass unnoticed. Although some of his poorer novellas have a smattering of socially tendentious propaganda, the majority use social elements merely as a distant backdrop. Stefanyk was far too much of an artist to subordinate his art to the needs of social reform, even those reforms which he, as a politician and a life-long member of the Radical Party, would have more than welcomed. The fact that he had little intention of mixing art with politics is further borne out by the definite split in his own life between the artist and the politician. It seems that his long silence was the direct result of the feeling that he should do something concrete to help remedy the situation of the impoverished peasants. Hence his involvement in politics and service as a member of the Austrian Parliament. He returned to the pen, however, to capture the anguish brought on by the madness of War.

It is clear from the study of his novellas in respect to content, that critics and scholars who would like to see in Stefanyk the great defender and lover of the peasants as well as a great nationalist are basing their case on very flimsy and minimal evidence. It is nothing more than an oversimplification to maintain that Stefanyk's prime concern was in delineating the socio-economic conditions or the struggle for independence. Even a quick perusal of his works will belie this contention by the sole fact that they are still powerful, interesting and meaningful today. Certainly, the powerful effect of the tragedy in "The Blue Book" is not derived from Stefanyk's description of a poor peasant but from the portrayal of a crisis in a man's soul when he is suddenly faced with the loss of all of his possessions, of his former way of life. In the same way, Semen's tragedy in "The Sons" affects the reader not because he lost his sons in the struggle for the independence of Ukraine, but because of the anguish he feels at losing them, no matter what the cause.

It is undeniable that there were influences on Stefanyk from other writers he read and from the literary milieu in which he lived while in Cracow. Yet it is doubtful that even a separate comparative study would reveal any influences of great significance. So far, claims for direct influences by such writers as Uspensky, Martovych, Cheremshyna, Orkan and others, are not very convincing. Some of the comparisons of Stefanyk to the other authors are often more misleading than illuminating. A comparison seems valuable only if all or the most important elements of the creative process can be compared, themes as well as technique. However, thematic similarities with such various writers as the Italian Verga and the Mexican Rulfo only serve to emphasize the universality of Stefanyk's theme.

In short, although Stefanyk is the greatest writer of short prose in Ukrainian literature, his preoccupation with the psychological experiences of his characters makes him a writer who steps out of the confines of his native literature. The fact that he managed to tune in on man's anguish makes him a great humanitarian, but only the fact that he portrayed this anguish in superbly crafted novellas makes him an artist of universal appeal. His lack of world recognition stems primarily from the fact that he is not easily translated into other languages. It is hoped, however, that this monograph and the novellas translated in the appendix will serve as an appropriate introduction to one of the great writers of the twentieth century.

APPENDIX

NOVELLAS IN TRANSLATION

The thirteen novellas selected and translated for this appendix are arranged in an order consistent with the presentation of Stefanyk's novellas in Chapter V of this book. Each novella is preceded by the original title, the date it was written and the collection in which it appeared. Some novellas appeared only in collected works and are so noted.

They were chosen for the non-Ukrainian reader primarily as illustrations of Stefanyk as seen by the author of this work. Although Stefanyk is extremely difficult to translate, it is hoped that these translations will convey at least partially the flavor of the originals.

LOSS

("Shkoda," 1898, *Synya knyzhechka*)

Romanykha's cow became ill. She lay on the straw and looked about sadly with large grey eyes. The nostrils quivered, the hide wrinkled; she was all aflame with fever. There was a smell of sickness and dumb pain about her. In such instances it's a real pity that the beast can't speak and complain.

"You can see it in the eyes that she's a goner. One could, perhaps, help her if it was the blood, but it ain't that; someone's cast an evil eye on her, may his own eyes pop, and now there's no way out for her. Turn to God, maybe He'll console you a bit . . . ," so spoke Ilash, the one who knew about cattle.

"Oh, Ilash, my friend, I can see that she's gonna go, but if she goes I might as well go too. I worked all my life to get a cow. I was left without a husband, my son died in the army, and I sweated blood day and night. The winter nights are so long and I'd get home only in the morning, tired so my fingertips were swollen and my eyes felt as if there was sand in them. God alone knows how I saved the money until I had enough . . ."

"It's always like that for the poor. Even if you work your hands down to your elbows—nothing will come of it. That's the way it is and what can one do about it? You got to live somehow and that's all . . ."

"I just don't know what to do; where to turn; who can help me?"

"Hire yourself out for a day or so; so's you can at least have money for a mass and to cook some dinner. Or you can make an offering to Ivan Suchavsky; they say he helps a lot."

"Oh, I've already hired myself for a day and have made an offering to Our Lady of Zarvanytsa and to Ivan Suchavsky."

"Well, as I've said, maybe God will help you if you turn to Him. May He grant you all of the best."

And Ilash left.

Romanykha sat by her cow and watched so that she wouldn't die. She gave her all the best she had, but the cow wouldn't eat. She only looked at the old woman and caused her grief.

"My little one, my precious one, what ails you? Don't leave an old woman without a drop of milk. Make me just a bit happy."

And she petted the cow over the head and under the throat and lamented over her.

"Where, oh where, can I get enough for another one? I can no longer put my fingers together nor thread a needle; how can I look for a cow in my old age?"

The cow shivered, and Romanykha covered her with her own fur jacket and sat next to her unprotected in the frost. Her teeth were rattling, but she did not leave the cow.

"And maybe it's for my sins, that God's punishing me so? For many a time I've sinned on account of you. I'd let you graze someone's furrow, or let you grab someone's pumpkin or a side-shoot here and there. But I never begrudged anyone any milk. If some child were sick, or some woman delivering, I'd go with a pot of milk. And I gave people cheese for their cornmeal. Oh, God, don't punish me, a poor widow. I won't touch anything that isn't mine, but please, spare my cow!"

Romanykha lamented thus over her cow far into the night. She sprinkled her with holy water; but nothing helped. The cow stretched her legs out across the whole stall, her sides pumped and she moaned. The old woman petted her, embraced her, talked to her, but really could do nothing.

The moon lit the stall through the door and the old woman could see every movement the cow made. Finally the cow stood up. She could hardly stand on her legs. She looked over the stall as if saying good-bye to every little corner.

Then she fell on the straw and stretched out like a string. Romanykha kneeled by her and rubbed her down with a handful of straw. She was no longer aware of what was happening to her. Then the cow moaned loudly and started kicking with her legs. Romanykha felt hot; she saw yellow spots in her eyes and bloodied she fell. The cow was kicking the old woman to pieces.

They were struggling with death together.

A STONE CROSS

("Kaminnyy khrest," 1899, *Kaminnyy khrest*)

1

For as long as people in the village remembered, gazda Ivan Didukh always had only one horse and a small wagon with an oak shaft. He harnessed the horse on the left side and himself on the right; for the horse he had leather breeching and a breast collar, and on himself he placed a small rope breeching. He had no need for a breast collar for with his left hand he pushed perhaps even better than he would with a collar.

Whenever they pulled sheaves from the field or manure to the field, then likewise, both on the horse and on Ivan, veins protruded, likewise for both of them going uphill the traces tightened like strings, and likewise going down, they dragged over the ground. Upwards the horse climbed as if on ice, and on Ivan's forehead such a vein swelled up as if someone had lashed him with a switch. From above, the horse looked as if Ivan had hung him by the breast collar for some great crime, and Ivan's left arm was wound in a net of blue veins, like a chain of blue steel.

Often in the mornings, still before dawn, Ivan rode to the field on a dirt road. He did not have breeching on him; instead he walked on the right side and held the wagon shaft under his arm. Both the horse and Ivan carried themselves firmly, for both had rested during the night. And when they had to go down a hill, they ran. They ran down and left behind the tracks of the wheels, hoofs and Ivan's wide heels. Grass and weeds by the side of the road swayed, rocking in all directions after the cart and threw dew on these tracks. But sometimes during the greatest momentum Ivan would start limping and holding back the horse. He'd sit by the road, take his foot in his hands and wet it with his spittle to find the place where a thistle had rammed itself in.

"You should scrape this foot with a hoe instead of washing it with your spittle," spoke Ivan querulously.

"Gramp Ivan, git that one on the right with a whip, make

145

him run if he eats oats," someone who saw Ivan's troubles from his own field was trying to make a joke of him. But Ivan was long used to such jokers and calmly continued to pull out the thistle. When he could not dislodge the thistle, he hit it with his fist and drove it deeper into the foot and got up saying:

"Don't worry, you'll rot and then you'll fall out by yourself, and I have no time to play around with you . . ."

People also called him Broken Ivan, for he had a fault in his back, and always walked around bent over as if two iron clamps pulled his body to his feet. A draught of wind did it to him.

When he returned home from the army, he found neither father nor mother, only a small, crumbling shack. And all the wealth his father left him consisted of a piece of the highest and the worst land in all of the village. On this hill the women used to dig for sand and it yawned toward the sky with gullies and caves like some awful giant. Nobody ploughed it or seeded it and there were no marked boundaries on it. Ivan alone took to ploughing and seeding his pitiful share. Together with the horse he carted manure up to the hill, but Ivan alone carried it to the top in a sack. Sometimes his shouts fell to the lower fields:

"Boy, am I gonna slam you down. You'll fall apart thread by thread, you're so damn heavy."

But apparently he never did slam it down for he did not want to waste the sack, and therefore he always lowered it down slowly. And once in the evening he told his wife and children of an event:

"The sun was burning, no, not burning, but spewing fire and I was kneeling my way up to the top with the manure so that the skin was peeling off my knees. Sweat trickling down every hair and my mouth so salty it was bitter. I hardly made it to the top. And on top such a breeze blew over me, such a light breeze. And in a minute it got me right across the middle, like knives pricking me. I thought I was a goner."

From then on, Ivan always walked around bent at the middle, and the people called him Broken.

But even though that hill broke him, it nonetheless gave good harvests. Ivan drove stakes and poles into it, brought turf to it and covered his part of the hill with it so that autumn and spring rains wouldn't wash away the manure into the gullies. He spent his whole life on that hill.

The older he got, the harder it was for him, broken in half, to get down that hill.

"Such a bitchy hill, always pulling one down head over heels."

Often when the setting sun caught Ivan on top then it

carried his shadow together with that of the hill far over the fields. Over those fields Ivan's shadow spread, like a shadow of a giant bent in half. Ivan then pointed his finger at his shadow and spoke to the hill:

"Oh, boy, did you ever make an arc out of me. But as long as my feet carry me, you have to bear bread for me. You can't just eat the sun and drink the rain for nothing."

On the other fields which Ivan bought for the money he brought back from the army his sons and wife worked. Ivan spent most of his time on his hill.

They also knew Ivan in the village for the fact that he went to church only once a year at Easter and for the fact that he "drilled" his chickens. He got them so trained that not one of them dared get into the yard and scratch the manure; if one as much as once scratched with her leg then she died from the shovel or a stick. Even if Ivan's wife layed herself out in a cross of supplication it didn't help.

And also perhaps for the fact that Ivan never ate at the table but always at a bench.

"I was a servant, and then spent ten years in the army and therefore I never knew a table and now food just doesn't pass my gullet at a table."

Such was Ivan. Strange both in character and in work.

2

Ivan's house was full of guests; *gazdas* and their wives. Ivan had sold everything he had. His sons and wife decided on Canada and the old man finally had to agree.

Ivan invited the whole village.

He stood in front of his guests, held a measure of whisky in his right hand, and it seems, turned to stone for he could not say a word.

"I thank you nicely, *gazdas* and *gazdynyas*, that you had me for a *gazda* and my woman for a *gazdynya.*"

He did not finish his speech and drank to no one, but kept starring dully in front of himself and shook his head, as if he were saying a prayer and nodding his head in agreement with every word.

Just like when some underwave dislodges a huge stone from the water and places it on the shore, then that stone sits on the shore heavy and spiritless. The sun chips off pieces of old sediments and draws on it small phosphorous stars. That stone blinks with dead reflections from the rising and the setting of the sun and with its stone eyes it looks at the live water and longs for the weight of the water which no longer presses it as it had for ages. It looks from the shore at the water as if it were some lost happiness.

So Ivan looked at the people, as the stone upon water. He shook his grey hair, like a mane forged from steel threads, and continued:

"And I thank you nicely, and may God give you what you wish. May God give you health, grampa Mykhaylo . . ."

He gave Mykhaylo the measure and they kissed each other's hands.

"My friend Ivan, may God give you few more years on this world and may merciful God lead you successfully to your place and may He with His goodness help you again to become His *gazda.*"

"May God will it . . . . *Gazdas*, please, drink up . . . I thought that I'd sit you around the table when you came for my son's wedding, but it turned out different. It's already like that. What our granddads and our fathers knew nothing about, we now have to know. It's God's will. But content yourselves, *Gazdas*, and forgive the rest.

He took another measure of whisky and went over to the women who sat at the other end of the table, near the beds.

"Tymofikha, friend, I want to drink to you. I look at you and, as someone said, I recall my youth. Where, where, oh whe-e-re? Oh, you were a strong girl, you were beautiful. I lost many a night because of you; and how you danced, straight like a top. Where, my friend, are those years of ours. Well, live through and forgive that in the old age I recalled our dancing. Please . . ."

He looked at his old woman who was weeping among women and took out a handkerchief from his pocket.

"Here, my old one, here's a kerchief for you; dry yourself nicely so that I don't see any weeping here. Look after the guests; you'll have plenty of time still for weeping; you'll weep so much that your eyes will flow out."

He went over to the men and shook his head.

"I'd say something but I'd better keep quiet in respect of the holy icons in the house and you, my good people. But still don't let any good person have a woman's brain. See how she weeps, and because of who, me? Are you crying because of me, my *gazdynya*? Was it me who uprooted you in your old age from your own home? Keep quiet, don't sob, for I'll pluck your grey braids right out and you'll go to that Hamerica like a Jewess."

"Ivan, my friend, leave your wife be. You know she means you no harm, nor her sons; she's just missing her people and her village."

"Timofikha, if you don't know all there is, then don't say a word. So she's missing, and what about me, am I roaring to go?"

He gnashed his teeth as if mill stones, threatened his wife with his fist, like a club, and struck his chest with his fist.

"Here, take an axe and drive it here into my liver and maybe this bile will burst out, for I can't take it anymore. My people, such sorrow, such sorrow that I don't know what's going on around me."

3

"Please *gazdas*, don't stand on ceremony, drink up and excuse us, for we are already travelers. Don't be surprised at old me for rubbing my wife, but it's not for nothing, not for nothing. This would never have happened, if it were not for her and the sons. The sons, mind you, are literate, so when they got ahold of some paper, some map, they got to their mother and worked at her, and worked at her until they broke her. For two years there was no talk in the house except about Canada and Canada. And then they got to me, and when I saw that they would keep on gnawing at me in my old age, then I sold everything to a button. The sons don't want to be servants after me, so they say: 'You're our father so take us to some land, and give us bread, for if you divide among us there will be nothing for any of us.' Let God help them eat that bread, and I'll perish anyway, here or there. But, *gazdas*, how am I, a broken man, to go wandering about? I'm a worn out has-been—my whole body is one callous, my bones moldy to the point where it takes several groans each morning to put them together."

"It's too late now, Ivan, and there's no point in paining your head. And perhaps if you show us the way we will all follow you. It's not worth filling one's heart with pain over this land. This earth can't endure so many people and so much misfortune. The peasant can't and it can't; both of them no longer can endure. There's no locust, but there's also no wheat. And the taxes keep growing, for what you paid a lev (dollar) now you pay five, when you ate salted pork, now you eat potatoes. Boy, they sure got to us, they latched onto us so well that no one can rip us out of their clutches anymore, except if one goes away. But someday a reckoning will come to these lands for the people will slaughter one another. You have nothing to miss when you leave."

"Thank you for these words, but I don't accept them.

Sure, the people will slaughter one another. For doesn't God get angry with people who speculate with their land? No one needs land anymore; all they want is promissory notes and banks. Now young *gazdas* have become very wise, such firemen that they don't burn on account of land. And look at that old fiddle (ref. to his wife)—should one speculate with her? She's no more than a hollow willow; just flick your finger and she'll fall to dust. Do you think she'll make it? She'll probably fall over into some ditch and the dogs will pull her apart, and we'll be pressed on so that we won't even have a chance to look at her. How is God to bless such children? Well, my old one, judge by yourself."

Ivan's wife, old and skinny, came up.

"Well, Kateryna, what is going on in that head of yours? Where will I find a grave for you? Or should the fish make a meal of you? But a good fish won't even have enough for one bite. Look at her."

And he pulled the skin on his wife's arm and showed it to the people.

"Skin and bones. Where is this bag of bones to go from her warm place by the stove? You were a good and proper *gazdynya*, you worked hard, you did not waste time, and in your old age you decided on a journey? You see, over there, there's your journey, there's your Canada? See."

And through the window he showed her a grave.

"You did not want to go to this Canada, then we'll go into the world and be blown about in our old age, like a leaf over the fields. God alone knows how it will be with us . . . and I want to do my parting with you in front of all these good people. We were wed before their eyes, so now let's part for death before them. Maybe they'll throw you into the sea, so as I won't even see you; or maybe they'll throw me, so that you won't see it, so forgive me, my old one, for often enough have I given you a hard time, for probably I hurt you sometime, and forgive me the first time and the second time and the third . . ."

They kissed. The old woman fell into his arms and Ivan spoke:

"For I'm taking you, my dear, on a long journey . . ."

But no one heard these words anymore for from the women's table weeping rose like a wind taking off from among sharp swords and all the peasants' heads slumped to their chests.

4

"And now go on among the women, and see to it that each

gets her due and have a drink, for God's sake, so that at least once in my life I'll see you drunk."

"And you, *gazdas*, I still have two favors to ask of you. Perhaps someday our sons will leave word through the village post that we have gone. Then I'd ask you that you have a mass said in our favor and that you get together like today, for dinner, and say an Our Father for us. Maybe the Lord God will write down fewer sins for us. I will leave the money for the mass with Yakiv, for he is a young and proper man and won't steal an old man's money."

"We'll have the mass, we'll have it and we'll say an Our Father for you . . ."

"Don't wonder at and don't laugh at an old man. I myself am ashamed to tell you this, but it seems to me that I'd have a sin if I didn't tell you. You know that I put up a little stone cross for myself on my hill. Bitterly I carted it, and bitterly hoisted it to the top, but I placed it there. It is so heavy that the hill won't be able to throw it off; it'll have to carry it on its back like it carried me. I wanted to leave at least so much in memory of myself."

He clenched his fists and pressed them to his lips.

"I long so for that hill like a child for teat. I spent my life on it, and am crippled because of it. If I could I'd take it and hide it in my pocket and take it with me into the world. I long for the smallest speck in the village, for every child, but I will never stop missing that hill."

His eyes glimmered with a great hurt and his face quivered, like the black field quivers under the sun.

"Last night I lay in the shed and thought and thought: God all merciful, what great sin have I committed that you are chasing me past the world's waters? All my life, all I did was work, and work, and work. Often when the day was ending, I would fall on the field and earnestly pray to God, Lord, never deny me a piece of black bread and I will always work except if I can no longer move an arm or a leg . . . ."

"Then such longing came upon me that I chewed my knuckles and plucked my hair, I rolled on the straw like cattle. And then the evil spirit touched me. I don't know how or when but I found myself under the pear tree with an ox harness. In a little while I would have hung myself. But the merciful Lord knows what he is doing. I remembered my cross, and it all left me. I ran, I ran up my hill. In an hour I was already sitting under my cross. I sat there, I sat there for quite a while, and somehow it became much easier for me."

"Even now as I stand in front of you and am telling you this, that hill is constantly before my eyes. I see it, and I really

151

see it, and when I'll be dying I'll still see it. I'll forget everything, but it I'll never forget. I knew songs and on that hill I
forgot them; I had strength and on it I lost it."

One tear rolled down his face like a pearl over a ragged
cliff.

"So I entreat you, *gazdas*, when on a holy Sunday you will
be going to bless your land, that you never omit my hill. Let
some young one run up and sprinkle the cross with holy water,
for you know that the priest will not climb up the hill. I beg
you very nicely that you never leave out my cross. I will pray to
God for you in the next world, but only fulfill an old man's
wish."

It was as if he wanted to spread himself in front of them,
as if he wanted with his good grey eyes to bury into the hearts
of his guests his wish.

"Ivan, friend, leave off grieving, throw it aside. We will
remember you once and for all. You were a good man, you
never bothered anyone without a reason, you never ploughed
over into another's field, nor sowed over, you never touched
even a grain of someone else's. No. People will always remember
you and they will not omit your cross on the holy Sunday."

So Mykhaylo cheered Ivan.

5

"I've already told you, fellow *gazdas*, everything there was
to say, and now all who like me will drink with me. The sun is
close to the grave and you haven't yet drunk a portion of
whiskey with me. While I'm still in my house, and have guests
around my table I will drink with them, and all who like me will
do likewise."

The drinking began, such drinking which makes out of
peasants crazy boys. Soon, Ivan, by now drunk, said to call the
musicians to play for the young people who filled the whole
yard.

"Boy, you have to dance so that the earth shakes and not a
blade of grass remains in the yard."

In the house all drank, all talked and no one listened. Talk
went on for its own sake, for it had to come out even if only
the wind listened to it.

"When I polished him, then he was polished; if he was
black then like if someone had sprinkled silver on black, if
white then like snow covered with butter. My horses were
always in order, the Kaiser himself could ride them. And did I
have money. Boy-oh boy . . ."

152

"If I'd only land in the middle of such a desert where there's only God and I. Let me walk like a wild animal as long as I don't see neither those Jews, nor lords, nor priests. Then one could say that I'm a real master. And let this earth fall through, let it fall through right now, no skin off my back ("tom ne zhoriv"). Why? They tortured and beat our fathers, enslaved them and now they don't even give us a piece of bread. Oh, if only I could have it my way . . ."

"There's never been yet such a tax collector who could get anything out of him. The Czech tried, the German, the Pole—and all took shit, excuse the expression. But when the Mazur came then he found even the stuff that was buried under ground. I tell you, Mazurs are an evil, even if you burn out their eyes there's no sin for it . . ."

There was all sorts of talk, but it flew into various directions like rotten wood in an old forest.

Into this noise, racket, and yelps and into the sorrowful joyness of the violin, into all of this broke in the singing of Ivan and old Mykhaylo. This singing which often one can hear at weddings when old men get up courage and desire to sing old songs. The words of the song go through the old throat with difficulty, as if there were callouses not only on the hands but also in the throat. The words of these songs flow like yellow leaves in the fall when the wind chases them over frozen ground and they stop over and over again in every gully and tremble with torn edges as if before death.

Ivan and Mykhaylo sang thus about youth which they tried to catch again at the cedar bridge, but did not want to come back to them even for a visit.

When they reached a high note then they pressed each other's hands so hard that the joints cracked, and when they came across a very sorrowful place then they bowed to each other and pressed forehead against forehead and grieved. They embraced each other, kissed, struck with their fists their breasts or the table, and with their rusty voices drove each other to such sadness that finally they could say no more than: Oh, Ivan, my brother, Oh, Mykhaylo, my friend.

6

"Father, do you hear, it's already time to go to the train and you sing as if for the good of the world."

Ivan's eyes bulged, but so strangely that the son turned white and stepped back. Ivan placed his head in his hands and for a long time tried to remember something. Finally he got up and walked over to his wife, took her by the sleeve.

"OK. Old one, let's go. March, eintz, zwei, drie. Let's go. We'll dress like the lords and we'll go and rule."

Both left.

When they reentered the house the whole house wept. As if a cloud of rain which hung over a village had fallen through, as if people's grief had torn asunder the Danube dam—such was the weeping. The women clasped their hands and raised them above old Ivan's wife as if to protect her from something falling and crushing her on the spot. And Mykhaylo seized Ivan by the scruff of the neck and wildly shook him and screamed as if mad.

"If you're a *gazda* then throw those rags off or I'll slap you like a whore."

But Ivan did not pay attention. He took his old lady and started to dance with her.

"Play a polka for me, just like for the lords; I have money."

The people froze, and Ivan threw his wife about as if he had no intention of ever letting her get out of his hands alive.

The sons ran in and forcibly carried both of them out of the house.

In the yard Ivan continued to dance some sort of polka and his wife latched onto the threshold and moaned:

"I walked you down. I chewed you down with these very feet."

And with her hand she kept showing in the air how deep she had gouged the threshold.

7

The fences by the road creaked and fell—all the people were accompanying Ivan. He walked with his wife, hunched, in a cheap, grey factory suit and every few minutes danced the polka.

Until they all stopped in front of the cross which Ivan had placed on the hill, then he came to and showed his wife:

"You see, my old one, our cross? Your name is also chiselled on it. Don't worry—there's both mine and yours . . ."

154

SUICIDE

("Stratyvsya," 1897, *Synya knyzhechka*)

The train rushed into distant lands. In the corner on a bench sat a peasant and cried. So that no one would see him cry, he hid his head in an embroidered bag (*taystra*). The tears fell like rain, the kind of a sudden rain that starts quickly and soon passes.

The hard beat of the train pounded like a hammer into the peasant's soul.

"I dreamed about him just the other day. Somehow I was pulling water out of a well and he appeared somewhere way at the bottom in a torn jacket, my God was it torn. It seemed he would drown any minute. Nykola, my son, I say to him, what are you doing here? And he answers me:

"Oh, daddy, I can't take the army anymore."

I say to him: suffer, be patient and learn as much as you can, and keep yourself clean. And now, now he's already learned . . .

One large tear streaked down his face and fell on the *taystra*.

"I'm going to him, but I know that I will not find him anymore. But will there be anyone to come back to? She ran after me through the fields, begging me with bloody tears, to take her along. Her feet turned blue from the snow, she screamed as if she were touched in the head. But I chased the horses on . . . Maybe she's freezing to death somewhere there in the field . . . I should have taken the old woman along. What do we need now? Let the money go, let the stock die from hunger. For such corpses like us, there's no need. Let her sew us bags and we'll go begging among people in the city in which Nykola's grave is."

He pressed his face to the window and his tears flowed down the glass.

"Oh, my old one, such is the wreath we waited out for our grey hair. You're probably beating your head against the walls, weeping to God."

The old man sobbed like a child. The weeping and the train bounced the old head as if it were a pumpkin. Tears flowed like water from a spring. The peasant seemed to hear the voice of his old woman as she runs barefoot and begs him to take her along. But he whips the horses, whips them. One can only hear a yelp in the field, but far, far away.

"For certain I won't find her when I get back. If only they would put me away together with Nykola into the grave. Let us rot together at least, since we could not live together; let even the dogs forget to bark for us, but let us be together. How can he be all alone here in this foreign land? The train rushed on.

"It's a darn shame that you grew up like an oak. No matter what he took up, it seemed to burn in his hands. I should have cut one of them off while he still was a kid . . ."

The train reached a big city.

He got off the train together with the other people. But he remained all alone on the street. Walls, walls, and in between walls—streets; and over the streets thousands of lamps, all strung on one rope. The lights sank and quivered in the darkness. It seemed that any minute now the light would fall and a black hell would descend.

But the lights sank their roots into the darkness and did not fall.

"Oh, Nykola, if only I could see you. Even if you're dead. I too will die here."

He sat under a wall. He placed the embroidered bag on his knees. Tears no longer fell on it. The walls bent, one toward the other; the lights all fell together and played with color like a rainbow. They closed in on the peasant, in order to see him better for he had come here from very distant lands. It began to rain. He huddled even more and began to pray.

"Mother of Christ, you help out all good people, St. Nicholas . . . ," and he pounded his fist against his chest in contrition.

A policeman came by and showed him the way to the barracks.

"Mister soldier, is it here that Nykola Chorny died?"

"He hung himself among the alders behind the city. Now he is lying in the morgue. Go down this street and there someone will show you."

The soldier returned to his guard. The peasant lay in the street and groaned. Once he had regained a little strength he went down the street. His legs doubled over and stumbled as if wind-blown.

"My son, oh, my son, so you killed yourself. Tell me son what pushed you into your grave? Why did you destroy your soul? Oh, will I ever bring happy news for your mother from you. We will perish uselessly."

In the morgue on a white slab lay Nykola. His beautiful hair swam in blood. The top of his head fell off like a piece of shell. On his stomach there was a cross, for they had cut him up and sewn him together.

The father fell on his knees and prayed. He kissed his son's feet and repeatedly struck his head against the slab.

"Oh, child, mother and I were preparing a wedding for you, ordering the musicians, and you went and left us . . ."

Then he picked up the corpse, embraced it by the neck and asked as if consulting:

"Tell me how many services am I to order, how much to give for the poor, so that God may forgive you your sin?"

Tears fell on the corpse and on the cold white slab. Weeping, he was dressing his son for death: a white embroidered shirt, a large embroidered belt and a hat with peacock feathers. He placed the embroidered bag under his head and at his head he placed a candle to burn for a lost soul.

Such a handsome and nice young man in feathers. He lay on a cold marble slab and, it seemed, smiled at his father.

SONS

*I dedicate this story to my
friend Levko Bachyns'ky.*

("Syny," 1922, *Zemlya*)

With good young horses old Maksym was harrowing spring
wheat. The harrow flew over the earth like feathers. Maksym
threw his hat down on the earth; the shirt opened and fell on
his shoulders. A cloud of dust flew from under the harrow and
covered the grey hair on his head and on his chest. He grew
angry and clamoured so that people in the next fields said to
themselves:

"The old dog is always angry; but he can still hold them
young horses, the giant. He was well fed all his life, but since
the time that he lost both his sons he keeps shouting both in the
field and in the village."

Maksym stopped the horses.

"Old bones are like old birch: they're good for the fire,
but they're worthless when it comes to walking after a horse.
When your feet give way while working or dancing, then it's
best not to say what such feet are worth. Get on the stove, you
old bag of bones, the time has come."

But he shook his grey hair under the black manes of the
horses and kept on shouting:

"Oh, brother, I can still make it on top of the stove all
right, but the stove is all chipped and cold. The icons have
dimmed and the saints look at the empty rooms like hungry
dogs. The old woman decorated them all the time with perriwinkle and sweet basil and gilded the doves around them so that
they'd be kind, so that the rooms would be bright, so that the
children would grow. But even though there's so many of them,
these saints are all good for nothing. My sons are gone, I
covered the old woman with earth, and you gods have to forgive
the lack of perriwinkle; you should have taken better care . . .
Well, Starhead, let's go and work 'til God has willed; let's take
care of this soil, brother."

And they went from one end of the field to the other, swaddled with dust; and the harrow bit at the earth, grumbled, tore it to pieces, so that the grain would have a soft bed.

"You, Barefoot, you're not a horse at all; you're a dog. You have chewed up my shoulders, inch by inch. Don't yank me, don't yank me, for life has yanked me so that I can hardly stand on my own feet. Before dawn I give you oats, not having eaten anything myself; I comb you, I wash you with my old tears, and you, you bite me. Now Starhead, there's a horse for you: he follows me with his black eyes; he wipes the old man's tears with his mane; but you, you're rotten; you don't have a heart. Just the other day you tore out a whole bunch of my grey hair and you threw it on a pile of manure. You shouldn't do that. And even though you're a very nice horse—for that you're rotten. I can't sell you to the Jews, but if Saint George were to come to me I'd give you to him, so that you'd go with him to kill the dragons. You're not good at working the soil; there's no peace in you."

And he spat on his fingers, washed his wound in the shoulder and sprinkled it with earth.

"Hey, horses, let's go, go."

The harrow quieted down, the earth gave in, fell apart. Maksym's feet felt the softness under them; that softness that so rarely enters the peasant's soul. The earth gives him that softness and for that he loves it so. As he was throwing a handful of grain he kept repeating: "I've made a soft crib for you, grow up to the sky."

Maksym quieted down; he no longer shouted but suddenly he stopped the horses.

"Why the devil do you hurt, you old bone you? You screech in every joint, you crooked one."

He looked back and saw a long thread of red blood, and he sat down.

"Glass, the mother ...! Now go and harrow, and you can't leave an unfinished field unless you bust. And you, field, you're not going to have much of a boon from this old blood, for old blood is like old manure—doesn't fertilize at all. I have a loss and you get no gain."

Limping, he unharnessed the horses and led them to the wagon and placed some hay in front of them.

"You, sun, don't be angry with the old man for making his lunch too soon; he's got nothing to walk on."

He took out of the bag some bread, pork fat, a bottle, and washed his wound with whiskey. Then he tore off his sleeve and bandaged his foot, tying it down with a piece of rope.

"Now you can hurt or stop, or as you like, but you'll

159

continue to harrow."

He drank some whiskey, took a piece of bread and chewed it; again he became angry and shouted:

"Is this bread? It's only good for combing a Jewish horse, for it would tear the skin off a good horse. They come to me in hordes, those sluts. Granddad, they say, we'll bake for you and wash for you, but deed some land to us. These torn bitches think that I held the land for them? When I die then let flowers grow on my fields and let them say an Our Father for the old man with their little heads."

In anger, he threw the bread far onto the field.

"Teeth shudder from this bread. Drink, Maksym, whiskey goes down smoothly . . ."

"Oh, shut up, don't bark over my head; for whom are you singing? For this dilapidated and chewed up old man? Fly away into the sky and tell that God of yours not to send me a stupid bird with its song, for if He's so strong then let Him send me my sons. For it's on account of His will that I'm left here alone on this earth. Tell your God not to fool me with songs, get away!"

And he threw a lump of earth at the lark, and the lark began to sing even more beautifully above his head and didn't want to fly to God.

"You, little bird, you don't understand a damn thing. When my young Ivan ran after you trying to catch you, when he was searching for your nest and played on his reed, then, little bird, you were wise to sing; that's the way it should have been. Your singing and Ivan's reed floated over the ground, and above you the sun, and all of you were sowing God's voice over me and over the shiny plows, over the whole world. And through the sun, as if through a golden sieve, God showered us with lightness, and the whole earth and all of the people shone with gold. So the sun leavened spring on earth, as if in a huge trough . . ."

"And from that trough we took out wedding cakes, and the cakes stood in front of the musicians, and the young couple, full of love, went to get married, and the spring rolled on, like the sea, like a flood; then, little bird, your singing flowed into my heart like spring water into a new pitcher . . ."

"Go away, little bird, into those lands, where they haven't taken away the wedding cakes, and where they haven't slaughtered the children . . ."

He took his grey head into his hands and bowed it down to the earth.

"You should be ashamed of yourself, grey hair, that you're whining and singing like an old crybaby, for nothing in this world will help you anymore . . ."

160

"Oh, my sons, my sons; where have you lain your heads to rest? Not only all my land, but my soul I'd sell just to be able to get to your grave on my two bleeding feet. God, the golden books in churches lie that You had a son, they lie. They say You resurrected Your son. And I don't ask You to resurrect them; all I ask is that You show me their graves so that I can lie by them. You can see the whole world, but over my graves You grow blind."

"May Your blue dome burst just like my heart."

"Why doesn't one of you come to the old man; as if you didn't embrace them, my sons, as if you didn't lie between white sheets with them? They were like curly oaks ... Go ahead, bring the little bastard children; don't be ashamed, come. Grandfather will spread all the carpets under your feet, he'll cut up all of the best linen for the diapers for the little bastard. For your walking about unwed and your weeping from derision."

And the old man raised his two arms high and called to the whole world:

"Come on, daughter-in-law, come to the house; we don't need a priest."

He wept loudly, lay close to the earth and with it, as if with a handkerchief, he wiped his tears and blackened himself. But he continued to entreat:

"Or you, lover, come, even without a child. On your neck I will see his arms, and on your lips his lips will redden, and from your eyes as from a deep well I will fish out his eyes and hide them in my heart like in a little box. Like a dog, I will sniff out his hair on your palm ... Come lover, come and save the old man."

"You're still in the world and they're no longer here; so find your way to me and bring me news. Pour some cold dew on my hair, for each strand burns me so as if a hot wire. My head is aflame from that fire."

And he tore hair out of his head and threw it on the earth.

"Grey hair burn the earth; I can no longer endure your weight ..."

Totally exhausted he lay on the ground and for a long time remained silent and then spoke gently:

"The last time my Andriy came to me—he was my learned one—he says, father, now we are going to go and fight for Ukraine. What Ukraine? And he picked up a lump of earth with his sword and says: this is Ukraine, and here, and he pointed his sword at his chest, here is her blood; we are going to take our soil away from the enemy. Give me, he says, a clean shirt, give me some water so that I can wash myself, and so long. When that sword of his glistened, it blinded me completely. Son, I say, I have a younger one, too, Ivan, take him with you for this cause; he's a big one; let me bury both of you in this soil so that the enemy cannot tear it out of these roots. Good, Dad, he says, we'll both go. And when the old woman heard this, then I saw right away that death wound herself around her neck with a white sheet. I stumbled to the threshold for I heard how her eyes dropped out and rolled on the floor, like dead rocks. It only seemed to me that way, but the light on her forehead went out forever.

And in the morning both of them were leaving, and the old woman leaned against the gate and didn't speak and looked from afar as if from heaven. And when I was dropping them off at the railway station then I said: Andriy, Ivan, never retreat, but don't forget me, for I'm alone; your mother died by the gate . . ."

Till late in the evening Maksym led the horses over the field but he no longer shouted; he was completely silent. The children, herding sheep; people, ringing with plows as they went by him, did not greet him out of fear. Covered with mud, tattered, limping—he seemed to be sinking into the earth.

Late at night, when Maksym saw to the cows and horses, when he milked the sheep, he entered the house.

"You've grown completely silent, you wretch. You're so dead as if someone had stuck a knife in you; you can't utter a word, but I'll get some fire into you yet."

He cooked some cornmeal, put on a white shirt, ate and sat quietly. Then he kneeled on the ground and prayed:

"And you, Mother of God, you be my houselady; you with your son in the middle, and next to you Andriy and Ivan on both sides . . . You gave one son, but I gave two . . ."

CHILDREN'S ADVENTURE

("Ditocha pryhoda," 1916, *Zemlya*)

"Vasyl'ko, take Nastya to your uncle's; there, follow that path by the woods, you know. But hold her by the hand gently and don't yank her, for she's still very small; and don't carry her, for you can't lift her."

She sat down; it hurt very much; she lay down.

"Am I supposed to know where to lead her at night? You go ahead and die, and we'll stay by you till morning, and then we'll go."

"You see, Nastya, a bullet buzzed by and killed mother, and it's your fault. Why were you crying when the soldier wanted to embrace mother? That wasn't going to hurt you. We were running away and a bullet whistled . . . And now you're not going to have a mother, and you'll go and serve . . ."

"She's not talking anymore, she died already. I could really give you a good spanking now, but you're already an orphan. But what's a girl like you worth? When Ivanykha died near us, then her girls lamented all the time: mother, ma, where are we to look for you, from where will you come to us . . . And you don't know how; and I'm a boy and it's not right for a boy to lament . . ."

"Do you see how the army is sending light from the other side; it's like water through a sieve. The light blinks and right away you can see where a soldier is, and bang him with a bullet and he'll lie down like our mother. Lie down quickly by your mother, for the bullets will fly right away. Hear how they're whistling?"

"Look, look how the soldiers are throwing about fiery bullets there across the Dnister. But high, so high; and the bullet burns, burns and then it dies. They're playing with them . . . look how many of them, look."

"There, listen to the cannon, boom, boom, boom; but it's not shooting at people, only at churches or houses or schools."

"You don't have to be afraid of a cannon. It's got a bullet as big as I am, and its wheels are the size of mill stones. But you don't know a thing; you barely know how to walk; but I can trot around like a horse . . ."

"Hide behind your mother. Oh, again it's sending out lights; so white, so white, white as a sheet; it's going to turn on us right away. See how white we are, and again the bullets whistle. So what, if a bullet gets me, then I'll lie down next to mother and I'll die, and you won't find your way to uncle all by yourself. So better that the bullet kill you, for I know my own way and I'll let uncle know and he'll come and bury both of you."

"Already you're crying, as if a bullet hurt. It'll only buzz and drill a hole in your chest, and your soul will escape through that hole and that's the end of you. It's not like at home when you're sick and they have to rub you down with whiskey . . ."

"You want to eat, thank God! And what am I going to give you to eat, when mother's gone? Let mother do it? OK, tell mother, go ahead, tell her to give you food. And what does mother say? Go ahead, go ahead, take her by the hand, and it'll fall; see, didn't I say so? Stupid girl, the soul has left mother and it's the soul that talks, and gives bread and spanks . . ."

"Nastya, honest to God, I'm gonna spank you; what am I gonna give you to eat? Look at the war; it's really nice, and in the morning we'll go to our uncle and we'll eat borshch . . . Or wait a minute, mother probably has some bread in her pockets . . . Quiet, there's bread in mother's pocket; here, eat it, you greedy girl . . ."

"Again it's sending out the sheet, white like snow. It's coming our way, oh! Nastya, and what happened to you? Why your whole mouth and hands are covered with blood. A bullet shot you? Oh, you poor wretch, go ahead, lie down by your mother . . . what else can you do . . ."

"Ech, that wasn't a bullet, that was the bread; it got soaked in blood while it was in mother's pocket. Boy, you're a dirty girl; you eat everything, like a pig. You smeared your face and hands with blood . . . And how am I going to lead you through the village in the morning, covered with blood like that? But wait, I'm going to go by the stream and I'll wash you in such a cold water, you'll scream something awful and I'll spank you yet."

"Have you finished eating? Then lie down by mother, and I'll lie down by you so that you can be in the middle and the wolf won't get you. Sleep and I'll watch the war . . . Go ahead, warm yourself by me . . ."

"Maybe a bullet has killed father too there in the war, and maybe by morning it'll kill me also, and Nastya, and there'll be nobody left, nobody . . ."

He fell asleep. Till the white of day, a light cover trembled over him and at the same time ran away over the Dnister.

164

ALL ALONE

("Sama Samis'ka," 1897, *Synya knyzhechka*)

The shack looked like an overturned ladybug on the hillside. The old woman lay inside on a burlap sack and a hard black pillow. There was black bread and a crock of water on the dirt floor beside her. The young people left them in the morning when they went to the fields. There was nothing else to leave for the old woman. Things were going badly. And to sit by the sick woman in these hot days was really impossible. God knows.

The flies buzzed in the house. They sat on the bread and ate it; they got into the crock and drank. When they were full, they sat down on the old woman. They climbed into her eyes, into her mouth. The old woman groaned, but she was helpless against the flies.

She lay on the ground and with blank eyes stared at the cross that was cut out in the girder. With great effort she forced her lips open and drew her white tongue over them.

The sun's rays came through the panes. Colors of the rainbow crawled among the wrinkles of her face. They made her look awful. The flies were busy. Together with the different lights they teemed over the old woman. Her lips cracked. A white tongue showed.

The room was like the cave of a cursed sinner: suffering from the beginning, suffering until Judgement Day.

It was later. The sun slid down among the old woman's feet and the rope that tied her sack together. The old woman rolled, groped for the crock.

"Look . . . . . Look . . ."

The old woman sat up quietly: she chased flies vaguely with her hand.

A devil climbed up from the pots in the stove. He had a long, long tail. He came and sat facing her. The old woman turned away from him with great difficulty. The devil shifted to face her. He took his tail in his hands and with it began stroking the old woman's face. The old woman only squinted and clenched her teeth.

Suddenly a black cloud of little devils blew out of the stove. They hovered around the old woman like locusts clouding the sun, or a swarm of crows over a forest.

They pounced on the old woman.

They crawled into her ears, her mouth. They sprawled on her head. The old woman protested. The thumb sought the middle finger and the arm tried to reach the forehead to make the sign of the cross. But all the little devils sat down on her arm and would not let the sign be made. The old demon menaced with his tail to stop this foolishness.

The old woman struggled for a long time, but she could not cross herself. Then the devil embraced her. He burst out in such a laugh that she fell to her knees facing the window.

Through the window riders charged. In green vests, with pipes in their mouths, on red horses, they flew at her. The end for the old woman!

She closed her eyes. The dirt floor cracked open and she fell. She fell down and down. Somewhere on the bottom the devil caught her, slung her onto his back and flew with her, fast as the wind.

The old woman lunged and hit her head against the table.

Blood rushed forth, she gulped and died. Her head rolled to the side. She lay near the foot of the table and with a dead, wide stare she looked cockeyed at the room. The devils ended their games. Only the flies licked the blood with pleasure. They bloodied their little wings. The flies multiplied—all were red.

They left bloody traces upon the black pots in the stove, upon the plates stacked against the wall: on the plates were horsemen in green vests, with pipes in their mouths.

The flies carried the old woman's blood everywhere.

THE AGONY

("Skin," 1899, *Doroha*)

When bare autumn came, when all the leaves fell in the forest, when black crows covered the whole field, then death came to old Les'.

Everyone must die, and death itself is not frightening, but a long illness—that is suffering. And Les' suffered. Throughout his agony, he would fall into some other world and then come out of it, again and again. And that other world was painfully strange. Les' could not hold that world at bay with anything but his eyes. And so he clung with them, tired and glistening, to the little lantern. He latched onto it and held fast, always afraid that his eyes would shut and he would fall through, head over heels, into the unknown world.

In front of him his sons and daughters slept in rows on the floor, for they could no longer go sleepless for so many nights. He held on to the lantern with all his might and resisted death. His eyelids hung heavily on his eyes.

He sees many small girls in the yard, each one holding a bunch of flowers. All of them are looking at a grave, awaiting death. Then all the eyes turn to him. A cloud of eyes, blue and grey, and black. That cloud floats to his forehead, soothes and cools him . . .

He rubbed his eyes; took hold of the vein on his neck, for it made his head roll off his shoulders, and thought:

"See, these are angels appearing before death." But while he was thinking, the lantern fled from his eyes.

A field, straight and far away, bakes under the sun. It is begging for water, trembles and gathers all the undergrowth toward itself to drink water from it. He is ploughing and cannot hold onto the handles of the plough for thirst is burning his throat. It is burning the oxen too, for they are muzzling the earth. His hands drop off the handles and he falls onto the field and it burns him like coal.

The lantern brought him out of that world.

"More than once did I die on the field without water; it is

all noted down in God's book."

And again he fell through.

Near the end of the table sits his dead mother singing a song. Softly and sadly the voice carries through the house and reaches him. It is the lullaby his mother sang to him when he was a baby. And he cries, and his heart aches, and he catches tears in his palms. And his mother keeps singing straight into his soul, and all the sufferings in his soul cry together with that singing. His mother goes to the door and after her follow the song and the sufferings from the soul.

And again the lantern appeared.

"Mother is supposed to come from the other world and cry over her child. God gave this right."

His feet were bursting with cold and he wanted to throw a fur over them and again his eyes lost their light.

Sonorous bells ring above him, touching his head with their rims. His head is falling apart, his teeth shake loose from his mouth. The clappers tear loose and fall on his head and wound him . . .

He opened his eyes, gaping, frightful and unconscious.

"I promised to buy a bell for the village, to warn of fire, but the years were very tight and I always kept putting it off. Forgive me, Merciful God."

And again he rolled down a precipice.

From a hill, from a huge hill sheaves of barley fall and pile on top of him. Aristae fill his mouth, push into his throat. They burn like red hot needles and all come together in his heart, and burn with a hellish flame, cutting the very heart . . .

He pried open his eyes, already dead and senseless.

"We did not give Martyn the barley he earned and that barley is bringing me death."

He wanted to shout to the children to give Martyn his barley, but the shout could not rip through his throat, but instead spread over his body like hot tar. He thrust out his black tongue, pushed his fingers into his mouth to let his voice out of his throat. But his teeth clenched shut and closed on his fingers. His eyelids descended with a thunderclap.

The windows in the house open. A white cloth is sucked into the house, an endless immeasurable cloth. Brightness flows from it as if from the sun. The cloth swaddles him like a little baby, first the feet, then the arms, the back. Tightly. He feels light, light. Then it crawls into his head and tickles his brain; it is being sucked into every gland and softly covers everything. And finally it swaddles the throat, always tighter and tighter . . . Like a breeze it flows around the neck and swaddles, and swaddles . . .

THE THIEF

("Zlodiy," 1900, *Doroha*)

In the middle of the room stood two huge, strong men. Their shirts ripped, their faces bloodied.

"Don't let it cross your mind, man, that I'll let go of you."

Both were tired and out of breath and trying to catch some air in their lungs. Near the bed leaned a young woman, frightened and sleepy.

"Don't stand there, but get Mykhaylo and Maksym and tell them to come right away for I've caught a thief."

"If you had hit on a weak one, you could have taken his life right by his house."

He approached the bench, took a quart of water and drank so greedily that one could hear the gurgling of water in his throat. Then he kept wiping his face with his sleeve and, looking at the thief, said:

"I don't have to go to the village medic anymore; you've let out enough blood as it is."

He no sooner finished saying these words when the thief hit him with his fist smack between the eyes.

"So you're hitting. Then I'll hit too; let's see who's better at it."

He swung a thick beech log and the thief fell to the ground. Blood was gushing from his legs.

"Run away now, if you can. I won't stop you."

They were silent for a long time. The dim candle could not tear into the corners and the flies began to hum timidly.

"Stop your bleeding, man, or all your blood will run out."

"Give me some water, *gazda.*"

"I'll give you some water; get your strength back, for you don't know what awaits you."

A long silence.

"I see, you're a strong one, *gazda.*"

"I'm strong all right, you poor wretch; I can lift a horse on my shoulders. You weren't lucky to have come upon me."

"And are you soft-natured?"

"I'm soft, but I never let a thief get out of my hands alive."

"Then I'm supposed to die here?"

"How do I know whether you're soft or hard. If you're hard—then maybe you'll survive . . ."

And again silence took hold of the low house.

"Stop your bleeding."

"What for? So that it hurts more when you begin to beat me? Blood is nothing but pure pain."

"When I beat you then it's got to hurt, unless you give up your spirit."

"Aren't you going to fear God?"

"Were you afraid of God when you were getting into my stores? All my possessions are in there and, if you had taken away from me, you would have wounded me forever. Why don't you pick on a rich man instead of choosing the poor to rob?"

"What's the use; go ahead, beat me, and there's no sense talking about it."

"You're damn right I'm gonna beat you."

On the floor a puddle of blood appeared.

"*Gazda*, if you've got any conscience then don't kill me slowly, but take that log again and hit me over the head like you got me in the legs and you won't have to worry about me anymore, and it'll be easier for me too."

"You'd like that, wouldn't you. Wait a bit, take your time; wait till the people come."

"So you want to give a show for your good neighbors?"

"Here they come."

. . . .

"Glory to Christ!"

"Forever Glory!"

"Something happened at your place, Georhiy?"

"Yes, a guest came and he has to be entertained."

"There's no question about it."

Maksym and Mykhaylo filled out the whole room, their heads reaching the low ceiling and their hair reaching to their waists.

"Sit down and forgive me for ruining your night for you."

"Is that him on the floor there?"

"That's him."

"He's big as an ox. Did you have a hard time getting him into the house?"

"He's big, all right, but he came on a bigger one. But before we go any further, sit down and ask the guest to join you."

Georhiy left and in a while came back with some whiskey, bacon, and bread.

"Why don't you ask him to join you at the table."

"He says he can't get up."

"Then I'll help him."

And the *gazda* picked up the thief under the arms and sat him at the table.

"So you already had an argument with him in the house, eh, Georhiy?"

"Well, he wanted to knock me out; and when he got me with his fist right between the eyes I thought I would keel right over. But I felt a log under my hands and I got him in the legs and he sat down quiet as can be."

"Don't be surprised at him; everybody wants to protect himself."

"I'm not saying anything."

The thief sat at the table, white and apathetic; next to him sat Maksym and farther on Mykhaylo. Near the stove stood the wife in a sheepskin.

"Georhiy, what are you gonna do with him? Folks, reason with him; he wants to kill a man."

"Woman, I can see that you're afraid, so why don't you go to your mother and spend the night there and tomorrow you can come back."

"I'm not gonna leave the house."

"Then you'll drink whiskey with us; but don't whine, for I'll tan your hide too. Better get on the stove and sleep, or watch, or do what you want."

She did not move away from the stove.

"A woman's a woman. Georhiy, don't be surprised; she's afraid of a fight like a Jew."

"Eh, why pay any attention to her. Here's to your health, man. I want to drink to you. I don't know who's going to have a sin for whom: you for me, or me for you? But there's going to be sin. It came about so that we can't avoid it. Well, drink."

"I don't want to."

"You must drink when I'm asking you. The liquor will pick you up a bit, for you're way down."

"I don't want to drink with you."

All three *gazdas* turned to the thief. Their spiteful eyes foretold his doom.

"OK, I'll drink, but five portions at once."

"Go ahead, drink; if we run out, we'll send for more."

He poured one at a time and drank six. Then Mykhaylo and Maksym drank. They ate a bit of the bread and bacon and drank again.

171

Mykhaylo:

"Tell us, man, where did you wander into our village from; are you from far away or nearby?"

"I'm from the world."

"And what are you, a peasant like us, or are you a burgher or a gentleman? For we'll approach you differently in each case. One beats a peasant like so: you take the heavy end of a wagon-wheel axle and you hit him over the head about three times, then several times you smack him across the face so that he falls. For a peasant is hard and one has to use hard methods with him; but once he's on the ground then it's easy . . . And if it's one of the gentry, then you go about it quite differently. Don't even show him the wheel axle for he'll die right away of fright; just scare him with a whip handle. And when he is trembling all over his body, then give it to him twice in the kisser, but not too hard, and he's already at your feet. Walk over him for a while, a minute or two, and his ribs will be worn to shreds, for it's a white bone he's got and thin as paper. And if it's a Jew you're dealing with, then first of all you grab him by his sideburns; he will jump, spit, and contract like a spring. But don't pay any heed to that, just take your thumb and place it between your two fingers and with this hit him a few times in the ribs. This is light beating, but it's very painful . . ."

The *gazda's* laugh was heavy and dull. Mykhaylo pushed his head behind Maksym and waited for the thief to answer.

"So to which class do you belong?"

"All I know, *gazda*, is that if you're drinking booze, you're not going to let me out of here alive, no matter what I am."

"You're telling the truth, the honest truth; I like you for that."

"But before you kill me, give me some more whiskey so that I can drink enough not to know when and how."

"For that, go ahead and drink all you want; but why did you have to come upon me, may you be damned. For I'm hard, I'm like stone and no one will tear you out of my hands alive."

The thief drank five more shots.

"Beat me as much as you want; I'm ready now."

"Wait a minute, brother, I'm glad you're ready, but we're not quite up to you yet: for every five you drank we had only one. When we catch up to you, then we'll talk."

Mykhaylo looked about very happily, Maksym had some thought on his mind but was afraid to express it, and Georhiy was restless.

"I can see, people, that there's going to be trouble. I'd get out of it, but something pulls me to him as if by chains. Well, let's drink and eat . . ."

172

"*Gazda*, let me kiss your hand," the thief said to Maksym.

"Oh, man, you're really scared; that's not nice at all."

"Honest to God, I'm not afraid of you; a hundred times I'll swear that I'm not scared of you."

"Then what?"

"I feel a lightness in my soul and I want to kiss this *gazda's* hand: he's a grey haired man—could be my father . . ."

"Leave me alone, man, for I've got a soft conscience. Just leave me be."

"But give me your hand, for you'll have a sin; I want to kiss you as if you were my own father."

"I'm very soft, man; don't kiss me."

Mykhaylo and Georhiy opened their mouths wide and stopped drinking. They couldn't believe their own ears.

"Trying to confuse us or what? You think you're clever, but, brother, we know all about that."

Maksym, his eyes popping like a ram's, sat there not understanding what was going on.

"He figured out that I was soft; he guessed it right off . . ."

He spoke to justify himself in the eyes of Mykhaylo and Georhiy.

"Give, give me your hand, *gazda*, but give it with a sincere heart; I'll kiss it and it will be easier for me; I can see that I'm not going to be in this world for long, so I'd like to ask your forgiveness."

"Don't kiss it, for I'll soften completely. I'll forgive you anyway."

"But I'm really begging you, for I'll have a hard death; I've never kissed anybody's hand before, at least not so sincerely. I'm not drunk, honest to God, but I want to so."

"Quiet, stop your wailing; don't try to come around from the side, for I'll let you have one so that you won't even move."

"You keep thinking that I'm trying to cheat you, but I'm really telling the truth. You see, when I drank some booze, my head opened up and it became quite clear that I have to die and kiss this *gazda's* hand, so that God will lessen my sin. Give me your hand, *gazda*; tell him to give it to me."

"What does this man want from me. I can't help it that I'm so weak that I can't stand this . . ."

Maksym didn't know what to do with himself, where to hide; he was ashamed like an innocent girl.

"It's always like that with softies. They're always a laughing stock; it's such rotten nature. You know that when I drink a bit, I weep; you know that. You shouldn't have called me here, for I'm, you know, soft as yarn . . ."

The thief wanted to take Maksym's hand in order to kiss it.

"This thief wants to trick us. Get out of here, Maksym; get away from him."

"Let's drink, Georhiy, let's drink three at a time so that we can build up some venom," said Mykhaylo.

"Don't go, Maksym, don't go for I'll die soon. I'm not afraid, honest I'm not, but such anxiety is bothering me . . ."

He started trembling all over; his lips trembled as if they were alive. Mykhaylo and Georhiy were drinking and not paying any attention to him.

"Don't be afraid; it's nothing to fear. I'll let you kiss my hand. I'll let you now. Let them kill me if they want; here, kiss it, if you want."

The thief latched onto the hand and Maksym kept blinking as if someone were hitting him in the face time after time.

"It's not good to be a softie. A soft man is good for nothing."

Mykhaylo opened all his fingers in his hand and showed them to Georhiy.

"Look at them; look how big they are and are they ever greedy for a fight, are they ever. If they grab you, they'll pull you apart meat and all."

And Georhiy didn't say a word; spat in his palms and poured more whiskey.

"That's enough, enough. Let go of me so that I can leave, for there's no God here; I can't look at it. Let go of me; don't embrace me, no, for I'm so ashamed that I don't know where to hide."

"I want to kiss the holy picture and the threshold and all, everybody in the whole world," the thief screamed.

The wife jumped off the stove and ran out. Mykhaylo came from behind the table, dark and drunk as night itself; Georhiy was standing there trying to recall what it was that he had to do.

"Maksym, you get out of here fast, so that I don't see you here or I'll kill you like a bird; go ahead, get out."

"I'm going, Georhiy, I'm not telling you anything, but don't be mad at me, for you know that I'm a soft man. I think that you are gonna have a sin . . . but I'm going . . . ."

"Go ahead, get out, for you're not a man but a slimy woman."

"All I'm saying is that this is not for me . . . I . . ."

Maksym got up and left the table.

"Well, take care and don't miss me, for I'm, as has been said, I'm not good for this . . ."

The thief alone remained at the table, somewhat pale but happy.

"Are you going to get away from the table, or do we have to drag you away?"

"I'm not going to get up; I know I'm supposed to sit here under the icons."

"Oh, yes, you will, you'll get up; we're going to entreat you."

And they jumped on him like hungry wolves.

SIN

("Hrikh," 1927, *Povne zibrannya tvoriv*, 1949)

Kasiyanykha is thinking about what will happen. Yesterday her husband came back from the front, drank some water and is sleeping. One can smell railway soot on his clothing. On the shelf a candle is blinking. Near her, time after time a biggish girl, her daughter in marriage from before the war, keeps uncovering herself. And a little Russian bastard son keeps searching for her breasts. Her round breast, like a hill, and the lips of the bastard seem like those of a greedy serpent. She thinks that this boy is like a vampire who has sucked into himself all of her feminine honor and now is sucking at her blood.

* * * * *

"How is it going to be when he gets up; boy, will he grab and wind about his hands those long braids of mine, will he ever drag my white body over the floors. Then he'll drag me to the threshold and the body will stay in the house but the head will roll off into the yard, so that dogs can lick blood off it. That's how you're going to atone your sin, you bitch. And this little puppy of mine will perish in dirt and derision; no one will give him a shirt to wear, and if unfortunately he manages to grow up, then he'll wander without me as a servant; he won't even know about his father who somewhere there in the open steppe knows nothing of him. Oh, my God, why have you punished me so severely that you took my reason away when he was looking into my eyes and when he rubbed his chest with my braids. You, God, are at fault for having taken away my reason. You wink at me with those bright stars and You laugh. May You be damned as I am."

"My mother stood for two days near the door, sad, with her honor injured, and my sisters washed the diapers of the bastard with their tears. And father didn't come into the house for weeks, stayed outside and there ate his dry piece of bread. The priest cursed me in church, the people avoided me. Even a mountain could not endure such a heaviness upon it. I didn't jump into the Danube only because my little bastard son laughed at me with his silken eyes."

She grabbed the child and tightly held it to her breast and kept on saying:

"Who'd give me such a strength now so that I could go outside, sharpen a knife and plunge it into his chest, right into his heart. Oh, God, You give the temptation for sin, but You don't give the strength to wash away that sin. I won't kill you, you poor wretch, even though I feel inside me that I should; my heart quivers like a spider web in the wind. Oh, if I could only rip my heart out and shove it into your throat so that you'd die with two hearts and I without any."

* * * * *

Morning.

"Who's child is this?"

"You know it's not yours, only mine."

"We'll manage to feed this one too."

"No, I don't want you to feed my child, I will feed it myself."

She held the boy to herself with a steel grip and thought that he was going to strike them with an axe and wanted to make sure that she died first so that she wouldn't have to watch the quivering of the little hands.

. . . .

"Ah, so you're a sissy; you're not joking; it's easy for you to carry the disgrace of your wife."

"You know that ever since I became a whore every bum in the village knocks on my windows at night; I'm no longer a wife for you; you don't need such a wife."

"I'm leaving Kateryna for you; she's bigger, and she's yours; I'm going away with my child."

From the chest she took out her dowry. For herself she took two shirts and a sheepskin.

"The rest," she says, "is for Kateryna; she is very smart and a good girl and you'll manage with her very well."

She walked down the street with her child.

Her mother, father, sisters and all the neighbors shouted after her:

"Don't go, don't go!"

But she was almost running and when she got on top of the hill and saw the pillars of huge mountains and the bright rivers below, then she took a deep breath, gave her breast to her son and whispered:

"My sin, my sin. I will atone you, and you will grow up for me strong and big, my son."

LES' FAMILY

("Leseva familiya," 1898, *Synya khyzhechka*)

Les', as usual, stole some barley from his wife and was taking it to the tavern. He didn't just carry it, but ran with it to the Jew and constantly kept looking back.

"Yes sir, here she comes with the brats, may they break their necks. If only I could reach the tavern, for if she catches me again, there'll be a row for the whole village to see."

And he ran on with the sack over his shoulder. But his wife with the boys was catching up. Just before the tavern she clutched at the sack.

"Don't run away, don't run, don't squander my work for the children."

"You wretch, again you want to cause a row in front of all the people! Where's your face, for crying-out-loud!"

"With such a man I never had a face and never will have one!! Give me back the sack and be damned. Or else we'll beat you, together with the kids I'll beat you right here in the middle of the village. May contrition fall on the whole world. Gi-i-ive it to me!"

"You old bitch, you crazy or something? I'll hang you and those brats of yours!"

"Andriy, my son, hit him in the legs, only in the legs, so that he don't squander your bread at the Jews'. Hit him so that you break his legs. Somehow we'll manage to support a cripple, but a drunkard—never."

She spoke to her boys who stood with sticks in their hands and timidly gazed at their father. Andriy was already ten and Ivanko only about eight. They did not dare approach and hit their father.

"Go ahead, Andriy, hit him; I'll hold his hands. Hit him in the legs only, only in the legs."

And she hit Les' in the face. He fixed her one even better, so that blood started to flow. Now the boys ran up and started pounding their father in the legs.

"Better break his legs, sons, so that he drags them after

178

him like a dog."

And she spit blood and turned blue, but held onto his hands.

The boys became more courageous and ran up like little yelping dogs, and hit him in the legs and ran away, and then came at him again. They were almost playing, almost laughing.

Several people ran out from the tavern.

"Boy, as the world is old, no one has ever seen anything like it. Look at the hitting. Look at them. The teat has not dried yet by their mouths! This is perdition for the whole world!"

The boys attacked like mad dogs, and Les' and his wife stood petrified, bloody, and did not move.

"Watch it, fellows, or you'll strain yourselves from hitting your dad . . ."

"You should've taken longer sticks, so that you could reach 'im better . . ."

"Hit 'im over the head, where his brains are, in the soft of the skull . . ."

So some drunkard out in front of the tavern encouraged the boys.

Les' threw the sack to the ground and stood there stupified. He never expected such an attack and did not know what to do. Finally he laid down and took off his jacket.

"Andriy, and you Ivanko, now hit me; I won't even twitch. You're still small and it's hard for you to keep running up like that. Go on, beat me . . ."

The boys stood a little to the side and looked strangely at their father. Slowly they dropped their sticks and looked at their mother.

"Why aren't you telling them to beat me. You see that I've lain down; go on, beat me!"

Les' wife bawled for the whole village to hear.

"How am I to blame, folks? I break my back at the potato fields with the kids, on dry bread, and all that I bring in he takes away to the tavern. Folks, I can't do anything because of him; I can't leave the house on account of 'im. He has left us without even a rag in the house. Whatever he gets a hold of he takes to the Jews for whiskey. I can't support both the kids and the Jews. I don't care what happens, but I can't go on any more . . ."

"Go ahead, beat me, I won't lift a finger."

"May merciful God beat you, you wretch; for you've squandered our life and orphaned the children. You have beaten us so much that we've never ceased being black and blue. I can't even keep a dish in the house, for you break everything. And how many times have the children and I slept out in the frost; how many windows have you broken? I don't want anything from you; may God punish you for me and the children. Oh, have I ever prayed out a fate for myself . . . People, folks, don't be surprised for you don't know half of it."

She picked up the sack, threw it over her shoulder and stumbled on home with the kids, like a winged bird.

Les' lay on the ground and did not move.

"I'm gonna go to jail, forever to jail. Once! No one has ever seen or heard anything of the kind. I'm gonna do something which is going to make the earth shake."

Les' lay there and whined audaciously.

. . . .

Les' wife took everything out of the house and carried it to the neighbors. For the night she and the kids bedded down in the weeds in the garden. She was afraid of Les' when he came home drunk at night. For the kids she spread out a sack and covered them with a fur jacket. She herself watched over them in a jacket of wool.

"Oh, my children, my children, what are we going to do? I have fixed it for you today for the rest of your lives. You'll die and still you won't rid yourselves of the disgrace. I can't pray this away from you . . ."

And she wept and listened for Les' approaching.

The sky trembled together with the stars. One fell and Les' wife crossed herself.

NEWS

("Novyna," 1899, *Synya knyzhechka*)

The news spread through the village: Hryts' Letyuchy has drowned his younger daughter! He'd wanted to drown the elder, too. But she begged her way out of it.

From the time Hryts's wife died he has suffered ... Couldn't handle the kids without his wife. No one would marry him—he had kids, he was poor.

Hryts' suffered two long years with his children. No one knew anything about him—how he lived, what he did, except possibly his closest neighbors. They used to tell stories about how he didn't heat his house all winter, but would spend the nights with his daughters on top of the stove.

And the whole village started to talk about him.

One day he came home and found the girls on the stove.

"Daddy, we want to eat!" said the older, Handzunya.

"Go ahead! Eat my arm! What else can I give you? ... Here. Here's a piece of bread. Stuff yourselves!"

And he gave them a chunk of bread. The girls grabbed it and gnawed: starved dogs on a meatless bone.

"She made you! Then she left you on my hands! May the earth cough her up! Dammit, somewhere there's a plague—but it won't come and get you ... Even the plagues are afraid of this house!"

The girls didn't listen to the old man's prattle. The same thing went on every day, every hour. They were used to it. They ate the bread on the stove. They were a pitiful, frightening sight. God alone knows how those brittle bones held together. Only their four black eyes—only these were alive—had weight. The eyes were lead-weighted, and but for the eyes, the rest of their limbs would have blown off like feathers in the wind. And now, as they ate dry bread, it seemed as if their jaws would snap.

Hryts' watched them from his bench. He thought, "corpses." And he broke out in a cold sweat of fright. He felt strange: something had put an enormous stone on his chest. The

181

girls slobbered down their bread loudly. Hryts' fell to the
ground and prayed. But something drew his eyes toward his
daughters and he thought again, "corpses."

After a few days Hryts' was afraid to stay at home. He
wandered among his neighbors, and they said with stupid
concern: "He's worried." He grew pale. His eyes deepened in
their sockets. They no longer looked at the world. They stared
only at the stone pressing upon his chest.

One evening Hryts' came home and cooked some potatoes,
salted them, and tossed them to the girls on the stove. When
they had eaten, he said, "Get off the stove. We're going for a
visit."

The girls climbed down. Hryts' wrapped them in rags,
picked up the younger girl, Dotska, and took Handzya by the
hand and walked out with them.

He led them for a long time through the meadows. When
they reached the hill he stopped. In the valley, the river
stretched off in the moonlight like a snake of living silver.
Hryts' shuddered. The sight of the river froze him and the stone
on his chest grew heavier. He gasped and could barely carry the
tiny Dotska.

They went down to the river. Hryts' ground his teeth so
hard that he felt the sound reverberating across the fields, and a
hot pain scalded his chest and burned his heart.

Drawing near the river, he broke into a run and left
Handzya behind. She ran after him. Hryts' raised Dotska over
his head and with all his strength hurled her into the water.

He felt better.

He spoke quickly: "I'll tell the gentlemen there was no
way out. There was nothing to eat, no fuel for the house,
couldn't wash clothes or wash their heads. Couldn't. Nothing.
I'll take the punishment. Because I'm guilty. Then to the
gallows."

Handzya stood next to him. She was speaking fast:
"Daddy, don't drown me! Don't drown me . . . Don't!"

"Well, you are begging, so I won't . . . But it'll be better
for you. For me it's all the same—one or two. You'll suffer as a
child. And then you'll hire yourself to a Jew and you'll suffer
some more. But, as you wish . . ."

"Don't drown me! Don't!"

"No. No, I won't. But Dotska is better off than you now.
Go back to the village. I'm going to give myself up . . . Take
that path there, all the way up to the hill, and when you get to
the first house, go inside and say 'My father wanted to drown
me, but I begged myself out of it, and I want you to put me up
for the night.' And tomorrow see if they'll take you as a

house-girl. Go on. It's dark."

And Handzya went.

He called after her, "Handzya, Handzya: here. Here's a stick. If a dog spots you on the way he'll rip you to pieces. You'll be safer with a stick."

Handzya took the stick and went away across the meadows.

Hryts' rolled up his pants to cross the river, for that way lay the path to the town.

He went into the water up to his ankles and stopped dead.

"In the name of the Father and of the Son and of the Holy Ghost, Amen. Our Father who art in heaven and on earth . . ."

He climbed out of the water and went to the bridge.

MOTHER

("Maty," 1927, *Tvory*, 1933)

Old Veryzhykha was walking to her daughter's house, leaning on a stick longer than herself, and thought: the autumn is rich this year; all the sparrows are smooth like butter and even poor children are growing fat.

"Glory to Christ."

She sat on the bench at her daughter's and, looking at her, thought: she's so beautiful.

"Well, what are you doing, my daughter. You've forgotten us and your boy that won't leave his granddad's lap and won't let him work."

Only a green leaf before a storm trembles so, as her Kateryna did.

"Daughter, light the fire and cook me some of that Russian tea; I hear that this tea is very helpful."

The fire burns.

"And show me those gifts which that great Russian of yours gave you."

With trembling, beautiful hands, she began to place in front of her mother silk scarfs, skirts, pearls, thin shoes and many other expensive things.

The fire was burning well. Old Veryzhykha sat in front of the stove and from her lap she threw into the fire these expensive gifts.

Kateryna, white as a wall, stood near the bed in front of her mother as if in front of a vampire.

"You whore, you. While your husband is pulling cannons out of the mud, you've thrown your son on my bed, like a bitch that leaves her pups. Everyday like a peacock you strut about with an officer. You drive about in carriages and people hide from your drives. The wheels of your carriages drive over my heart and cut it to shreds. You whore, you've put a flower of disgrace into my grey hair."

The goods burned down and the old woman climbed the bed to get at the shelves. From the shelves she took down embroidered shirts, blankets, towels and thin sheets.

"Kateryna, you slut, you prefer stolen Jewish goods to my dowry which I collected for you with honest hands from the time you came to this world."

The old woman looked like an executioner sitting on the pile of the dowry, and Kateryna already atoning for her sin had the light of the forgiving sky on her.

"Your life, my dear, has ended among us; I paid dearly for this poison; pour it into the Russian tea, drink it and you'll atone for your sins immediately. I will dress you nicely and we will bury you as proper; only then you will wipe the shame off us and off your boy."

Kateryna, white as a ghost, went out into the hallway and disappeared. The mother sat for a long time on the thin materials and bright covers. She picked up her walking stick, closed the house and going home whispered:

"Oh, God, for what sins do you punish me and my children?"

And near the church all the people avoided old Veryzhykha, for they heard that on her prompting Kateryna hung herself. And Veryzhykha says to them:

"So when my Kateryna lived, then a hundred of you came to me every day and you kept at it: she's shaming us, she's taking the best horses going with that Russian to town, she's telling him who has money, who has cattle, she's sleeping under Jewish covers, she's tinkling with Jewish pearls . . . My old man didn't come into the house for weeks out of shame in front of the holy icons. And now when I sent her to her death, now, you bitches, what do you want from me? As soon as I raise her boy, I'll go the same way she went . . ."

THE PIOUS WOMAN

("Pobozhna," 1897, *Synya knyzhechka*)

Semen and Semenykha had come from church and were eating dinner: dipping cooled cornmeal into sour cream. The husband ate so that his eyes were just about ready to pop, but the wife ate more delicately. Time after time she wiped herself with her sleeve, for her husband was showering her with spit. It was his way to smack his lips while he ate and send a shower of spit into people's eyes.

"Can't you close that trap a bit? Can't even eat one's bread in peace . . ."

Semen went on eating without closing his trap. His wife had hurt him a bit by using that word but he kept on hauling the sour cream from the bowl.

"He smacks like four swine. My God, Christ! You've got such a disgusting snout; like an old horse."

Semen remained silent. He felt a bit at fault and besides first of all he wanted to get something under his belt. Finally he got up and crossed himself. He went outside, gave the swine some water and came back to lie down.

"Will you look at him? He's stuffed himself and now he's gonna lie there like a log. D'you think he'd show his puss someplace? No, he rots like that every holiday and Sunday."

"Why are you itching for it? I'll give you such an itch you'll be scratching for the rest of your life."

"Every Sunday I'd eat you alive."

"If only pigs had horns . . ."

"He stands there in church like a near-dead ram. Other men are like men; but he's as sloppy as dishwater. My face burns on account of a man like that."

"Oh, poor me; I'll probably miss the Heavenly Kingdom for that. Work your head off all week and then stand at attention in church. You stand there for me and I'll get to hear the Lord's word without it."

"You sure listen to the Lord's word. You don't know one word of what the priest said in his sermon. You stand there in the middle of the church like a sleep walker. No sooner are you there than your eyes go blank, your mouth opens as wide as a gate, and the spittle starts running out of it. And I look at you and the earth is about ready to swallow me up with shame."

"Leave me alone, you pious female, so that I can get some shuteye. It doesn't matter to you if you go on squawking like that, but I'm dead tired."

"Well don't stand there in church like a pole. No sooner does the priest start to read than you pop your eyes like two onions. And you wag your head like a horse in the sun, and you dribble spittle threads as thin as a spider's web; you just about snore. And my mother told me it's the evil spirit sneaking up on a man that snags him into sleep so that he won't hear the Lord's word. There's no God near you, honest to God there isn't."

"The hell with you, woman. Leave me alone. You're a holy one! So you've joined some 'archroman' sisterhood and you think you're a saint already? Boy, will I tan your hide until it has blue lines, just like a book! So the ladies've formed a sisterhood? No one's ever seen or heard anything like it; one had a kid while she was still a girl, another while she was a widow, a third had one without a husband; real respectable ladies you've got together. Boy, if those priests knew what kind of a crowd you are, they'd chase you out of church with a whip. Look at the pious females; all you need is a tail. They read books, they buy holy pictures; they want to get into Heaven alive."

Semenykha, on the verge of tears, trembled with anger.

"Then you shouldn't have taken me when I had a child. So-oo what a fate I found for myself! Even a bitch wouldn't have gone for a bull like you. You should thank God that I ruined my life with you or you'd still be hanging around alone till you died."

"Because I was stupid and greedy for land, I took a witch into my house. Now I'd even add some of my own land to get rid of you."

"Oh no you won't. You won't get rid of me. I know, you'd like to have another wife with land, but don't you worry, you're not going to get rid of me that easy. I'll live and you'll have to put up with me and look at me and that's that."

"Go ahead—live till there's sun and a world to live in."

"And I'll keep going to the sisterhood and you can't do anything about it."

"Well, we'll see about that. You're not going to belong to any sisterhood as long as I'm around. I'll throw those books of yours to the wind and I'll tie you up. No sir, you're not gonna keep bringing me any of that wisdom from the priests . . ."

187

"Oh, yes I will, yes I will and that's that."

"Lay off woman, cause I'm gonna grab something and I'll latch onto you, but good."

"Oh mother, did you ever marry me off to a Calvin; look at him there, he's planning to beat me on a Sunday!"

"Well, did I begin the fight? And she still thinks she's holy! Oh, my dear, if you're gonna carry on like that then I'll have to take you down a peg or two, I'll have to close that mouth of yours a bit, or I'll have to leave my house because of this pious female. But whatever happens I'll beat you."

Semenykha was running out of the house, but her husband caught up with her in the hallway, and he beat her. He had to beat her.

BIBLIOGRAPHY

The bibliography is divided into three sections: the first is a list of Stefanyk's works used in the preparation of this study, the second deals with bibliographical guides to Stefanyk, and the third enumerates all of the critical literature which was consulted.

I Primary Sources
(In Chronological Order)

Stefanyk, Vasyl'. *Povne zibrannya tvoriv.* 3 vols. Kiev, 1949-54.
_____. *Tvory.* Kiev, 1964.

II Bibliographies
(In Alphabetical Order)

Genyk-Berezovskyj, Julian. "Die Sprache V. Stefanyks (Phonetik)." Unpublished Ph.D. dissertation, Karl-Franzens University, Graz, Austria, 1947. Pp. 30-46.

Kravtsiv, B. "Zlydni radyans'koyi bibliohrafiyi." Review of *Vasyl' Stefanyk. Bibliohrafichnyy pokazhchyk*, compiled by O. P. Kushch, *Suchasnist'*, 1962, No. 6, pp. 110-14.

Kushch, O. P. *Vasyl' Stefanyk. Bibliohrafichnyy pokazhchyk.* Kiev, 1961.

Lewanski, Richard. *Slavic Literatures: The Literatures of the World in English Translation.* New York, 1967. Pp. 400-1.

Rudnyts'ky, Mykhaylo. *Vid Myrnoho do Khvyl'ovoho.* L'viv, 1936. Pp. 432-33.

Plevako, Mykola A. *Statti, rozvidky y bio-bibliohrafichni materiyaly.* New York - Paris, 1961. Pp. 694-96.

Ukrayins'ki Pys'mennyky. Bio-bibliohrafichnyy slovnyk u p'yaty tomakh. V (Kiev, 1963), pp. 192-210.

III Critical Literature
(In Alphabetical Order)

Atamanyk, Vasyl'. "Suchasna halyts'ka literatura." *Zakhidna Ukrayina*, 1927, pp. 215-36.

Avidyenko, Semen. "Spivets' krashchoyi selyans'koyi doli." *Doroha*. Supplement to *Hromads'kyy Holos*, 1931, No. 17. Reprinted in T. Kobzey, *Velykyy riz'bar ukrayins'kykh selyans'kykh dush*, Shevchenko Scientific Society Ukrainian Studies, Vol. XXI. Toronto, 1966. Pp. 240-44.

Avrakhov, Hryhoriy. "Problemy suchasnoyi novely." *Radyans'ke literaturoznavstvo*, 1966, No. 8, pp. 7-8.

Bates, H. E. *The Modern Short Story*. London - New York, 1941.

Bennett, E. K. *A History of the German Novelle*. 2d ed. revised and continued by H. M. Wadison. Cambridge, 1965.

Bilets'ky, F. M. *Opovidannya. Novela. Narys*. Kiev, 1966.

Bilyavs'ka, O. O. "Pryntsypy naukovoho vydannya tvoriv V. Stefanyka," in S. D. Zubkov, ed., *Pytannya tekstolohiyi*. Kiev, 1968. Pp. 243-301.

Blavats'ky, Volodymyr. "Moyi zustrichi z Stefanykom," in T. Kobzey, *Velykyy riz'bar ukrayins'kykh selyans'kykh dush*, Shevchenko Scientific Society Ukrainian Studies, Vol. XXI. Toronto, 1966. Pp. 185-87.

_____ . "Stefanyk u teatri—Storinka z istoriyi teatru 'Zahrava,'" *Kul'turno-mystets'kyy Kalendar-Al'manakh Ukrayins'koho Slova na 1947 rik*. Regensburg, 1947, pp. 66-67.

_____ . "V Rusovi—rodynnomu seli Vasylya Stefanyka," *Novyy chas*, No. 191 (August 28, 1937). Reprinted in T. Kobzey, *Velykyy riz'bar ukrayins'kykh selyans'kykh dush*, Shevchenko Scientific Society Ukrainian Studies, Vol. XXI. Toronto, 1966. Pp. 188-90.

Cheremshyna, Marko. *Tvory*. Kiev, 1960.

Current-Garcia, Eugene, and Walton R. Patrick. *What is the Short Story?* Chicago, 1961.

Dan'ko, M. "Kray skorby," *Ukrayins'kaya zhizn'*, 1913, No. 1, pp. 59-67.

Denysyuk, Ivan. "Problemy suchasnoyi novely," *Radyans'ke literaturoznavstvo*, 1966, No. 8, pp. 5-6.

Doderer, Klaus. "Novelle." *Lexicon der Weltliteratur*. II (1961), 546-48.

Dontsov, D. "Poet tverdoyi dushi," *Literaturno-naukovyy vistnyk*, XXVI (1927), No. 42, Bk. 2, pp. 142-54.

Doroshenko, V. "Vasyl' Stefanyk," *Zhyttya i znannya*, X (1937), No. 1, p. 2.

Doroshkevych, Ol. *Pidruchnyk istoriyi ukrayins'koyi literatury*. 3d ed. Kiev, 1927. Pp. 194-97.

Dzyuba, Ivan. An interview with *Nove Zhyttya* (Preshov, Czechoslovakia), January 14, 1967. Reprinted in *Ukrayins'ki visti* (Edmonton, Alberta), March 2, 1967.

Erlich, Victor. "Notes on the Uses of Monologue in Artistic Prose," *International Journal of Slavic Linguistics and Poetics*, 1959, Nos. 1-2, pp. 223-31.

Fashchenko, Vasyl'. *Iz studiy pro novelu*. Kiev, 1971.

_____. "Novelistychna kompozytsiya," *Ukrayins'ka mova i literatura v shkoli*, 1968, No. 7, pp. 18-23.

Franko, Ivan. *Tvory*. Vol. II, New York, 1956.

Garborg, Arne. "Zahublenyy bat'ko," Translated by V. Stefanyk. *Literaturno-naukovyy vistnyk*, V (1902), No. 17, pp. 144-65, 254-63.

Gordon, Donald Keith. "The Short Stories of Juan Rulfo." Unpublished Ph.D. dissertation, University of Toronto, 1969.

Hamorak, Yu. "Pershe kokhannya V. Stefanyka," *Nashi dni* (L'viv), 1942, No. 7, pp. 7-8.

_____. "Vasyl' Stefanyk—Sproba biohrafiyi," in V. Stefanyk, *Tvory*. 2d ed. Regensburg, 1948. Pp. iii-xlii.

Hetsztynski, Stanisław. *Przybyszewski*. Cracow, 1958.

Hemingway, Ernest. *The Short Stories of Ernest Hemingway*. New York: Charles Scribner's Sons, 1953.

Hladky, V. M. "Do pytannya pro psykholohiyu tvorchosti Vasylya Stefanyka," *Ukrayins'ke literaturoznavstvo*, No. 4, 1968, pp. 76-79.

_____. "Lysty V. Stefanyka do S. Morachevs'koyi," *Ukrayins'ke literaturoznavstvo*, No. 2, 1966, pp. 138-44.

Hranychka, L. "Stefanykove slovo," *Vistnyk*, V (1937), Bk. 5, pp. 361-75.

_____. "Stefanykovyy svit," *Vistnyk*, V (1937), Bks. 3-4, pp. 221-30, 262-74.

_____. "V. Stefanyk u literaturniy krytytsi," *Vistnyk*, V (1937), Bk. 2, pp. 124-32.

Hrebenyuk, H. "Pokuts'ka hrupa pys'mennykiv," *Chervonyy shlyakh*, 1929, No. 4, pp. 111-27.

Hrinchenko, Borys. Letter to V. Stefanyk from Chernihiv, October 16, 1899, published in *Literaturna Ukrayina*, January 28, 1964.

Hrushevs'ky, Oleksandr. "Suchasne ukrayins'ke pys'menstvo u yoho typovych predstavnykakh: Vasyl' Stefanyk," *Literaturno-naukovyy vistnyk*, XLIII (1908), Bk. 7, pp. 25-30.

Hrytsay, Ostap. *Vasyl' Stefanyk. Sproba krytychnoyi kharakterystyky*. Vienna, 1921.

Hrytsyuta, M. S. "Vasyl' Stefanyk," in Ye. P. Kyrylyuk and others, eds., *Istoriya ukrayins'koyi literatury u vos'my tomakh*. V (Kiev, 1969), 223-58.

Ivchenko, M. "Tvorchist' Vasylya Stefanyka," *Ukrayina*, 1926, Bks. 2-3, pp. 183-96.

Kachurovs'ky, Ihor. *Novela yak zhanr*. Buenos Aires, 1958.

Kenihsberh, Mariya. "Perespektyvy zhanru," *Dnipro*, 1968, No. 4, pp. 139-43.

Keyvan, Ivan. "Vasyl' Stefanyk u moyikh spohadakh," in T. Kobzey, *Velykyy riz'bar ukrayins'kykh selyans'kykh dush*, Shevchenko

Scientific Society Ukrainian Studies, Vol. XXI. Toronto, 1966. Pp. 191-213.

Khmara, V. "Vasyl' Stefanyk–Spivets' selyans'koyi doli," in Vasyl' Stefanyk, *Vybrane.* Zaltsburg, 1946. Pp. 78-86.

K-k, Iv. "Cheremshyna pro Stefanyka," *Nove zhyttya* (Preshov), September 28, 1969.

Klynovy, Yuriy. "*Kaminnyy khrest* V. Stefanyka. Peredistoriya tsiyeyi noveli ta yiyi heroyiv," in T. Kobzey, *Velykyy riz'bar ukrayins'kykh selyans'kykh dush*, Shevchenko Scientific Society Ukrainian Studies, Vol. XXI. Toronto, 1966. Pp. 117-26.

Kobylyans'ka, Ol'ha. *Tvory.* Vol. V, Kiev, 1963.

Kobzey, Toma. *Velykyy riz'bar ukrayins'kykh selyans'kykh dush*, Shevchenko Scientific Society Ukrainian Studies, Vol. XXI. Toronto, 1966.

Kochur, Ivan. Letter to Miss M. Skorupsky, Kiev, October 18, 1969. In the personal files of Miss Skorupsky in New York.

Kokovs'ky, Frants. "Vasyl' Stefanyk pro sebe," *Nasha kul'tura* (Warsaw), 1937, Bk. 5 (25), pp. 245-47.

Kolberg, Oskar. "Pokucie, obraz etnograficzny," in his *Dzieła wszystkie.* Vol. XXIX. Worcław, 1962.

Koryak, V. "Mizh dvoma klasamy," in V. Stefanyk, *Tvory.* 2d ed., Kharkiv, 1927. Pp. 5-24.

_____. *Narys istoriyi ukrayins'koyi literatury.* Kharkiv, 1929. Pp. 533-36.

_____. *Selyans'kyy Betkhoven.* Kharkiv, 1929.

Koskimies, Rafael. "Die Theorie der Novelle," *Orbis Litterarum.* XIV (1959), 65-88.

Kostashchuk, Vasyl'. *Volodar dum selyans'kykh.* L'viv, 1959.

Kotsyubyns'ka, Mykhaylyna. *Obrazne slovo v literaturnomu tvori.* Kiev, 1960.

Kotsyubyns'ky, Mykhaylo. *Tvory v shesty tomakh.* Vols. V-VI, Kiev, 1962.

Kovalyk, Ivan. "Do kharakterystyky movy V. Stefanyka," *Ridna mova*, 1937, No. 4, pp. 160-64.

Koziy, D. "Spynys', khvylyna! Ty prekrasna!" *Lysty do pryyateliv*, XV (1967), Nos. 171-73, Bks. 7-9, pp. 26-30.

Kozoris, M. "Sotsiyal'ni momenty v tvorchosti V. Stefanyka," *Zakhidna Ukrayina*, 1931, Nos. 4-5, pp. 140-72.

Kravtsiv, Bohdan. "Yuriy Stefanyk–biohraf 'Poeta tverdoyi dushi,'" *Svoboda* (Jersey City, N. J.), February 15, 1969.

Krushel'nyts'ky, Antin. "Vasyl' Stefanyk," in his *Ukrayins'ka Novelya. Vybir narysiv i novel'.* Kolomyya, 1910. Pp. iii-x.

Kruszelnickyj, A. *Szkice z ukraińskiej literatury współczesney.* Kolomyya, 1910. Pp. 34-41.

Kryzhanivs'ky, Stepan. "Pislyavoyenna tvorchist' Vasylya Stefanyka," *Vitchyzna*, 1946, No. 5, pp. 183-96.

Kryzhanivs'ky, Stepan. "Publitsystyka Vasylya Stefanyka," in V. Stefanyk, *Publitsystyka*. Kiev, 1953. Pp. 3-14.

         . "Spivets' halyts'koho sela," *Dnipro*, 1946, No. 5, pp. 122-26.

         . *Vasyl' Stefanyk. Krytyko-biohrafichnyy narys.* Kiev, 1946.

Kunz, J. "Geschichte der deutschen Novelle vom 18. Jahrhundert bis auf die Gegenwart." *Deutsche Philologie im Aufriss.* II (1966), 1795-1895.

Kurylenko, Y. M. "Spivets' znedolenoho halyts'koho selyanstva," *Literatura v shkoli*, 1951, No. 2, pp. 28-35.

Lepky, B. "Koly my shche buly molodymy," *Dilo*, January 7, 1927.

         . *Nezabutni. Literaturni narysy.* Berlin, 1922. Pp. 78-82.

         . "Stefanyk u Krakovi," *Novyy chas.* 1937, Nos. 14-16, reprinted in T. Kobzey, *Velykyy riz'bar ukrayins'kykh selyans'kykh dush*, Shevchenko Scientific Society Ukrainian Studies, Vol. XXI. Toronto, 1966. Pp. 129-36.

         . *Try portrety: Franko, Stefanyk, Orkan.* L'viv, 1937.

Lesyn, Vasyl'. "Problemy suchasnoyi novely," *Radyans'ke literaturoznavstvo*, 1966, No. 8, pp. 4-5.

         . "Shche raz pro movu Stefanyka," *Radyans'ke literaturoznavstvo*, 1965, No. 9, p. 48.

         . *Tvorchist' Vasylya Stefanyka.* Kiev, 1965.

         . *Vasyl' Stefanyk i ukrayins'ka proza kintsya XIX st.* Chernivtsi, 1965.

         . *Vasyl' Stefanyk: Mayster novely.* Kiev, 1970.

         . "Velykyy mayster realistychnoyi novely," in V. Stefanyk, *Tvory.* Kiev, 1964. Pp. 3-30.

         . "V. S. Stefanyk—talanovytyy uchen' Franka," in *Radyans'ka Bukovyna*, Chernivtsi, 1965. Pp. 75-90.

Lukiyanovych, D. "Nova faza tvorchosty Vasylya Stefanyka," *Literaturno-naukovyy vistnyk*, LXXXIX (1926), Bk. 2, pp. 177-81.

Luts'ky, Ostap. "Literaturni novyny v 1905 r.," *S'vit*, I (March 9, 1906), No. 2, pp. 24-26.

         . "Syn chornozemu," *Novyy chas*, December 14, 1936. Reprinted in T. Kobzey, *Velykyy riz'bar ukrayins'kykh selyans'-kykh dush*, Shevchenko Scientific Society Ukrainian Studies, Vol. XXI. Toronto, 1966. Pp. 159-61.

M., G. Review of V. Stefanyk, *Rasskazy*. Translated by V. Kozinenko, St. Petersburg, 1907. *Vestnik Evropy*, 1907, Bk. 7, pp. 369-71.

Makovey, Osyp. Letter to V. Stefanyk from L'viv, March 9, 1898. Published by M. Hrytsyuta in *Literaturna Ukraina*, November 27, 1964.

Mikhaylov, A. V. "Novella," in A. A. Surkov, ed., *Kratkaya literaturnaya entsyklopediya.* V (Moscow, 1968), 306-7.

Moraczewski, Wacław. "Wasyl Stefanyk," *Pamiętniki warszawskie* 1931,

Nos. 10, 12, pp. 177-82.

Murashko, Pavlo. "Druhyy naybil'shyy pys'mennyk zakhidnoyi Ukray-iny," *Duklya*, 1967, No. 2, pp. 55-57.

Myronets', Iv. Review of V. Stefanyk, *Tvory*. Introduction by V. Koryak, 3d ed. Kharkiv, 1929. *Krytyka*, June 1929, No. 6, pp. 157-59.

Nenadkevych, Ye. O. "Iz studiy nad stylem Frankovoyi i Stefanykovoyi novely," *Zapysky Volyns'koho Instytutu Narodnoyi Osvity im. Ivana Franka*, 1927, Bk. 2, pp. 81-109.

O., Yu. Review of V. Stefanyk, *Tvory*, ed. by I. Lyzanivs'ky, Kharkiv, 1927. *Literaturno-naukovyy vistnyk*, 1928, Bks. 7-8, pp. 355-59.

Ohiyenko, Ivan. "Hovirka chy literaturna mova?" *Ridna mova*, 1937, No. 3, pp. 121-24.

Petrovsky, M. A. "Kompozitsiya novelly u Mopassana," *Nachala*, 1922, No. 1, pp. 106-27.

Pohrebennyk, Fedir. "Debyut Vasylya Stefanyka," *Radyans'ke literatur-oznavstvo*, 1967, No. 1, pp. 52-62.

_____. "Maksym Hor'ky i Vasyl' Stefanyk," *Radyans'ke litera-turoznavstvo*, 1968, No. 3, pp. 37-41.

_____, ed. *Vasyl' Stefanyk u krytytsi ta spohadakh*. Kiev, 1970.

_____. "Zv'yazky Vasylya Stefanyka z Radyans'koyu Ukrayin-oyu," *Prapor*, 1968, No. 9, pp. 98-100.

P[odiuk], I. "Vasyl' Stefanyk zblyz'ka," *Likars'kyy visnyk*, IX (1962), No. 3, pp. 44-47.

Polgar, Alfred. "Peter Altenberg," in Peter Altenberg, *Der Nachlass*. Berlin, 1925. Pp. 149-54.

Ragusa, Olga. *Verga's Milanese Tales*. New York, 1964.

Remak, Henry H. H. "Novella," in Wolfgang Bernard Fleischmann, ed., *Encyclopedia of World Literature in the 20th Century*. II (New York, 1969), 466-68.

Rubchak, Bohdan. "Probnyy let." Introduction to Yuriy Luts'ky, ed., *Ostap Luts'ky—Molodomuzets'*. New York, 1968. Pp. 9-43.

Rudnyts'ky, Mykhaylo. *Pys'mennyky zblyz'ka*. L'viv, 1958. Pp. 107-37.

_____. "Vasyl' Stefanyk," in his *Vid Myrnoho do Khvyl'ovoho*. L'viv, 1936. Pp. 238-49.

_____, "Yoho slovo. Vasyl' Stefanyk pro sebe," *Dilo*. January 7, 1927.

Rusova, S. "Stare y nove v suchasniy ukrayins'kiy literaturi" (translated and edited by Ivan Franko), *Literaturno-naukovyy vistnyk*, XXV (1904), pp. 66-84.

Sadovy, I. "Stefanyk zblyz'ka," *Novyy chas*, 1936, No. 278. Reprinted in T. Kobzey, *Velykyy riz'bar ukrayins'kykh selyans'kykh dush*, Shev-chenko Scientific Society Ukrainian Studies, Vol. XXI. Toronto, 1966. Pp. 179-84.

Scherer-Virski, Olga. *The Modern Polish Short Story*. The Hague, 1955.

Shcherbak, A. "Zhyve slovo Stefanyka," *Vitchyzna*, 1951, No. 6, pp. 176-79.

Shevelov, George Y. *The Syntax of Modern Literary Ukrainian.* The Hague, 1963.

Simovych, Vasyl'. Review of the "Zahrava" performance of "Stefanykova Zemlya" in *Nazustrich*, 1934, No. 2.

Smal'-Stots'ky, Stepan. "Moyi spomyny pro Stefanyka," *Novyy chas*, 1937, No. 50. Reprinted in T. Kobzey, *Velykyy riz'bar ukrayins'-kykh selyans'kykh dush*, Shevchenko Scientific Society Ukrainian Studies, Vol. XXI. Toronto, 1966. Pp. 174-78.

Stefanyk, S. V. "Vasyl' Stefanyk i rosiys'ka literatura," in N. J. Zhuk, ed., *Materiyaly do vyvchennya ukrayins'koyi literatury*, IV (Kiev, 1961), 316-20.

Stefanyk, Yuriy. A private interview with D. Struk in Edmonton, Alberta, June 1967.

_____. "Trahediya i triyumf rodu Stefanykiv," *Ukrayins'ki visti* (Edmonton), May 15, 1969.

Sulyma-Blokhyn, O. "Zahal'ni teorytychni pytannya novelistychnoho zhanru," in her Kvitka i Kulish. *Osnovopolozhnyky ukrayins'koyi noveli.* Munich, 1969. Pp. 3-20.

Tomashevsky, B. *Teoriya literatury: Poetika.* Moscow, 1931. Pp. 191-97.

Trusch, Jwan. "Wassyl Stefanyk (Eine Silhouette)," *Ukrainische Rundschau*, 1909, No. 5, pp. 219-26.

Trush, Ivan. "Vasyl' Stefanyk," in N. Y. Zhuk, ed., *Materiyaly do vyvchennya ukrayins'koyi literatury.* IV (Kiev, 1961), 312-16.

Ukrayinka, Lesya. "Malorusskie pisateli na Bukovine," in her *Tvory.* VIII (Kiev, 1965), 66-80.

Uspensky, Gleb. *Sobranie sochineniy.* 9 vols. I-II. Moscow, 1955.

"Vasyl' Stefanyk v dvadtsyayatu [sic] richnytsyu smerty," in *Ilyustrovanyy Kalendar "Prosvity" no 1956 rik.* Buenos Aires, 1956. Pp. 75-78.

Velyhors'ky, Ivan. "Mova tvoriv V. Stefanyka," *Ridna mova*, 1937, No. 3, pp. 115-22.

Verga, Giovanni. *Little Novels of Sicily.* Translated by D. H. Lawrence. Oxford, 1925.

Verves, H. D. "Vladyslav Orkan i Vasyl' Stefanyk," in his *Vladyslav Orkan i ukrayins'ka literatura.* Kiev, 1962. Pp. 137-74.

Vytanovych, E. "The Western Ukrainian Lands Under Austria and Hungary, 1722-1918," in V. Kubijovych, ed., *Ukraine: a Concise Encyclopaedia.* Toronto, 1963. Vol. I. Pp. 697-707.

Vytvytsky, S. and S. Baran. "The Period of the Directory," in V. Kubijovych, ed., *Ukraine: A Concise Encyclopaedia*, Toronto, 1963. Vol. I. Pp. 754-781.

Wyka, Kazimierz. *Modernism polski.* Cracow, 1968.

Yarema, Ya. Ya. "Vasyl' Stefanyk i Hlib Uspens'ky," *Radyans'ke literaturoznavstvo*, 1954, No. 17, pp. 114-38.

_____. "Vasyl' Stefanyk i Vatslav Morachevs'ky (1895-1897)," *Mizhslav'yans'ki literaturni vzayemyny*, 1963, No. 3, pp. 78-92.

Yarema, Ya. Ya. "Zv'yazky Vasylya Stefanyka z Stanislavom Pshyby-shevs'kym i Vladyslavom Orkanom," *Mizhslav'yans'ki literaturni vzayemyny*, 1958, No. 3, pp. 166-69.

Yefremov, S. "V poiskakh novoy krasoty," *Kievskaya starina*, LXXIX (1902), No. 11, 394-401.

Yevshan, M. "Vasyl' Stefanyk," in his *Pid praporom mystetstva*. Kiev, 1910, Bk. 1, pp. 103-8.

Zerov, Mykola. "Marko Cheremshyna y halyts'ka proza," in his *Vid Kulisha do Vynnychenka*. Kiev, 1929. Pp. 142-73.

Zhuk, A. A private interview with D. Struk in Vienna on May 25, 1966.

Zhuk, N. Y. *Vasyl' Stefanyk. Literaturnyy portret*. Kiev, 1960.

_____. "Vasyl' Stefanyk," in Vasyl' Stefanyk, *Vybrani tvory*. Kiev, 1962. Pp. 3-18.

INDEX

Altenberg, Peter, 45, 46, 47, 55, 69.
"Anhel" (Angel), 110, 124, 125.
Augenblick, 77.
Ausspartechnik (Omission Technique), 46.
Avdiyenko, S., 36.

Bachyns'ky, Lev, 16, 17, 18, 19, 24.
"Basaraby" (Basarabs, The), 66, 72, 110, 131.
Bennett, E. K., 68, 69, 70, 77.
Bilets'ky, F. M., 66, 70.
Blavats'ky, V., 28, 74.
Boyko, V., 36.
"Brattya" (Brothers), 111.
Budzynovs'ky, V., 21.

Chekhov, A., 45, 55, 65, 68, 69.
Cheremshyna, Marko (pseud., Semaniuk, Ivan), 26, 43, 44, 45, 48, 49, 52, 55, 81, 140.
"Chervonyy Shlyakh," 27.
"Chervonyy veksel'" (Red Bill of Exchange, The), 110.
"Confiteor," 22.

Dan'ko, M., 24
"Davnyna" (Good Old Times, The), 111.
Denysyuk, I., 67, 70.
"Did Hryts'" (Grandpa Hryts'), 111.
"Ditocha pryhoda" (Children's Adventure), 121, 122, 123, (163-164).

"Dity" (Children), 125, 126.
"Dlya ditey" (For the Sake of the Children), 117.
Dontsov, Dmytro, 40, 41.
"Doroha" (Road, The), 22, 41, 43, 111; *Doroha*, 23, 64.
Doroshenko, V., 36.
"Durni baby" (Stupid Women), 110.
Dzyuba, Ivan, 46, 47.

Erlich, V., 79.
Esenwein, J., 67.

Fashchenko, V., 67, 70.
Fed'kovych, Yuriy, 48.
Franko, Ivan, 23, 27, 35, 44, 45, 49, 54, 57, 62, 63, 66, 73; "Khlops'ka komisiya" (Peasant Commission, A), 49, 54, 73.

Garborg, Arne, 22; "Den Burtkomne Faderen" (Lost Father, The), 22.
Gorky, Maksim, 27, 45.

Hamorak, Ol'ha, 17, 19, 22, 23, 80.
Hamorak, Yuriy, 16, 27, 28, 42.
Hauff, Wilhelm, 70, 72.
Hauptmann, G., 18; "Die versunkene Glocke," 18.
Hemingway, Ernest, 46, 47.
Hladky, V., 97.
Hranychka, L., 34, 35, 36, 37, 41, 53, 55.

Hrebenyuk, H., 48, 49, 75.
"Hrikh" (Kasiyanykha . . .), 132,
(176-177).
"Hrikh" (Sin, The), 129.
Hrinchenko, B., 80, 81.
Hrushevs'ky, Mykhaylo, 28.
Hrushevs'ky, O., 57.
Hrytsay, O., 41.
Hrytsyuta, M. S., 77.

Ivchenko, M., 34, 64, 87.

Kachurovs'ky, Ihor, 65, 66, 67,
72, 81.
Kalytovs'ka, Yevheniya, 22, 23,
24, 25.
"Kaminnyy khrest" (Stone Cross,
The), 55, 71, 104, 116, 117,
(145-154); Kaminnyy khrest,
23, 64.
"Katrusya," 134.
Khvyl'ovy, Mykola, 130.
"Klenovi lystky" (Maple Leaves,
The), 55, 72, 79, 116, 121,
123.
Kobylyans'ka, Ol'ha, 22, 24, 48,
63, 65.
Kobzey, Toma, 42.
Kochur, Ivan, 47.
Koryak, V., 36, 37.
Koskimies, Rafael, 65, 68, 69.
Kostashchuk, Vasyl', 42.
Kosynka, Hryhory, 28.
Kotlyarevs'ky, Ivan, 23.
Kotsyubyns'ky, Mykhaylo, 23,
24, 27, 43, 44, 45, 63, 66,
114; "Fata Morgana," 114.
Kozoris, M., 38, 39.
Kvitka-Osnovyanenko, H., 62.
Kravtsiv, B., 34.
Krushel'nyts'ky, Antin, 35, 36.
Kryms'ky, A., 28.
Kryzhanivs'ky, S., 37, 52.
Kurylenko, Y. M., 37.

"Lan" (Potato Field), 39, 78, 109.
L. M., 16.
Lepky, B., 18, 35, 45, 55, 105.
"Leseva familiya" (Les' Family),
54, 132, (178-180).
Lesyn, V., 16, 19, 29, 37, 87, 107,
108.
Literaturno-naukovyy vistnyk
(LNV), 21, 22, 23, 64, 76, 113.
"Lumera," 16.
Luts'ky, Ostap, 43.
"Lyst" (Letter, The), 110, 114.
Lyzanivs'ky, Ivan, 27, 28, 81.

Maeterlinck, M., 18, 43.
Makovey, Osyp, 76, 77, 114.
"Mamyn synok" (Mommy's Boy),
112.
"Mariya," 41, 73, 74, 120, 121.
Martovych, Les', 16, 17, 44, 45, 48,
49, 55, 110, 140.
"Maty" (Mother), 134, (184-185).
"May" (May), 38, 78, 130.
"Mayster" (Master Craftsman), 110,
116, 118.
"Mezha" (Boundary, The), 40, 110,
130.
"Moloda Muza" (Young Muse), 63.
"Młoda Polska" (Young Poland),
17, 43, 64.
Moraczewski, Wacław, 17, 19, 21,
52, 56, 57, 80.
Moraczewski, Sofia (neé Okunevs'ka),
17, 19.
"Morituri," 74, 111.
"Moye slovo" (My Word), 22, 24,
43, 111; Moye slovo, 24, 64.
Murashko, P., 26.
Myrny, P., 47, 62, 63.
Myronets', I., 10, 34, 36, 38.

Nechuy-Levyts'ky, I., 47, 62, 63.

"Nechytal'nyk," (Non-Reader, The), 16.
Nenadkevych, Y., 49, 52, 54, 73, 74, 77.
"Novyna" (News), 78, 133, (181-183).
"Nytka" (Thread, The), 128.

O'Faolain, S., 67, 70, 75.
Ohiyenko, Ivan, 81, 82.
Okhrymovych, Volodymyr, 25.
Orkan, W., 17, 52, 54, 140.
"Osin'" (Autumn), 116.
"Ozymyna" (Winter Crop), 110, 125, 127, 128.

"Paliy" (Arsonist, The), 35, 38, 39, 71, 72, 114.
"Pidpys" (Signature, The), 110.
"Pistunka" (Baby-sitter, A), 110.
"Pluh" (Plough, The), 28.
"Pobozhna" (Pious Woman, The), 74, 82, 108, 110, 134, (186-188).
Pohrebennyk, F., 29.
"Pokohoron" (Funeral, The), 109.
Polgar, Alfred, 45.
"Portret" (Portrait, A), 24, 110, 124.
"Pratsya," 21, 23, 92.
Przybyszewski, S., 17, 22, 43, 44.

Remak, H., 65, 68.
"Rosa" (Dew, The), 111.
Rubchak, B., 43.
Rudnyts'ky, M., 53, 56.
Rulfo, Juan, 56, 141.
Rusova, S., 35, 57.

"Sama samis'ka" (All Alone), 78, 125, 128, (165-166).

"Sertse" (Heart, The), 22.
Scherer-Virski, Olga, 68, 69, 88, 91.
Shevelov, George, 95, 98.
"Shkil'nyk" (Schoolboy, The), 121.
"Shkoda" (Loss), 116, (143-144).
Simovych, V., 81.
"Skin" (Agony, The), 110, 128, (167-168).
"Slovo o polku Ihorevi" (Tale of Ihor's Campaign, The), 41.
Smal'-Stots'ky, S., 21, 47.
"Son" (Dream, The), 116.
Stanivs'ky, M. F., 78.
Staryts'ky, Mykhaylo, 23.
"Stratyvsya" (Suicide, The), 110, 116, 119, 120, (155-157).
"Sud" (Judgment), 24, 39, 114.
"Svyatyy vechir" (Christmas Eve), 94, 125, 127.
"Svit," 27.
"Syny" (Sons, The), 74, 121, 140, (158-162).
"Synya knyzhechka" (Blue Book, The), 38, 56, 78, 88, 89-91, 94, 95, 98, 99, 100, 103, 104, 116, 140; *Synya knyzhechka*, 21, 22, 35, 47, 64.

"Takyy ranok" (Petty Squire, A), 38, 112.
Thoma, Ludwig, 22, 67; "Das Sterben" (Death), 22; "Solide Köpfe" (Hard Heads), 22.
Tomashevsky, B., 66, 67, 69, 70.

Ukrainian Radical Party, 24, 25, 26, 113, 140.
Ukrayinka, Lesya, 23, 27, 43, 48.
"Ukrayins'ka khata" (Ukrainian House), 63.
"U nas vse svyato" (We Always Have a Holiday), 111, 112.

Uspensky, Gleb, 52, 53, 54, 140;
"Nravy rasteryaevoy ulitsy,"
52, 54.

"Vaplite," 27.
"Vechirnya hodyna" (Evening
Hour), 76, 124.
Verga, Giovanni, 55, 56, 141.
Verlaine, P., 18, 20, 21.
Verves, H., 54.
"Vistuny" (Heralds, The), 108.
"V korchmi" (In the Tavern), 108,
110, 130.
"Vona—zemlya" (She—The Earth),
74, 117; *Vona—zemlya*, 27, 64.
Vovchok, Marko, 44, 45, 62.
"Vovchytsya" (She-Wolf), 114.
"Voyenni shkody" (War Casual-
ties), 110.
Vynnychenko, V., 66.

"Vyvodyly z sela" (Village Send-
Off, The), 119, 120.

Wyka, K., 44.

Yatskiv, M., 23.
Yarema, Ya., 52, 53, 54.
Yefremov, Serhiy, 28, 48.

"Zasidannye" (Meeting, A), 39,
113.
"Zemlya" (The play "Earth"), 74.
Zerov, M., 10, 48.
"Z mista yduchy" (Coming from
Town), 76, 113.
"Zlodiy" (Thief, The), 40, 50, 54,
73, 74, 75, 76, 77, 79, 94, 131,
(169-175).
"Z oseny" (From Autumn), 21.
Życie, 17, 80.